W9-AFU-026

# THE
# WORLD-CLASS
# EXECUTIVE

# THE WORLD-CLASS EXECUTIVE

---

*How to Do Business Like a Pro*
*Around the World*

---

NEIL CHESANOW

RAWSON ASSOCIATES • *New York*

Library of Congress Cataloging in Publication Data

Chesanow, Neil.
   The world-class executive.

   Includes index.
   1. International business enterprises —Management.
   2. Americans —Foreign countries.   I. Title.
   HD62.4.C44   1985        658'.049        83-43106
   ISBN 0-89256-258-7

Published simultaneously in Canada by McClelland and Stewart Ltd.
Composition by Westchester Book Composition, Inc.
                Yorktown Heights, New York
Manufactured by Fairfield Graphics
                   Fairfield, Pennsylvania
Designed by Jacques Chazaud
First Edition

For the people listed
in the acknowledgments,
as well as
David Chesanow and Vicki Fabry.

"Negotiation is a field of knowledge and endeavor that focuses on gaining the favor of people from whom we want things. It's as simple as that."

—HERB COHEN,
*You Can Negotiate Anything*

# CONTENTS

———

# ACKNOWLEDGMENTS

I'm grateful to the following people who shared their international negotiating experiences and knowledge, and to a number of others whose names do not appear here because they wished to remain anonymous. Thanks, everyone.

*Marjorie K. Alfus*, marketing director, K-Mart Trading Services (merchandising) . . . *Henri Alster*, president, Alster International (real estate investment and development)

*Alan L. Bain*, president, World-Wide Business Centres (office leasing) . . . *Linda Miller Bain*, vice-president, World-Wide Business Centres (office leasing) . . . *T.O. Beidleman*, professor, New York University (anthropology) . . . *Zenus Block*, former vice chairman, DCA Food Industries (fast food), professor, New York University (entrepreneurship) . . . *Elio Boccitto*, president, Berlitz Schools of Languages of America (foreign-language instruction, interpretation, and translation) . . . *Rita Boehm*, contracts manager, Hartman Systems (military display and control systems) . . . *Marguerite Borchardt*, president, American Society of Interpreters (interpretation and translation) . . . *Rodrigo K. Briones*, senior associate, The Globecon Group (business analysis), adjunct professor, New York University (Latin American and Caribbean studies) . . . *Peter Van Brundt*, director, program operations and strategic planning, Save the Children Foundation (charity)

*Juanita Caspari*, classified advertising manager, *International Herald Tribune* (newspaper) . . . *John R. Celentano*, manager, marketing/international licen-

sing, United Media Enterprises (publishing, syndication, merchandising)...
*R. Britton Colbert*, partner, Laventhol & Horwath (accounting)...*Deborah
L. Coon*, manager, publication services, Center for International and Area
Studies, Brigham Young University (publishing)

*Christine Daher*, program designer (cross-cultural training)...*George Daher*,
former communications advisor, Ministry of Defense, Saudi Arabia, lecturer
(cross-cultural training)...*Nicholas L. Deak*, chairman, Deak & Co. (currency exchange and precious metals)...*Lesley Dorman*, president, Small
World (cross-cultural training)

*Federico Fahsen Ortega*, vice minister, foreign affairs, Guatemala (diplomacy)...*Lawrence V. Fairhall*, senior consultant, Korea Trade Promotion
Center (trade promotion)...*Robert C. Fisher*, publisher, Fisher Travel Guides
(publishing), author, *Fisher Travel Guide to Japan*...*Constance Fitzgerald*,
manager, strategic planning, American Express Travel Related Services (travel
services)...*Monique Fong*, conference interpreter, United Nations and other
organizations (interpretation)...*Felix E. Forestieri*, public relations director,
Latin America, Eastern Airlines (air transportation)...*Howard Frith*, marketing director, J. Pask Associates (advertising)

*Michael V. Georgopolis*, vice-president, director of licensing, United Media
Enterprises (publishing, syndication, merchandising)...*Lewis Griggs*, general partner, executive producer, Copeland Griggs Productions (film production)

*Young-soo Hahm*, manager, Korea Trade Promotion Center (trade promotion)
...*Denise Hamon*, president, Executive Language Services (foreign-language
instruction)...*Oliver W. Harris*, president, World Wide Relocation Assistance (cross-cultural training)...*Philip R. Harris*, president, Harris International (management psychology), coauthor, *Managing Cultural Differences*
...*David S. Hoopes*, senior editor, Intercultural Press (publishing)...*Lucille
M. Hoshabjian*, press relations manager, North and Central America, Luf-
thansa German Airlines (air transportation)...*Emanuel T. Huarte*, regional
director, Inlingua (foreign-language instruction, interpretation, and translation)...*Joanne M. Hvala*, manager, editorial programs, General Electric
International Trading Operations (manufacturing)

*Sandra L. Jaco*, vice-president, Berlitz Schools of Languages of America
(foreign-language instruction, interpretation, and translation)...*Brij M.
Jairath*, manager, communications, General Electric International Trading
Operations (manufacturing)...*Werner D. Jurgeleit*, partner, BJR Communications (advertising)

Scott Kalb, business and political analyst, Harvard University (East Asian studies)...*Fredric M. Kaplan*, president, Eurasia Press (publishing), coauthor, *The China Handbook*...*Arne J. de Keijzer*, owner, A.J. de Keijzer & Associates (China negotiations), coauthor, *The China Handbook*...*James H. Kober*, vice-president, Latin America/Caribbean Travel Division, American Express Travel Related Services (travel services)...*Neil Krupp*, vice-president, international services, Runzheimer and Company (management consulting)...*Thomas Kutzen*, vice-president, Chase Manhattan (banking) ...*Robert H. Kwon*, senior partner, Coopers & Lybrand (accounting)

*James R. Ladd*, managing partner, Japan, Deloitte Haskins + Sells (accounting)...*Alison R. Lanier*, publisher, *Living Abroad* (newsletter), author, *Living in the U.S.A.*...*William J. Lederer*, coauthor, *The Ugly American*, author, *A Nation of Sheep*...*David J. Lewis*, director, international marketing & sales, Crane U.S.A. (manufacturing)...*Lars-Erik Lindblad*, president, Lindblad Travel (travel services)...*Sven-Olaf Lindblad*, president, Special Expeditions (travel services)

*W. Peter Mahler*, corporate director, marketing, Hilton International (hotels) ...*Stuart Marks*, partner, Kaye, Scholer, Fierman, Hays & Handler (law) ...*Rose Maginniss*, manager of license services, Energy Program, Grumman International (manufacturing)...*Hugh McCandless*, public information director, Deloitte Haskins + Sells (accounting)...*Linda McGlathery*, former deputy director, Peace Corps (Guatemala), owner, Palopó (fashion exports) ...*Marvin Miller*, president, Miller Supply Company (capital goods imports) ...*Teresa Miller*, public relations consultant, Korean Cultural Service (trade and tourism promotion)...*Joan Mills*, associate editor, International Editions, *Reader's Digest* (publishing)...*Mercedes Miranda*, regional sales director, Pearl Cruises of Scandinavia (travel services)...*Robert T. Moran*, director, Cross-Cultural Communication Program, American Graduate School of International Management, coauthor, *Managing Cultural Change*...*Harriet Mouchly-Weiss*, chairman, Ruder Finn & Rotman International Partners (public relations)...*Francis I. Mullin III*, president, Canada Dry U.S.A. (soft drinks)

*Al Nadler*, acting director, New York District Office, U.S. Department of Commerce (federal agency)

*Patrick J. Oliver*, vice-president, Latin America and Florida Division, Pan American World Airways (air transportation)

*Nicholas C. Papadopoulos*, vice-president, Irving Trust (banking)...*Raphael Patai*, Arabologist, author, *The Arab Mind*...*C. Wolcott Parker*, director,

International Council to Management, American Graduate School of International Management (cross-cultural training)... *Elena Paz*, executive director, The Language Lab (foreign-language instruction, interpretation, and translation)... *Ann Himes Pedersen*, professor, Massey University, New Zealand (management), consultant, The World Bank (cross-cultural training)... *Paul Pedersen*, chairman, Counseling and Guidance Program, Syracuse University, consultant, The World Bank (cross-cultural training)... *Margaret D. Pusch*, president, Intercultural Press (publishing)

*Claire Quinn*, assistant vice-president, Benelux, Irving Trust (banking)

*Ellen Raider*, former research scientist, U.S.–U.S.S.R. Trade Negotiation Project, president, Ellen Raider International (trade and diplomatic negotiations)... *Arnoldo A. Ramirez*, vice-president, Irving Trust (banking)... *John B. Ratliff*, assistant dean, External Programs, Foreign Service Institute, U.S. State Department (School of Language Studies)... *Kathleen K. Reardon*, associate professor, University of Connecticut (communication science), author, *International Gift-Giving Customs*... George W. Renwick, president, Renwick and Associates (cross-cultural training)... *Stephen H. Rhinesmith*, former president, Moran Stahl & Boyer (management consulting)... *Barbara Roder*, president, American Association of Language Specialists, conference interpreter, United Nations and other organizations (interpretation)... *Otto E. Roethenmund*, vice-chairman, Deak & Co. (currency exchange and precious metals)

*Joseph M. Saggese*,...group vice-president, Asia/Latin America, Can Machinery/Export, Borden International (manufacturing)... *Andrew L. Salad*, vice-president, marketing, Technical Translation International (translation)... *Sol Sanders*, International Outlook editor, *Business Week* (publishing)... *Michael A. Seamark*, vice-president, operations, Canada Dry International (soft drinks)... *Charles M. Silver*, vice-president and associate treasurer, International Telephone and Telegraph Corporation (communications)... *Morris G. Simoncelli*, manager, press relations and publications, Japan Air Lines (air transportation)... *Ernest M. Sinauer*, president, International Training Institute (cross-cultural training)... *Richard Smith*, group vice-president, American Steel Export (manufacturing)... *Stephen Soule*, president, Stephen Soule Importers (capital goods imports)... *Arthur South*, international marketing manager, Technical Translation International (translation)... *Deanna Stone*, consultant, Government of Peru (tourism)... *Michael Strumpen-Darrie*, vice-president, curriculum and training, Berlitz Schools of Languages of America (foreign-language instruction, interpretation, and translation)... *Richard B. Swank*, president, Reuben H. Donnelley (Yellow Pages advertising sales)

*Tibor Taraba*, advertising director, Reuben H. Donnelley (Yellow Pages advertising sales)...*Carol Thomas*, associate director, Business Council for International Understanding Institute, The American University (cross-cultural training)...*Michel Thomas*, president, Michel Thomas Language Centers (foreign-language instruction, interpretation, and translation)...*Michael F. Tucker*, vice-president, international services, Moran Stahl & Boyer (management consulting)

*John L. Ufheil*, chief operating officer, Malinckrodt (manufacturing)

*Doris Walsh*, editor, *International Demographics* (newsletter)...*Richard Webber*, controller, Borden International (manufacturing)...*Norman Weissman*, president, Ruder Finn & Rotman, New York (public relations)...*Margaret C. Weitz*, research affiliate, Harvard University (Center for European Studies)

*Patrick Yau*, president, Inter Pacific Tours International (travel services)...*Tae-wan Yu*, former director, Korean Cultural Service (trade and tourism promotion)...*Byung-gook Yuk*, vice consul, Korean Cultural Service (trade and tourism promotion)

*David Zable*, director of manufacturing, E.P. Dutton (publishing)...*Diane Zeller*, executive director, Society for Intercultural Education, Training and Research (cross-cultural training)

# THE
# WORLD-CLASS
# EXECUTIVE

# The Bottom Line

You're probably reading this book for one of three reasons:

1. You're about to go abroad on business for the first time, and you're wondering if what you know about your field of expertise in the U.S.— be it marketing, sales, licensing, or operations—is sufficient to effectively negotiate elsewhere in the world. *It isn't, not even in Western Europe.*

2. You've already negotiated overseas. Perhaps you've even lived abroad as a managerial expatriate. You're curious to see if what you learned about differences between our and other business cultures is confirmed in the pages to come. *You'll have to check, but be prepared for some surprises.*

3. Right now your job does not take you abroad. But you love to travel. And you're savvy enough to foresee that in a commercial world growing ever more interdependent, the time is not far off when executives without international negotiating skills will be like those who know nothing about computers today: They are rapidly becoming obsolete. You're hoping this book will start you off on the right track, giving you knowledge to compete for a position that does involve international travel. *This is precisely what it will do.*

There are a variety of books that discuss doing international business.

But there never has been one like this. What makes *The World-Class Executive* special is its unique *practicality*.

*It's written with one reader in mind.* This book is specifically for U.S.-based business travelers who make short but frequent negotiating trips to foreign parts. Executive expatriates will also find it useful.

*It recognizes business travelers come in two sexes.* Each chapter includes special tips and guidelines for international business*women*— from what to wear to establish professional credibility to how to ward off a pass without alienating a foreign businessman with whom you must still successfully deal.

*It covers more than one country.* The World-Class Executive discusses not one but *four* of the most heavily trafficked regions in global commerce: Western Europe, the Arab world, East Asia—including Japan, the People's Republic of China, and South Korea—and Latin America. So many places have never before been squeezed between the covers of one book. Yet this is what most business travelers want and need as most don't seek contracts in only one foreign place. The person dealing in Tokyo today may be in Seoul next week, in Beijing next month, in Abu Dhabi next season, and in São Paulo before the year is out. However excellent, a book about doing business in only one country overseas is of limited use.

*It's short and sweet.* This book is written with a plain fact of business life paramount in mind: Businesspeople are extremely *busy.* If you're typical, you're already overburdened with "required reading." The last thing you want to do is wade through page after page of arcane text to get a bottom-line piece of advice. *The World-Class Executive* is not a scholarly work. It's not a book for thinkers; it's a book for *doers.*

*It will help you do the job.* The World-Class Executive is not the last word on its subject. Far from it. A multivolume encyclopedia would barely serve as an introduction to the cultural differences in international negotiating. Here you get the *distilled essence* of what you really need to know to deal effectively around the world. However, the insights, tips, and guidelines to come *will* give you a definite negotiating edge over any competitor—whether he comes from Tallahassee or Tokyo—who does not know what you're about to learn. Most *won't.*

*It's a quick read.* This book is organized into concise blocks of information. Each block is clearly titled. You can read *The World-Class Executive* from cover to cover if you wish. Or you can just skip around at random, finding precisely the facts you need quickly and absorbing the information at a glance, or refinding a bit of advice you wish to recheck without a lot of flipping.

*Over a hundred heads are better than one.* When it comes to matters of business culture, no one—no matter how impressive his credentials—can be the final authority. The possible permutations of the subject are simply too vast. What gives *The World-Class Executive* extra authority is extra experts. Among the more than one hundred names listed in the acknowledgments, you'll find people who know the ropes in just about every area of global commerce: exporters, importers, corporate officers, middle managers, presidents of major multinationals, owners of medium-size and small concerns, former and current executive expatriates, international bankers, lawyers, and accountants, business-school professors, anthropologists, political and financial analysts, people in diplomacy and government—non-Americans as well as Americans—cross-cultural trainers, language experts, authors, and editors.

So, with this in mind, let's get down to the business of doing international business.

---

A WORD ABOUT QUOTES

This book is interspersed with quotes, letting international negotiators present advice and anecdotes in their own words. All quotes in which book titles, authors, and other publishing data are not immediately cited in the text are extracted from personal conversations between me and the people listed in the acknowledgments. When an individual's name is mentioned without reference to his or her title, it's because that person's name and title were cited earlier in the chapter. The acknowledgments have been alphabetized to enable you to easily recheck who said what. When an individual's name is not mentioned in conjunction with a quote, it's because he or she requested anonymity. Due to the delicacy of their global business dealings, many executives agreed to participate only on this basis.

# PART ONE

---

# US AND

# THEM

# CHAPTER ONE

---

# What Makes You
# a Typical American

"My first lesson abroad was that foreign executives
are not Americans in disguise."

A U.S. MANUFACTURER

*Caracas:* An American manager is in a rush to close a deal the Venezuelan
government has already told his firm it wants. By refusing to take time
to build good interpersonal rapport with a key minister, he loses what
should have been a certain sale. The price of his impatience: A sociable
Swede gets the goods—$2 million in new business.

*Tokyo:* An American marketer enters a conference room expecting
to begin superficial negotiations with the CEO. Instead, she faces a dozen
department heads who want to know everything about her offer from A
to Z. Unable to answer their minutely detailed questions, she loses face.
The tab for being unprepared: A German with the facts on hand makes
the $6 million sale.

*Riyadh:* An American exporter is trying to sell to a Saudi official.
As he sits back comfortably in his chair, he crosses his legs, exposing the
sole of a shoe—an insult. He passes documents to the Arab with his left
hand, which Muslims consider unclean. He refuses coffee, implying criticism of his host's hospitality. The cost of being a cultural klutz: A Korean
versed in Arab tact lands the $10 million contract.

Exceptions? If only they were. Such negotiating blunders happen
every day, the world over, time and again. Often they cost U.S. firms
multimillion-dollar contracts, and their negotiators a raise, a promotion,

sometimes even a job. As most Americans are chosen to represent their companies abroad precisely because they are successful at home, why do so many fail on foreign soil?

The reason is because they act like "typical" Americans. In fact, because our behavioral style *has* been so effective here, we commonly assume that business sophisticates the world over, admiring our methods and envious of our results, have reached the same inevitable conclusion: The American way of doing business is best.

It may come as a shock to executives dealing abroad for the first time to find this is anything *but* the case. What is sanctioned business behavior here is often regarded as unnatural, rude, and repugnant to no less sophisticated managers in other countries. Even the peoples of Western Europe, whose ideas of acceptable commercial conduct are often closer to ours than those of other non-Americans, differ significantly from us in what they consider the "right way" to do business.

This book is about what non-Americans consider the *right* way to negotiate. But before we can begin to understand them, we must begin to understand ourselves. We are intelligent, resourceful, imaginative, ingenious, inventive, progressive, thoroughly likable people who happen to inhabit the richest, most powerful, most successful country in the world. Since we like to think of ourselves as a nation of unique individualists, what is it about us that's viewed as "typical," traits that our foreign counterparts find so strange?

## Ethnocentricism

Just about everyone feels culturally superior to everyone else, but Americans are the only people who feel superior because of money. We assume our way of doing business is best because we make more money faster than anyone else, and we have the highest standard of living of any major power to prove it. In fact, so convinced are we of our money-making virtues that we consider them natural, logical, and desirable for everyone to adopt and universally approve. This conviction is so deeply instilled that we carry it with us wherever we try to deal, treating non-Americans around the globe as if they were American managers in the making—or should be. We expect them to do business over the telephone. We expect them to talk shop at any hour of the day or night. We expect them to accept our logic after we have taken pains to spell it out. We expect them to respond well to our aggressive, efficient, hard-sell style. We expect them to want short-term profits. And we expect them to make up their minds quickly, before our week-long trips have run their course. We expect all this because there's money to be made. And Americans believe that nothing should interfere with making money.

## English

If being called typical or ethnocentric irritates you, how many foreign languages can you speak fluently? Few Americans can speak any language other than their own. We have many reasons why, including boredom and lack of time. But probably the most widespread reason, which our international executives are the first to admit, is that there's no need to learn other people's languages: They've already learned *ours*. And it's true: English has become *the* language of global commerce. This is as it should be, or so many of us think. After all, the world needs us more than we need it. If a Korean or Brazilian already speaks English, why should we bother to learn Hangul or Portuguese? It's a duplication of effort. It's inefficient. Besides, time is money, and our time is worth more money than anyone else's in the world.

## Pressure

Americans are aggressive, dynamic, high-pressure businesspeople. We dislike taking no for an answer. It goes against our grain, especially when we're convinced that our logic is sound. We not only want people to say yes, we want them to agree on the spot. We come with facts. We spell them out. We add them up. We use case histories to prove our points. We even bring blank contracts ready to be filled in. If we sense interest but not yet commitment from a customer-to-be, we offer sweeteners—introductory offers, quantity discounts, no-risk trials, money-back guarantees—to pull fencesitters over to our side. We turn time into pressure: "If you want delivery by a certain date at a certain price, say yes right now." The sooner a deal is closed the better, and the more we're considered credits to our firms.

## Directness

Nobody can accuse us of beating around the bush. We make appointments, enter offices, take seats, and get to the point. We consider directness efficient, but we also feel it's polite. It's a sign of respect. It shows you know the person you've come to see is busy, and you don't want to waste his valuable time. So we're frank. There's nothing we're unwilling to put into words. In our culture the most effective salespeople perfect the art of putting *everything* into words as quickly, concisely, and convincingly as possible.

## Time

We can't afford to be indirect. It takes time, and time is money in the U.S. Time is a commodity. It has value. It can be saved or spent, invested or wasted, used or abused. And yet our attitudes toward time are ambivalent. For example, as businesspeople, our *personal* time may be disposable. *Company* time is all-important. If company business takes more time than was anticipated we work overtime, sacrificing personal time, often at the expense of family, friends, and self-renewal. We get to work early. We stay at the office late. We read reports at dinner or in front of the TV. This, we think, is how everybody is forced to operate, because all businesspeople have the same goal, which, by chance, was perfected by us: to get the most done in the least time to make the most money for the least cost.

## Deadlines

Who invented deadlines is unknown. While it probably wasn't an American—as a nation we're too young—we've refined the term to the point where its meaning is almost literal: Miss a deadline and you may be "dead." Miss a deadline and something bad is bound to happen. It may mean a black mark in your personnel file, cause you to be passed over for promotion, or even cost you a job. But Americans accept the need for deadlines. They're compatible with our intense sense of competitiveness. They're a yardstick for performance. And they're the nervous system of business. Without deadlines, few jobs would get done on time, profit predictions would be impossible to make accurately, and commerce as we know it might grind to a halt.

## "Quickies"

A acquaintance of mine in Shanghai calls us that. Another in Beijing refers to us as "Green Tigers." We think of projects that take three years to pay out as being long-term. Even a year may seem forever to many

Americans, particularly those who work for publicly owned firms where raises, perks, and promotions are pegged to quarterly earnings per share of company stock. To us, the benefits of short-term transactions are obvious—quick profits, less risk, instant gratification. No wonder many Americans go abroad believing this phenomenon is worldwide.

## People and Profits

Which matters more in business? Profits! People go with a whimper. Profits go with a bang. It's the deal that matters most to us, not the dealer. In a few industries, like the garment industry, everyone knows everyone else and negotiations may be concluded with a handshake, without a formal contract. But in most of Corporate America, buyer and seller are strangers and don't need to know each other to talk shop. Getting personally acquainted is all very nice, but it wastes time, which is money. If it's the right person, the right offer, and the right time, you deal; if not, you don't. Unless negotiators are incompetent or unusually obnoxious, their personalities seldom play a significant role in the ordinary conduct of U.S. business. If everything works out, if it seems like you'll do business together again, then—maybe—you'll decide to socialize. After, not before.

## Lawyers and Contracts

Lawyers and contracts are central to negotiating as we conduct it; to be efficient, we're forced to deal with each other as strangers. Nobody trusts a stranger, especially with money. That's why we have lawyers and contracts—to keep strangers honest. Here, as soon as an agreement is reached, lawyers are summoned—if they weren't present from the start—and everything is elaborately spelled out in what is often a voluminous document. In fact, you may be wondering right now whether or not a lawyer should accompany you in negotiations abroad.

## Profit

In the view of many Americans, the sole reason for being in business is to make a profit. The raison d'etre of a corporation is self-perpetuation made possible by a steady, acceptable flow of new income. In the process of trying to survive and prosper among the fittest, if a firm does something to benefit society or promotes peaceful coexistence between Americans and people of other cultures, fine! But altruism isn't our main motivation for doing business. It's a fortuitous but secondary by-product.

## Preparation

Americans who negotiate abroad tend to be owners of small firms or decision makers of larger corporations. Often they are generalists, not specialists. And, to further limit the scope of business knowledge, many companies today are tightening their business travel budgets, sending a single emissary overseas, not a team as in the past, to save money. The emissary's role may merely be to work out the terms of an agreement in broad brushstrokes. Later, subordinates back in the U.S. are expected to investigate the details in depth. It's assumed that some negotiating points will be irresolvable outside the U.S., but these can be worked out in mid-process, as bargaining sessions are drawing to a close.

## Non-People

Americans are often contradictory in their behavior. For example, we stress our individuality, but we may be individualistic when it suits us and mere numbers when it doesn't, enabling us to evade responsibility. In the U.S., a client contact often represents his firm only in a symbolic sense. As long as he's competent and reliable, who he is as a person is inconsequential. After all, it's the firm's money and integrity that are ultimately at stake, not that of an individual representative. The firm is all-important. The client contact is merely a pawn. If necessary, another "body" can easily take his place, with no disruption of the business relationship.

## Promises

The U.S. may be only two centuries old, but Americans weren't born yesterday. We know full well that human beings are fallible; sometimes they make promises that are not kept. Who among us can boast that they have never broken a promise? Too often Americans go abroad assuming this is universally understood and resignedly accepted. As a result, we may fail to think a business transaction through thoroughly and say yes prematurely. Or we may say yes as a tactic, *knowing* we can't meet some terms, but why let a lucrative deal fall through over minor points that can be resolved later on, when everyone is too deeply committed to back out?

## Job Mobility

American managers-to-be are often raised to impressively succeed when they're young. The fastest, most efficient road to success is to change jobs, and it's accepted practice here for competing firms to woo top talent away from rivals. Because U.S. job mobility is the world's highest, client-contact relationships are frequently impermanent. And why not? It's the buyer-seller relationship between companies that counts, not the one between their individual representatives. No one—not even the chief executive—is indispensable. Company presidents commonly get fired or resign to take new jobs. Ultimately, everyone—from the top down—can be replaced.

## Obsession

Americans have a monomania for talking shop. Many of us do it at every opportunity—at breakfast, lunch and dinner, over midnight drinks, at weddings and bar mitzvahs, on Thanksgiving, before and after sex. Often we think that talk of making money is as much a passion with people the world over and appropriate for discussion anytime or anyplace. We assume that company responsibilities come before all else, even family and friends. If it isn't an emergency, family and friends can wait; business can't.

## Traditions

We have traditions like everyone else, but they're not deeply ingrained. We observe traditions as long as they don't interfere with business or otherwise inconvenience us; when they do, we eliminate or ignore them. If dealing a certain way serves a logical, efficient purpose, that's how we deal. But we don't deal one way or another because it's how our forefathers dealt, let alone our professional predecessors. If another method comes to light that does the job better, we promptly change. Americans assume everyone shares this logic. We expect all peoples to accept our view of common sense—to make efficiency and progress more important than preserving outmoded customs for their own sake, particularly when they delay profits.

## Informality

We're the world's easiest people to know and like because we don't stand on ceremony. We're warm, casual, informal, and friendly. We think the best of everyone. We'll give anyone the benefit of the doubt. We're practically uninsultable. We automatically overlook innocent faux pas. A person's innocence is what matters to us most, not his ignorance. As there is no simpler way to be, we assume that our informality fits in anywhere. When local mores on politeness prevent foreign colleagues from making the truth known, we feel no constraints about our behavior and continue on in blissful ignorance, misinterpreting often deeply felt but unspoken criticism for acceptance.

# CHAPTER TWO

---

# The Business World
# As One World

"One world is said to resemble another."

WALLACE STEVENS,
*Three Academic Pieces*

Novice negotiators soon discover three truths about global commerce:

- Each of the world's businesspeoples is culturally unique
- Beneath their differences there are often key similarities
- The similarities are not ones that Americans typically share

In Chapter One we viewed the business world through red-white-and-blue glasses. Let's look at it again, but this time from a foreign point of view.

## Ethnocentricism

For most Americans, foreign trade is relatively new. For years after World War II, we had no need to sell abroad; domestic markets were big enough. But many non-Americans weren't blessed with our good fortune. Without sufficient domestic markets in which to sell their wares, often due to war-torn economies, they were forced to seek customers in other lands.

At first, most were probably in the same position that many Americans find themselves in today. They couldn't speak local languages. They didn't know how to play by local business and social rules. They made serious cultural faux pas, inadvertently insulting the natives. And their initial unschooled efforts probably cost them millions of dollars in lost business.

But now World War II is nearly four decades past. The Korean War is over three decades past. The Vietnam War is over a decade past. The world that we grew up in as children, and learned about at school, is not the world as it exists today.

Many non-Americans, or their corporate heirs, are no longer novices at international negotiating. Yet most Americans still are. Older and wiser, our foreign competitors now understand that business methods, manners, and motivations differ markedly from one region of the world to another, from one country to another, from one city to another within the same country, and from individual to individual within the same city.

Our foreign counterparts have also come to realize that such differences *can't* be ignored. Why? Because their potential customers abroad, often prepared to spend billions of dollars, simply won't deal with someone who fails to show respect for their national customs and values.

Today's global business sophisticates make every effort to learn how their foreign customers prefer to deal, but not out of nobility of heart or because they are amateur anthropologists. They do it for a reason that we as pragmatists should be the quickest to understand yet remain the slowest to accept: The competition is doing it, people the world over insist on it, so everyone must do it, particularly Americans who seek the same foreign customers.

Cross-cultural awareness is no longer optional. To meet the ever-growing challenge of competition from abroad, it often determines who flies home with the contract.

## English

Many people in foreign business and government speak English. But they aren't as accommodating as we often assume. It's true that other people learn our language because English is *the* language of global commerce. Yet non-Americans maintain a deep love for their mother tongues, and only 4 percent of the world beyond the U.S. speaks English as the first language of the land.

When non-Americans visit the U.S. on business, they speak English to communicate and to show respect for our language. When we visit their countries, many natives—though they may be too polite to make a public issue of it—resent our general unwillingness to reciprocate. They try to behave like Americans when they are here. Yet they are also forced to behave like Americans when we are there.

The implication is clear: We consider ourselves superior to them.

## Foreign Types

Americans make two common mistakes in appraising foreign colleagues, and they can be costly. First, when a non-American shows he can speak English, we assume that he also *thinks* like one of us. Second, when we learn a foreigner not only speaks our language but has been educated at one of our universities, we become convinced that he has clearly seen the superiorities of the American way of life and business and has become thoroughly Americanized.

Neither assumption is usually true. But to complicate life, they are not always totally untrue.

As the business world becomes increasingly homogenized, three types of non-Americans have emerged. Type One are strict cultural traditionalists. They are usually old-timers, a dying breed though often still the people who make the key decisions at home. Adding to their numbers, however, is a growing number of young people who are resurgent nationalists, who seek to curb or eliminate outside cultural influence to preserve the purity of their heritages and their national identities.

Type Two are non-Americans who have become Americanized or Westernized. Younger-generation people, they usually speak English and have been Western educated. More than a few become expatriates, remaining in the U.S. or Europe rather than returning home. This group is a minority.

Type Three, the largest and fastest-growing faction, lies somewhere in between. They may be young or middle-aged. They may speak English and hold Western university degrees. And they accept American business practices *up to a point*—a certain indefinable point that varies from individual to individual. They are attempting a cultural compromise by blending age-old customs with modern ideas in order to economically progress.

Expect to encounter any or all of these types of non-Americans in negotiations abroad, sometimes within the same meeting. Yet each may require different treatment. It's important to correctly match an individual to his type to avoid causing offense and to effectively make your case. Part Two of this book helps you do just that.

## Hard Sell

Beyond our borders the pace of life and business slows down, often considerably. Non-Americans are not usually eager to make quick decisions, no matter how convincing your presentation may be. Most are conservative, cautious, suspicious, indirect, subtle, patient, low-key, and formally mannered. They don't merely dislike American aggressiveness in selling; they *despise* it.

Many of us who sell overseas learn our lesson the hard way. We beat out the competition in quality and price. Yet we still lose lucrative business to foreign competitors by demonstrating to a native buyer that dealing with us will be professionally annoying and socially embarrassing, overly disrupting local life.

## Directness

Frankness, directness, and bluntless are not universally admired in the business world. Simply stating an unpleasant—or any—truth may violate local mores on politeness. You may get a circumlocutious yes for an answer that's really a no courteously disguised to save face for all concerned.

Americans are encouraged to be direct, frank, and concise in getting to the bottom line fast. If you're among them, you may have to adapt your presentation style to conform with local etiquette outside the U.S. It's important to know how to convey facts and opinions in roundabout ways, as well as how to recognize and correctly interpret a foreigner's indirect reply.

In *Never Take Yes for an Answer*, Masaaki Imai cites one of the many puzzles awaiting you abroad:

> A newcomer to Japan may never be able to recover from the initial culture shock of finding out that "yes" does not always mean "yes" in Japan until he realizes that there are some sixteen ways to avoid saying "no" and that to call a spade a spade is not in the Japanese tradition. (The Simul Press, Tokyo, 1975)

Compare this fact, which has analogs in many business cultures, with the American ideal which Harold Geneen, former president of ITT, expressed in a stern memo to his staff (quoted in *The Art of Japanese*

*Management* by Richard Tanner Pascale and Anthony G. Athos, Simon & Schuster, New York, 1981):

> Effective immediately, I want every report specifically, directly, and bluntly to state at the beginning a summary of the unshakeable facts. ... The highest art of professional management requires the ability to smell a real fact from all others—and moreover, to have the temerity, intellectual curiosity, guts and/or plain impoliteness if necessary to be sure what you have is indeed what we will call an *unshakeable fact*.

While this may be a virtue here, if you have the temerity, intellectual curiosity, guts and/or plain impoliteness to show your counterparts abroad the unshakeable facts, they may respond by showing you to the door.

## Efficiency

Americans are often surprised to find that time is not money the world over. That other peoples may not conform to our standards of efficiency is no reflection on their intelligence, ability, or even desire to make money. Usually it's a matter of different life priorities, and it's assumed by them that if you're serious about doing business on their native soil you understand, accept, and respect what those priorities are. Many Americans have no one but themselves to blame for their failures and frustrations overseas. Had they not jumped the gun, gone abroad culturally untutored, and brought with them expectations of efficiency that are realistic in the U.S. but elsewhere are not, they would have known how to design schedules, set deadlines, and plan trip goals that were practical to meet.

## Deadlines

Take the *dead* out of deadline and what have you got? Not much. Concepts of time differ the world over. When a Swede says he will meet you at 3:00 P.M., he may mean precisely that: not 2:59, not 3:01. When an Arab says something will be done at 3:00 P.M., he may specify the day but not the week. Outside the U.S., deadlines often don't have the sense of seriousness, urgency, and implied threat that we take for granted as being a universal business norm. This doesn't mean that predicting how long a foreign project will take is impossible. But it does require practice and experience to know how local time works abroad to make accurate job estimates and set deadlines apt to be met.

## Long-Term

The pressure to improve quarterly dividends is not a cross most foreigners have to bear. Beyond our borders continuity, stability, and security based on mutual trust often matter more than the short-term gains on which Americans thrive. The slow, patient building of an amicable, enduring relationship between prospective partners to ensure years of hassle-free repeat business may be prized above quick, possibly problematic one-shot deals.

In Japan, profit projections may span five or ten years. In economically unstable Latin America, secure, long-term relationships can be the only way to justify investment. In China, with a recorded history over 3,000 years old, a human lifetime may not be unduly long to wait for a project payout; by the Chinese clock only an instant may have lapsed.

## People

The U.S. is one of the few countries in the business world where profits come before people. Foreigners tend to be old-fashioned; they like to know whom they are dealing with before the dealing begins. Many insist on it. In many cultures, *who* makes an offer, and *how* it's made, may mean as much as—or more than—the offer itself.

A century ago, Americans were similar. With the Industrial Revolution, modernization took place with increasing speed. To keep abreast of the ever-faster pace of change—which, as pragmatists, we felt was only natural and right—Americans had to streamline, efficiently concentrating on business and processing the inefficient human element out.

Elsewhere, however, the human element is still stressed. Foreign business customs may be over a millennium old. Preserving them as they have always been may matter more than changing with the times simply for the sake of being modern. In other countries, *more modern* and *better* are not the synonyms they often are in the U.S.

Yet this rigidity has begun to change. Increasingly, non-Americans are seeking compromises by which they can progress without sacrificing their cultural identities. Be this as it may, few believe that change for its own sake is for the best, and one age-old custom that persists even in the wake of change is that people come *before* profits, not the other way around.

## Legalism

Lawyers may not participate in negotiations overseas. If they play a role at all, it may come after the nature of a business relationship has been established, and after mutual trust—based on repeated contact and interchange of personal as well as professional ideas—has been formed. Many natives are insulted when Americans appear to negotiate with lawyers before trust has paved the way. While every country has its lawyers, they don't replace the need for trust as they do in the U.S.

The importance of trust may also affect the forms contracts assume in other cultures. Sometimes you may not even have a contract; with trust, your word may be enough, and you're expected to feel likewise. If there is a formal document to describe the relationship, it may be shorter and more general than the detailed legal instruments we're so fond of here. In many cases the contract is symbolic, merely a token of good faith that carries little legal weight. It does not specify the obligations of each party in every possible future contingency. Trust established, it's assumed that future problems can be amicably ironed out among friends on an ad hoc basis.

## Money

Everyone in the business world seeks a profit. But many non-Americans are not in business solely to make money or even mainly to reap financial gains. Konosuke Matsushita, founder of the Matsushita Electric Company, among the world's fifty largest corporations, is a case in point. In *The Art of Japanese Management*, he's quoted thus:

> A business should quickly stand on its own, based on the service it provides the society. Profits should not be a reflection of corporate greed but a vote of confidence from society that what is offered by the firm is valued. When a business fails to make profits it should die—it is a waste of the resources of society. (Simon & Schuster, New York, 1981)

This is hardly how Americans think. Yet Matsushita is far from the only non-American, Japanese or otherwise, who doesn't believe that the be-all and end-all of business is profits.

## Preparation

While foreign contracts may seem simplistic and vague, the negotiations resulting in a general document may be anything but. In other cultures, every minor issue may be the subject of seemingly endless debate, even though the outcome of all these mind-wearing discussions may not appear in a contract clause or rider.

For example, the Greeks see delegating details to subordinates as a devious tactic because it happens outside the conference room where they can see it. To Latins, it may mean sacrificing personal power and authority. The Japanese negotiate with large teams of experts, and expect equal input from the American side. In China, many potentially lucrative deals fall through because Americans have neither the knowledge to answer technical questions nor authority to make on-the-spot decisions, particularly regarding changes in price.

Americans sometimes do insufficient homework to deal abroad where important answers may be expected at once, not researched and reported at a later date. This may be regarded as lack of forethought, competence, sincerity, and respect, and an insult to the intelligence of foreign negotiators who are thoroughly prepared.

## Symbols

You may be the sole negotiator whom they meet, but foreigners are aware that you aren't the sole employee of your firm (unless you run a one-man shop). The title on your business card gives them a good idea of where you stand in your corporate hierarchy. But they still may not consider you merely one among the many. You're the person they are dealing with face to face. Your personality and competence are on the line, no one else's. If you make a poor impression, most non-Americans couldn't care less how many top experts are on staff back in the U.S. If you shine, the number of mediocre people you must answer to at home is equally irrelevant. On foreign soil, you're not a symbolic representative of your firm. You *are* the firm.

## Accountability

Broken promises and business dishonesty are cultural universals. However, because most non-Americans won't deal with you without making sure you're trustworthy first, they don't usually give their word on a whim. In most cultures when a person gives his word, an intricate, deeply serious system of expectations, obligations, sanctions, and other behaviors begins. Breaking a trust bond—perceived or real, regardless of the reason—may end your business relationship at once and forever. When you deal overseas, the natives expect you to fully understand the commitments you make—and their implications—and to honor them with no excuses.

Many accusations by Americans that foreigners break *their* word often enough stem from two wrong assumptions. The Americans assume the natives do business in the American way. And the natives take for granted that the Americans know they don't. Other people have no intention of changing their business habits after centuries of preservation to suit American convenience.

One non-American business expectation found everywhere is accountability: keeping promises personally made. Many Americans learn the hard way that a commitment made abroad—even if it's only verbal, with no contract signed—had better be kept if they ever want to deal again with a given foreign firm or even in a given foreign place. In most cultures, news of treachery, particularly by Americans, travels fast.

## Familiarity

Americans are highly mobile geographically, socially, and occupationally. Most other peoples are not; often they remain in their places of birth, and with the firm by which they were first hired, throughout their lives. Being more sedentary, they place a higher premium on personal relationships in business than we ordinarily do. Many are perplexed and dismayed when an American representative whom they know and trust has been fired, changed jobs, or been promoted to a position that no longer involves client contact.

Personnel changes made midway through extended negotiations—which U.S. firms often do—can seriously retard progress. Failing to accept the importance of building and reinforcing trust bonds between its own personnel and that of a foreign firm may be the biggest blunder that an American company can make. Trust is based on familiarity, on deepening personal friendships that evolve over time, not on a corporate logo, no matter how prestigious. Non-Americans are only too aware of how the world works when it comes to money. Companies screw each other every day; friends don't.

## Shop Talk

Most other peoples feel that talk and thought of business should be contained, so that what is truly important and pleasurable in life is not ignored. To them, business often isn't the essence of life, it's something one must do to pursue what really counts in life, like enjoying one's family, cultivating friendships, and developing nonbusiness interests. We refer to these activities by adjectives like *extra*curricular and *a*vocational, implying that leisure pastimes matter less than professional concerns— which is not what U.S. psychologists maintain.

Americans are often unprepared for the elaborate socializing overseas that takes place before native colleagues will even consider discussing business. To insist on talking shop at such times, which many of us do, may be the height of incivility, a personal rejection by you of your host, who is trying to get to know you as a person so that he can trust you as a professional.

For this reason, Japanese and Koreans may take you out for an evening of drinking. Latins may invite you to a café before they invite you to an office. Arabs will offer you refreshments as soon as you sit down. All this is simply an excuse to size up your personal character. It's not a time for making proposals. Afterward, if it turns out that you're compatible as human beings, it may also be possible for you to be compatible business partners.

## Traditions

Americans understand traditions intellectually, but few of us appreciate their intense emotional hold on other peoples. Our traditions are disposable; if they get in the way of doing business, we change or eliminate them. But traditions are not so easily or willingly cast off outside the U.S. That doing business in time-honored ways may be impractical for reaping quick financial gains is not something non-Americans are unable to grasp. They know. Still it doesn't matter. Their values are different, and uppermost among them is to preserve the "old ways"—to foster cultural identity, historical continuity, and ancestral pride. To abandon these might leave them with bigger bank accounts, but in a world no longer worth living in—a non-world, an existential void. Is any business deal worth that price?

## Formality

Foreign codes of etiquette may be elaborate and inflexible in ways that have no analogs in the U.S. Particularly when there's money to be made, Americans will forgive anyone just about anything; it's practical. Elsewhere, however, it's expected that you know the proper way to behave inside the office and out. That you're a stranger in a strange land is not the excuse that it is here. Ignorance may be interpreted as disrespect for revered traditions and result in public humiliation for a native host, or be taken as a personal affront.

Non-Americans—including Western Europeans, Britons not excepted—can be especially intolerant of faux pas made by Americans, because of our long-standing international reputation for acting like we're better than everyone else. The world over, our mistakes, however innocent, are often taken as further evidence of typical American arrogance and feelings of superiority.

# CHAPTER THREE

---

# Ground Rules
# for Getting the Goods

"Subdue your appetites, my dears, and you've conquered human nature."

CHARLES DICKENS,
*Nicholas Nickleby*

This advice is good advice no matter where in the world you go to
negotiate.

## Ask Around

Every negotiator bound for foreign soil has a rich fund of free expert
advice at his disposal. Yet few people take advantage of it. They are
unaware that it exists, or they are too busy to seek it out. Or, because
they expect to deal abroad as they do in the U.S., they have no idea of
how the cultural engimas they are going to face will turn their hair prematurely gray.

Here are sources of expertise to prevent this from happening to you:

### Your Own Company

According to the U.S. Department of Commerce, at last count there
were some 3,500 U.S. multinational firms; 30,000 American manufacturers exporting their wares; 25,000 companies with branches or affiliates
overseas; and 40,000 concerns dealing abroad on an ad hoc basis—in all,
one-third of the total companies in the U.S.

At each firm, international negotiators can be found. At many, repatriated managers who have lived and worked abroad may be right down the hall or in the same building where you now work. If they can't give you the advice you seek, often they know a colleague who can and will.

If your firm is large and decentralized, with departments functioning independently of each other, and with few people knowing anyone else, there's one department in your company with a file on everyone: the *personnel* department.

### Another Company

If your firm is one with no experience in international trade, you may know someone at a corporation that has been dealing abroad for years who will contact his firm's personnel department on your behalf. This request is legitimate. While you do seek specific advice, you're not after company secrets.

### Salespeople

Your sales representatives, who may know of international experts in your industry whom you may not, can be good sources of leads, as are the sales reps of your suppliers.

### International Banks, Law Firms, and Accounting Firms

Part of global networks, they can telex an affiliate abroad on your behalf if international negotiating pros are not currently stationed at U.S. headquarters.

### Trade Publications

Most industries have such periodicals. Editors and salespeople of trade magazines may know of savants in your field and can often suggest whom to call next.

### A University

It doesn't have to be local, but it should have a graduate school of international business. Ask the average Ph.D. specific questions about his field of expertise, and he will often be generous with his time.

## America's Best-Kept Business Secret

A U.S. machine-tool manufacturer with sales limited to the Northeast is seeking to expand. Where is his best market: domestically in the Midwest, or abroad in China?

The marketing manager of a multinational giant must report on the prospect of building fisheries in Egypt. After weeks of searching, he's still empty-handed. Market research, he asserts, does not exist. Or does it?

Lured by cheap labor and a ten-year moratorium on paying local income tax, a textile broker considers building her own mill in Guatemala. But can a government that has changed hands by military coup three times in six years provide a sufficiently stable economic environment for long-term investment?

The questions are tough but the answers, surprisingly, can be easy to find if more Americans knew where to turn: the International Trade Administration (ITA) of the U.S. Department of Commerce. With forty-seven district offices nationwide and an army of experts in Washington, D.C., ITA is the key federal agency for American firms seeking advice on how to do business globally. Yet it's sadly underused.

Says Al Nadler, acting director of the New York District Office, the largest in the country: "If we were to poll the many firms in the New York area alone, I would conservatively estimate 75 percent don't even know that we exist, and only a fraction of the rest ever turn to us for help. Yet we are funded by U.S. tax dollars, and many of the support services we provide are free."

The International Trade Administration exists not only to foster foreign trade, but also to ensure that U.S. firms seeking to expand their markets abroad know what's involved, thus improving their chances of success. "We're set up almost like a service company," Nadler explains. "Our agents actually go out and knock on company doors, trying to get new firms to export, and showing others already engaged in foreign trade where market opportunities exist that they may have overlooked."

What can ITA do for you?

• The agency maintains a corps of Foreign Commercial Service officers around the world to advise U.S. traders, and to gather data on foreign commercial and industrial trends to benefit U.S. business.

• It manages the U.S. Commercial Service, a network of offices nationwide to counsel U.S. firms on exporting from A to Z: how to get started, how and where to find potential buyers or distributors overseas, and how to compete for foreign government contracts.

• ITA sponsors overseas commercial exhibitions of U.S. products, and conducts trade missions, catalog exhibitions, and sales seminars abroad to introduce U.S. manufacturers directly to foreign buyers.

• The agency collects and publishes commercial and marketing information on each region of the world and on individual countries to help U.S. firms conduct profitable business transactions in hundreds of specific markets, from selling coal in India to selling shoes in Malaysia.

• In addition, ITA maintains a Travel Advisory Center to which U.S. companies may bring specific problems arising from multilateral trade negotiations involving the federal government and from other federal international trade agreements.

While some ITA services are not free, those with price tags are equivalent to the fees charged by private consultants. ITA offers free literature that describes in detail its many services. Check your local telephone directory under U.S. Department of Commerce, or call Commerce Department headquarters in Washington, D.C.

## Foreign Trade Organizations in the U.S.

Most nations that seek to foster trade between American firms and their native public and private sectors have established embassies, consulates, missions, councils, institutes, chambers of commerce, and other organizations in the U.S. to make it easier for you to deal with them.

While most foreign trade organizations (FTOs) are located in New York or Washington, D.C., branch offices may exist in Miami, Chicago, Houston, Dallas, Los Angeles, San Francisco, and other major cities here. Check your local telephone directory for listings under the country name. If you don't have directories for New York and Washington in the office, a local library usually does.

FTOs will send you free literature—books, booklets, brochures, fact sheets, and such—that discuss the technical (and sometimes the cultural) aspects of trade with native companies and governments. There may be one all-purpose publication or dozens of titles explaining the specifics of importing and exporting for a multitude of industries.

The Japan External Trade Organization (JETRO), with offices in New York, Houston, Los Angeles, and San Francisco, offers more literature than any other FTO. JETRO will send you a catalog listing more than a hundred titles on the technicalities of trade in Japan (product design for the Japanese market, manufacturing, delivery, selling, distribution, pricing, patents, payment terms, after-sale service, joint venturing, licensing, etc.); status reports on individual industries (from toys to textiles to computer hardware); and on business culture (like how Japanese decision making works).

If you have questions, JETRO—and analogous agencies of other countries—exists to answer them. But request literature first, read it, and then ask about what you don't understand or find is omitted.

Not all foreign trade organizations will answer questions on matters cultural. When I called the British Trade Development Office in New York with questions on negotiating in the U.K., there was a baffled silence. But when I asked about *British Enterprise Zones*, and how they intend to encourage industrial and commercial investment from abroad by removing certain tax burdens and by relaxing or accelerating certain statutory and administrative controls that formerly hampered international negotiations, I learned all I wanted to know.

However, some FTOs exist specifically to answer questions on native business culture. When I wrote to the Korean Cultural Service in New York with a list of twenty questions on Korean business culture, Tae-wan Yu, then agency director, took the time to write me a personal letter, addressing each question point by point.

You may learn from an FTO that it's unnecessary for you to leave the U.S. to negotiate with a firm or government of the nation that it represents. The FTO, which already has professional credibility in native public and private sectors, may serve as a negotiating intermediary via telex. Ask if this is possible.

If it's necessary to take an overseas trip, an FTO may also see to your travel arrangements. Says Lawrence V. Fairhall, senior consultant to the Korea Trade Promotion Center in New York, the agency can arrange for airport transfers, hotel rooms, prearranged meetings with potential buyers, sellers, or partners, and private consultations with local experts on how to succeed in South Korea.

## Forgotten Questions

You can get so involved in asking technical questions of an FTO representative that basic—but no less important—questions may be overlooked.

For example, you usually need a commercial not a tourist visa to enter a foreign country to do business. If so, what's required in the way of technical and personal information, snapshots of yourself, etc.? How long does the visa take to process once you've met the requirements (an hour or a month)? How long is the visa valid (a year, a month, or only a week)? How long does it permit you to stay in the country per visit? (If negotiations are prolonged, your legal trip time may run out before you've accomplished your goals.)

Should you get certain shots, or pack certain medicines—like chloro-quinine for protection against malaria? Must you prove that you've taken mandatory medical precautions by getting a health certificate?

What are the customs regulations and duties for entering or leaving the country? These vary widely from nation to nation and are often based on idiosyncrasies of local culture. Not knowing them can cause you major hassles. One U.S. exporter was deported from Saudi Arabia, which forbids the drinking of alcoholic beverages, when a miniature bottle of airline Scotch was discovered in his jacket pocket by airport customs agents. An American engineer, who was to live and work in the same country on long-term assignment—the relocation cost to his firm was over $100,000— was expelled as soon as he deplaned when a copy of *Cosmopolitan* mag-azine was discovered in his wife's handbag at the customs desk. The charge: pornography smuggling. The Saudis consider pictures of women in diaphanous dress and showing bare arms and legs to be pornographic, according to Muslim precepts stated in the Koran.

If you plan to bring product samples or demonstration equipment into the country, is special customs clearance required? If so, how can it be obtained? The sales manager of a U.S. hospital diagnostic equipment manufacturer lugged $20,000 worth of high-tech gadgetry to a South American country. It was confiscated at the airport. It had never occurred to him that official papers were mandatory to bring it in and out. Without the equipment, his trip was a waste of time and money. Moreover, he never got the costly hardware back.

## Foreign Tourist Offices in the U.S.

U.S.-based foreign tourist offices are also in the telephone book. Most are in New York, but many have branches elsewhere. Because tourist offices offer free literature for leisure travelers—maps, brochures, illus-trated broadsides, and such—business travelers often assume it's not for them. Not so.

## Maps

Request as many maps as are available. Often there are separate maps of the region, the country, and each city you plan to visit. Maps will give you a good idea of where specific companies, government buildings, and factories are located in relation to your hotel, and will help you choose a place to stay that isn't miles away. A good map is also a valuable lesson in geography: local terrain, distances between major cities, infrastructural development (the existence and quality of airports, roads, and railway networks may affect the length of your trip), and geopolitical neighbors, particularly in parts of the world where military or guerrilla action is rife. For instance, many business travelers, ignorant of geography, perceive the entire isthmus of Central America to be a war zone; it's not. But many others should be more concerned about fireworks now taking place at their intended destinations and are not. Play it safe. Call the U.S. State Department in Washington to get the latest update on the safety of any foreign locale of which you have the slightest doubt.

## General Information Booklets

Every foreign tourist office in the U.S. has at least one of these "bibles." It's full of handy facts for business travelers: local currency denominations; business and banking hours; monthly temperatures and weather conditions; taxi fares; tipping customs; telephone dialing instructions, which can be complicated; business and government addresses and telephone numbers; glossaries of native-language words and phrases, and more.

## Cultural Literature

In addition to maps and general information booklets, separate booklets and brochures may exist on local culture: history, food, art, crafts, sports, performing arts, etc. This knowledge will introduce you to the people and place you'll visit. You may be surprised to find how often subjects like these come up in business conversations. Non-Americans may use your appreciation of their heritage as a yardstick to gauge your desirability as a potential business partner.

### Color Illustrations

When requesting literature, ask for a publication with color pictures. You may get photographs of smiling, seemingly joyous natives who you know are living in wretched poverty. But even they will help reduce culture shock by giving you a visual orientation as to what awaits you when you land.

### Advertising

Try to get samples of local ads, preferably a magazine with ads in color. The art of a business culture is its advertising, and the savvy learn a lot by studying it. If the text isn't in English, no matter. Focus on the visual images conveyed. Are they classy and sophisticated, or drab and utilitarian? This can be a useful guideline for how your own ads should look. If you book an overseas flight with a foreign country's national airline, you'll find in-flight magazines aboard with color ads.

## Patrons and Local Representatives

Outside the U.S., you can't usually pick up the hotel room telephone and set up appointments with local businesspeople or government officials who haven't met you in person. Many will refuse calls from Americans they have yet to personally meet, and will not personally meet with you as a total stranger unless you're introduced by a mutually respected third party, a patron who can vouch for your reputation and give you needed credibility.

Some foreign trade organizations in the U.S. can serve as patrons. The Korea Trade Promotion Center mentioned previously is one. Its personnel are known and respected in the country they represent, which is why they were sent to the U.S. If an FTO can't serve in this capacity, the International Trade Administration, described earlier, may direct you to a potential patron abroad.

Many U.S. firms seeking foreign patrons turn to an international bank. Citibank and Bank of America are among those with branches the world over. Irving Trust is linked to a network of correspondent banks around the globe. Barclay's, Dai-Ichi Kangyo (Japan), and the Hong Kong–Shanghai Banking Corporation are among many foreign banks with branches in New York and other U.S. cities. Their sources of native business intelligence regularly monitor the public and private sector match-making opportunities currently available.

While foreign firms may be willing to do business with you on a trial basis, expect initial orders to be small. Don't leave the U.S. with overly optimistic expectations and then feel disappointed. Non-Americans typically take a cautious, prudent, wait-and-see attitude, rather than rushing into things as Americans are prone to do. Most will probably want a long-term business relationship or none at all, justifying the extra time investment up front.

U.S. companies that pass the trial-order test will usually need a permanent local presence: an on-site office run by a native representative. He'll look after your interests in his country and see that relationships with local buyers, sellers or partners continue to run smoothly. Your local office should have a prestigious address. This shows you're sincere in your trade commitments, not a fly-by-night outfit. It conveys an image of corporate quality. And you'll need a credible image to attract qualified natives to your local staff. The best local managers may refuse to join a firm housed in a seedy building in a nonbusiness district. Would you?

The person who heads your foreign office needs the following qualifications:

• He should be a true native, not a repatriated national who was born or raised outside his own country. He should not merely be an expert on local culture. He should be the living embodiment of it.

• He should be male. Women the world over are increasingly entering local workforces, even in some Arab countries. But few non-American women are decision makers anywhere on the globe, including Western Europe. Most are receptionists, secretaries, typists, clerks, computer operators, technicians, teachers, nurses, etc., or occupy the lower to middle positions in management. Those who have risen higher are rare.

However, U.S. businesswomen have become a common sight just about everywhere. Not long ago, a Japanese businessman would have felt highly insulted if an American firm had sent a woman as its negotiating representative, and would probably have refused to see her. Today, he'll deal with her, as will businessmen from many other lands, excepting most Arabs.

But paradoxically, that same Japanese businessman who will now negotiate with an American woman will probably still refuse to deal with a qualified businesswoman of his *own* culture, even if she's representing an American firm. He's apt to consider it a sign of disrespect that a

Japanese man wasn't chosen instead. Such are the enigmas of other business cultures, and this one remains widespread.

• The male native who heads your foreign office should be old enough to deal respectably with local decision makers on the basis of age. He should have enough professional experience to have earned the credibility and trust of his peers—his credibility, or lack of it, will also be yours. A native man who is a business whiz but only twenty-six years old won't do.

• Your representative may be a government official (foreign government officials may moonlight as local representatives of U.S. firms, as in some Latin American countries), a local businessman, an attorney, a banker, an accountant, or a professional agent. But he must be someone with the ability to give you sound advice.

• A nongovernmental representative with prior government experience (preferably at the ministerial level), or who has political clout, can be useful in surmounting local government roadblocks to international commerce.

• However, an individual with strong political ties can do more harm than good if the current government may soon change through general elections or by being overthrown, and he's not in favor with the new regime. Expert analysis of the local political climate is a must in choosing an appropriate candidate to run your foreign office.

These are not questions you can pose to an interviewee and expect to get honest answers. Where do you find the best referrals? Consider sources in Brazil: the U.S. Embassy (Brasilia); the U.S. Trade Center (São Paulo); the U.S. Consulate (São Paulo); other U.S. consular offices (Belém, Pôrto Alegre, Recife, and San Salvador); the Ministry of Industry and Commerce (Rio de Janeiro); the American Chamber of Commerce for Brazil (Rio de Janeiro, São Paulo, Recife, Pôrto Alegre, and Santos); the Chamber of Commerce of Brazil (Rio de Janeiro and São Paulo, with branches in most other major cities); the American Society (Rio de Janiero and São Paulo); the Brazilian-American Society (Rio de Janeiro and other cities); and the University Club of North America (Rio de Janeiro). Analogous organizations can be found throughout the world.

• Your local representative should be more than totally fluent in the native language. He should speak it with no trace of accent and with full command of local idioms. For instance, Puerto Rican, Mexican, Venezuelan, Colombian, Bolivian, and Chilean Spanish have different accents, idioms, expressive styles, even different meanings for the same words with the same spellings. They promptly peg a person who doesn't get them precisely right as a cultural outsider.

• A suitable candidate should have sufficient command of English to discuss abstract concepts and technical details without your being confused. He may also have to serve as an interpreter and translator.

## Pre-Negotiating Trips

If you don't already have an established presence abroad, or it's your first personal visit, try to make a separate reconnaissance trip *before* the trip in which actual negotiations will occur. If what you stand to gain in potential profits does not justify the time and cost of a pre-negotiating trip, something is wrong. International negotiating is complex even when you know the facts. Without them—and you may only be able to learn them on site—the odds of success are against you.

### Trade Missions

There are two ways to make a pre-negotiating trip. One is to visit a target destination overseas as a member of a U.S. or foreign government–sponsored trade mission. The Foreign Trade Administration arranges these conclaves, as do many private U.S. and official foreign organizations. Most are located in New York or Washington, D.C. Check the telephone directories of those cities under the country name. Such outfits will send you schedules of annual events that may be suitable for your needs.

In a trade mission, representatives of different U.S. firms, often in different industries, travel together as a group to a foreign country. They are met by their non-American hosts, participate in seminars in which often tricky issues involving international trade are openly discussed, local plants are visited, native government officials are met, potential buyers, sellers, and partners on both sides are introduced, frequently amicable business relationships begin, and sometimes sales are made on the spot.

If your firm isn't a multinational giant, this does not preclude you from participating in a trade mission; it may make you a prime candidate. For example, in 1978, a 137-member American Export Development Mission, jointly sponsored by the U.S. Department of Commerce and the Japan External Trade Organization, visited Japan. The mission included three entities: a Spokespersons' Mission, which represented the group as a whole in meetings with Japanese government and business leaders; an Invest in the U.S. Mission, which made contacts with potential Japanese investors; and five industry groups from both countries—advanced scientific equipment, modern management equipment, food processing and packaging equipment, general industrial machinery, and original equipment automotive parts.

Of these five groups, on the U.S. side sixty-eight companies were represented. The majority (forty-four firms) were *totally new* to the Japanese market. In addition, most participants (forty-six firms) were smaller concerns with gross annual sales of under $50 million; fifteen had gross annual sales of *less than $15 million.*

According to then Assistant Secretary of Commerce Frank Weil, the mission was successful. He announced: "Seventy percent of the companies achieved their objectives, such as developing business prospects, making immediate sales, finding sales representatives or distributors, or exploring product sales potential. Another 15 to 20 percent accomplished some of their goals."

Moreover, the success rate of participants *new* to the Japanese market compared favorably with that of companies already established in Japan. About 75 percent were successful. This is how effective a well-run trade mission can be.

## Do-It-Yourself Reconnaissance

The alternative to a trade mission is to travel abroad on your own. Most people who do this spend a few days or a week walking around, talking with experts at local public and private sector organizations, arranging appointments for a future date, and getting a sense of the political, economic, geographic, and cultural environment in which they may deal. You can accomplish a lot traveling on your own.

• Investigate a potential partner or customer. Is the firm established? Does it have a good reputation locally? Does it pay its bills on time? Or is it a fly-by-night outfit?

• If the company seems like a good business prospect, what is the structure of its corporate hierarchy? Who are the key decision makers? Who is the person in the company with problems you're going to solve? (He may not be a top executive.) Ask about the personalities of the players. What are their likes and dislikes, personal as well as professional? Answers to such questions are often readily available if you ask at local U.S.

organizations and native business and government agencies, as well as in local American expatriate communities.

• If things go well, you may need a local representative. Ask about potential candidates. Take good prospects out to lunch. Get to know them better. Who seems most competent and reliable? Trust your instincts, but don't depend solely on them. Double and triple check everything you feel and hear. Business communities abroad are often small. Everyone knows everyone else. And people everywhere gossip. The more inquiries you make, the more you'll begin to hear the same facts and opinions repeatedly. If someone has misinformed you, it will stand out.

• You may need a professional interpreter and translator. If so, find out who is best locally for the jobs.

• Go sightseeing. Don't feel guilty about wasting company time and money. You're not. Sightseeing is important research. When actual negotiations begin, your knowledge of national and local prides may carry as much weight as your professional expertise.

• If your flight is transatlantic or transpacific, how long does it take to recover from jet lag? (It's different for everyone.) How are you affected—mentally and physically—by the local climate? By the local altitude? Mexico City, for example, is 7,000 feet above sea level. That's high. It may leave you short of breath, forcing you to slow your normal walking and working pace. And alcoholic beverages may affect your system more potently than at lower altitudes.

• Familiarize yourself with local currency. Never refer to it as "funny" money; implying that U.S. currency is the only money with any real value won't endear you to the natives. Is public transportation reliable? You should always be punctual for appointments. How long does it take to hail a taxi? It may take forever to get one—or to get where you're going due to rush-hour traffic. It may be faster to catch a subway or bus. Which hotels have the best locations for your business needs? Learn all you can about the practicalities of local life.

If making a pre-negotiating trip as a member of a trade mission or on your own is out of the question, arrive at your overseas destination two or three days before your first scheduled appointment. You still should try to get as much done as you can in what extra time you can spare—if you want to negotiate as fully prepared as possible. Which makes better sense: spending a week away from the office and losing business that might have been yours, or taking off ten days or two weeks and succeeding overseas? A few extra days may mean the difference.

## Language Lessons

If you aren't already fluent in the native tongue, is it important to take language lessons? *Yes.* Here's why:

• It's a sign of mutual respect, and appreciated by native colleagues who have taken the time to learn English.

• Many non-Americans who speak English as a second or third language speak better English than they actually understand, especially when it comes to the often subtle nuances of the language used in bargaining sessions. This can lead to stalled negotiations and contract disputes, because each party *thought* it knew what the other meant and didn't.

• Even foreign businessmen who understand English as well as they speak it may have wives who don't speak a word. A wife may be the power behind the throne anywhere in the world, even in "macho" Latin countries, particularly when the firm is family owned. In social settings, she had better not feel left out of English-only conversations. You may need her on your side to make a sale.

Most executives who consider language lessons wonder:

• *How many lessons must I take?* It varies with the individual. You should take at least enough lessons to learn polite, commonly used words, phrases, and idioms, and master their pronunciation well enough so that natives understand what you're trying to say. But the more you can converse, the better. With competitors after the same business, contracts can be won or lost on this basis alone.

• *Do I need a "human" instructor?* Yes. According to Elio Boccitto, president of Berlitz, very few people can learn to correctly speak a foreign tongue solely from tapes and texts. Tapes and texts are meant to enhance classroom instruction, not replace it.

• *Am I too busy to take language lessons?* Many executives voice this excuse. But you have time for lessons if you have time for lunch.

• *But aren't language lessons dull?* They may have been when you took them in high school or college. But now your variety of options are much wider and more enjoyable.

To gain conversational fluency fast in a foreign tongue, U.S. businesspeople are taking language lessons in a host of untraditional ways. Some check the Yellow Pages for a free-lance instructor. Others, particularly those with long commutes by car to work, are ordering self-

instruction courses to play on tape decks at home and on the road—
exercise in futility though this may be. A few large companies have even
set up in-house language departments. Most, however, send executives
to special schools designed to meet the immediate needs of the international
traveler or expatriate-to-be.

Some commercial schools are big in size as well as reputation. The
Language Lab, for instance, has one facility in New York with more than
seventy instructors on call. Madame Dulac, also in New York, has several
schools in the area. Michel Thomas, with luminaries like Woody Allen
and Warren Beatty among his graduates, has opened Language Centers
in New York, Washington, D.C., Miami, Beverly Hills, Encino, and
London. The industry giants, Berlitz and Inlingua, each with more than
200 schools worldwide (with at least one in most major U.S. cities), serve
lists of Fortune 500 clientele that are—well, nearly 500 companies long.

At Berlitz, the languages in highest demand are English (taught as
a second language to non-Americans working in the U.S.), Spanish, and
French, followed by Italian and German. Next come Indo-European tongues
like Greek and Russian. In the past decade, Japanese, Mandarin Chinese,
and Arabic have gained in popularity, reflecting global business-travel
patterns. But no language, the top schools maintain, is beyond their teaching ken. If you need Tagalog or Urdu and an instructor isn't in-house,
someone will be found, trained in the school's teaching methods, and put
to work.

To executives pressed for time, what commercial schools offer that
college courses usually don't are learning speed and proven results. As a
rule, programs for beginners are initially prepackaged, then customized
to individual needs, with job-specific vocabulary included. While they
can span any length of time, from a weekend to a year or more, most run
from several weeks to several months. The variables are individual ability,
the difficulty of the language (Oriental tongues may take twice as long as
European languages to master), how often a student attends forty-five- to
sixty-minute classes, and the degree of fluency sought—from being able
to direct a taxi driver to holding your own in social chitchat to negotiating
contracts. Be forewarned, you need a lot of lessons to negotiate on your
own.

Private or semiprivate lessons can generally be taken at a school or
on company premises. Some schools will send a teacher or teaching team
across the country or the world on request, as Michel Thomas has done
for Westinghouse in Madrid, where the Americans needed to learn Spanish
and the Spaniards English so they could work together. In addition, many

schools offer variations of what Berlitz terms "total immersion." You attend classes full time and become fluent in two to six weeks.

But each school has its own special way of serving corporate clients. While some combination of texts and tapes usually supplements conversational instruction, the Language Lab also uses foreign-language newspapers, magazines, and technical documents to build executive skills. With Madame Dulac you can even take lessons over the phone. Some departments of decentralized Citibank send their executives to Berlitz or Inlingua. Others use Denise Hamon, who has an office at corporate headquarters in New York, where she teaches bankers bound for French-speaking countries. Her company, Executive Language Services, serves firms in other industries as well.

Michel Thomas offers unparalleled learning speed. A noted philologist who speaks eleven languages, he asserts that without books, drills, memorization, or homework, his language centers can teach you to speak, read, and write a Western language in ten days flat—or an Oriental language in about twice that. Hard to believe? Among his graduates are executives from Boeing, Chase Manhattan, and other corporate giants, and they give his program rave reviews.

The international networks of Berlitz and Inlingua offer a benefit that smaller outfits can't: Students who start school in the U.S. can continue their lessons right where they left off in most major cities around the globe. Check a telephone book for locations near you.

## Interpreters and Translators

While globetrotting executives are taking language lessons in record numbers, the corporate need for *experts* who can speak and write foreign tongues perfectly is more pressing than ever. Many firms turn to the same language schools for interpretation and/or translation services. Others contact professional organizations like the American Association of Language Specialists (TAALS) and the American Society of Interpreters (both in Washington, D.C.), and the American Translators Association in Ossining, New York, with members nationwide.

Still, experts maintain, most companies that should use professional help fail to seek it out. While multinational giants like IBM and ITT say they generally rely on native personnel to do their interpreting, Barbara Roder, who often works at the United Nations and is president of TAALS, explains that contrary to popular myth, simply being bilingual does not qualify someone to interpret. Interpreting, she explains, is not merely a mechanical process of converting one sentence in language A into the same sentence in language B. Rather, it's a complex art in which thoughts and idioms that have no obvious analogs from tongue to tongue—or words that have multiple meanings—must quickly be transformed in such a way that the message is clearly and accurately expressed to the listener. At one international conference, Roder recalls, an American speaker said: "You can't make a silk purse out of a sow's ear," which meant nothing to the Spanish audience. Her interpretation was, "A monkey in a silk dress is still a monkey"—an idiom the Spanish understood and that conveyed the same idea.

There are two types of interpreters, simultaneous and consecutive, each requiring different talents. The former, sitting in an isolated booth, usually at a large multilingual conference, speaks to listeners wearing headphones, interpreting what a foreign-language speaker says as he says it—actually a sentence behind—a kind of mental gymnastics so taxing that simultaneous interpreters work in pairs on half-hour shifts, enabling one to recuperate while the other concentrates.

Consecutive interpreters are the ones most international negotiators use. They are mainly employed for smaller meetings without sound booths, headphones, and other high-tech gear. Equally taxing in its own way, consecutive interpretation also requires two-person teams. A foreign speaker says his piece while the interpreter, using a special shorthand, takes notes and during a pause, tells the client what was said. Every half-hour or so, a replacement then takes over.

A good teacher may not be a good interpreter or a crack simultaneous interpreter may be less than best at interpreting consecutively, and vice versa. And none of them, adds Arthur South, international marketing manager of Technical Translation International (TTI), a London-based firm with a New York office, may fill the bill as a translator. In fact, finding the right translator may be the most difficult job of all. He must not only be totally fluent in two languages but also write expertly in the appropriate technical style and have professional knowledge of the field a given document concerns—be it licensing, marketing, or law—not just in the country of the "source" language but in the country of the "target" tongue as well.

What happens when bilingual amateurs try their hand at translation is often a comedy of errors. General Motors, introducing the Chevy Nova in Latin America, was unaware that in Spanish, *no va* means "it doesn't go." Pepsico, out to conquer Taiwan, used a line that worked well here: "Come alive with Pepsi." But translated into Chinese the slogan became:

"Pepsi brings your ancestors back from the grave."

The cost of hiring a pro to avoid such mistakes can run from 15 or 20 cents a word for a short, nontechnical letter to six or seven figures for translating a set of volumes on building nuclear power plants from English into Arabic. Tracking down what may be one of three people in the world completely qualified to do an arcane job—someone, say, who is a native speaker of Mandarin, writes in English like James Michener, and knows the carpet-tufting business inside out—is the job of outfits like TTI and the Intercontinental Bureau of Translators and Interpreters (New York, San Francisco).

The most significant change in language services, say the experts, is not computer software—as many people think—but one of growing corporate consciousness. As more American firms expand their commercial interests beyond national borders, their executives are realizing that the ability to speak, read, and write English alone is no longer enough to survive in an increasingly competitive business world.

## How to Make the Most of Interpreters and Translators

Don't put off hiring one until the last minute. As in any other profession, there are some of top-notch practitioners, but the majority are so-so. It takes time to find someone who is first-rate. Also, interpreters and translators do their best work if it isn't a rush job, and rush jobs nearly always cost more for a service that already isn't cheap.

Even though it may seem costly—a top interpreter, for instance, may charge up to $200 a day, plus expenses—hire a pro. The English-speaking Japanese manager of your Tokyo office is not a pro. Many Japanese words have multiple meanings, and many Japanese idioms have no easy analogs in English. How well your bilingual manager can bridge the communications gap between two highly complex, often subtle, languages is anyone's guess. As in other areas of life, be prepared to pay for the quality you expect to receive.

Interpreters complain that too often they are not filled in on enough—or sometimes any—of the details prompting a meeting in which they will participate. Corporate clients commonly assume that all interpeters must do is to translate exactly what they hear and that's it. Hiring an interpreter is like hiring an attorney or an accountant. For one to give you the best possible service, he must know all relevant details of a meeting agenda. Meet with your interpreter beforehand, consider him part of your negotiating team, and brief him fully. Members of major industry associations observe a professional code of confidentiality, just like any other professional you hire to advise you on a confidential matter. Even though you may be meeting an interpreter for the first time, you can feel secure that company secrets are safe.

Interpreters should always be debriefed after each meeting. Body language, subtle shifts in tone of voice, or words and phrases that have several meanings, may signal clues to true communication that's not being expressed either by the foreign speaker or your interpreter's translation of what he says. Sometimes an interpreter has no choice but to withhold the truth until later on, in order to save face for all concerned. For instance, if a Japanese executive replies "It is difficult" in Japanese, your interpreter turns to you and says in English that you were just given an unequivocal "no," and then *his* interpreter translates the English remark, causing your Japanese colleague to lose face, it may jeopardize your business relationship.

A top translator is also expensive. Says Andrew Salad, marketing manager of TTI in New York, clients typically come to a translation bureau with a preconceived idea of what a given job will cost—which, of course, is usually low—with no comprehension of the work involved. Then, when they're given a fair but informed estimate, they're taken aback. A first-rate translation should be judged by its quality, not its cost. Every work of translation is also a piece of public relations. It's *your* corporate image, for better or worse.

## Cross-Cultural Training

Over 100,000 U.S. executives and their families are stationed overseas on extended assignment, and millions more are making short but frequent business trips to foreign parts. As a result, a little-known cottage industry is gaining increasing attention from Corporate America: cross-cultural training. Its purpose is to groom U.S. executives to negotiate, work, and live successfully around the world.

Cross-cultural training is not new. It was begun by the U.S. State Department after World War II to train its diplomats and consular officials bound for foreign soil, where the methods, manners, and motivations for doing business are a world apart from ours.

In the early 1960s, the Peace Corps developed programs of its own, because it was sending well-intentioned but culturally untutored advisors to Third World countries, initially with ineffective results. For example, a U.S. medical doctor and a civil engineer were dispatched to an Arab village where the residents suffered a high incidence of dysentery. The physician diagnosed polluted water from an ancient drinking well as the cause. The engineer proceeded to dig a new well with healthy water. But the villagers refused to drink from it, for its creation violated their notion of man's relationship to nature, which was one of harmony and integration, not of arbitrary manipulation of the environment to better serve mankind— a concept of American pragmatism that's far from universally approved.

The problem was only solved when the Peace Corps advisors stopped trying to impose "foreign" American values on the peoples of other cultures, sought to understand the Arab point of view, and addressed the problem with that knowledge paramount in mind.

The next logical step was to move from the cross-cultural training of State Department and Peace Corps personnel to those of multinational corporations who were encountering similar problems in trying to train, manage, motivate, and gain cooperation from their native staffs overseas. And yet, in the more than twenty years since, only a few hundred of some 3,500 U.S. multinational firms are committed to the cross-cultural training of their managers bound for foreign soil.

Meanwhile, the moment they step off the plane, these managers face many problems that cross-cultural training is designed to solve. Multimillion-dollar contracts are lost to foreign or American competitors who *have* been trained and know how to play by local rules. Cultural barriers to communication result in stalled negotiations, contract disputes, unintended insults, and employee enmity from native personnel, crippling productivity. Moreover, because most executives and their families receive no cross-cultural training, they may be unable to adapt to life outside the U.S. The result is often depression leading to alcoholism, drug abuse, family unrest, and divorce, forcing their early return. The irreclaimable relocation costs of early returnees can set a company back over $300,000 per family.

One reason U.S. firms have been slow to embrace cross-cultural training is lack of understanding of how the programs work. Most offer language lessons and include classes on native history, politics, religion, business customs, social etiquette, and such, supplemented by audiovisual presentations and readings that show trainees what to expect. Briefings by foreign nationals and recently returned expatriates are also standard features.

But the core of the best programs is videotaped role-play exercises. In these, trainees, playing members of different cultures, interact with each other (or with actual natives) in carefully designed business and social conflict situations they are apt to encounter abroad. Their filmed performances are then viewed on screen and professionally critiqued.

Finding out how role-play exercises work is no easy task. Designed to help private clients solve classified problems, they may be trade secrets. Paul and Ann Pedersen, who have served as cross-cultural consultants for the World Bank, reveal one exercise called "Outside Expert." In this scenario, managers who are designated outside experts leave the room. Those remaining become "natives" of a fictitious culture with a curious rule: If someone smiles when asking them a question, they must answer yes, even if they know the answer is wrong; if the questioner does not smile, their reply must be no.

When readmitted, the outside experts must figure out the unspoken ways in which this make-believe culture operates. While questioning the natives, they usually end up posing the same question twice in a row to the same person, one time unconsciously smiling but not the other, and getting a yes answer first then a no as a result. This baffles most trainees.

Solving the mystery of the contradictory replies is the goal, and the predicament is not as farfetched as it may seem. Says Paul Pedersen, who has lived in Taiwan, in many Oriental cultures people will tell you what they think you want to hear—often based on nonverbal cues, like smiling—whether or not it happens to be true. They are not trying to be devious, just polite, based on a very un-American concept of what politeness means. An American dealing in a foreign culture with an infinite number of tricky rules must know how to identify, analyze, and resolve such seeming paradoxes to effectively do his job.

The acceptance of cross-cultural training has also been slowed by program length. In fact, according to Stephen H. Rhinesmith, consultant to New York–based Moran Stahl & Boyer, the largest management consulting firm in what it terms "business mobility," how long a program runs may depend less on the complexity of the problems it must solve than on how much time a company will give its managers off from work. At MSB, most requests are for three- to six-day programs. The American University's Business Council for International Understanding Institute (BCIU) in Washington, D.C., now twenty-six years old, offers four types of standard-format programs that are customized for clients. Area and country studies are for expatriates-to-be. They range from three to twelve days, depending on whether language lessons are included. A three- to five-day program called "Assessing Alternatives for Working and Living Overseas" helps managers and their families who are considering a foreign assignment decide if they are really doing the right thing. For U.S.-based business travelers, there's a three- to five-day program in international negotiating. And a program in protocol, for corporate meeters and greeters of foreign guests in the U.S., takes two days. Going the other way, the American Graduate School of International Management's International Council to Management (Intercom) in Glendale, Arizona, has trained Japan-bound Westinghouse Electric engineers for fourteen weeks, and has designed programs for other clients that ran for the better part of a year.

However, for most trainers, programs running longer than a week or two are rare. Another reason why cross-cultural training has been slow to catch on is cost. At BCIU, the cost of training averages about $200 per person per day, but that's low. Most outfits charge closer to $1,000 per day for each participant. That's simply for tuition; it does not include other expenses (transportation, food, and lodging) if trainees must travel to an out-of-town location. Total it all up, multiply it by a week or two— even for just one trainee, let alone several—and you get a pretty hefty bill, particularly at a time when many companies are trying to tighten their training and business-travel budgets.

Still, a growing list of multinational clients apparently feels the time and money is well spent. Intercom, for example, has a client roster over 200 companies long, from Abbott Laboratories to W.R. Grace. Adds C. Wolcott Parker, Intercom's director, most are repeat customers. BCIU, which monitors the progress of its graduates every six months wherever they are stationed abroad, compiles statistics on its success. Says Carol Thomas, associate director: "The number of our graduates who return home early remains below 1.2 percent worldwide, compared with the 33 to 68 percent failure rate common for international personnel who haven't had our training."

One solution to the problems of time and cost is that offered by Brooklyn, New York–based Ellen Raider International. While most cross-cultural training is customized for private clients, Raider conducts a three-day public program in international negotiating, with individuals from different firms in the same class. The complete cost of the program is about $1,000, making it affordable to smaller companies as well as multinational giants. It's held several times a year in different cities; New York and Brussels are on the 1985 schedule.

But whether cross-cultural trainers will attract significantly greater numbers of corporate clients remains to be seen. (Of the nearly 100,000 U.S. firms now engaged in one form or another of international trade, only a fraction of one percent have an ongoing commitment to cross-cultural training.) Be this as it may, experts expect corporate requests for programs to increase, if slowly. But it may not be until the year 2000 (if then) that some sort of cultural preparation will be the rule rather than the exception for most managers who deal abroad.

You're already getting a headstart on the international competition by reading this book. If you choose a well-run program, cross-cultural training is a highly recommended next step.

## How to Pick a Good Program

Some people have been training managers cross-culturally for over two decades. But most firms have been in business only for a couple of years or less. They may boast names that sound established—with "Institute" or "Center" in the title—but often they consist of one or two people with office space and a phone. While the value of cross-cultural training is not in doubt among international business sophisticates, check out a few organizations as early as possible before you sign up with one. Find out how long each has been in business, how its programs work, how long they take to design and run, what the trainers' qualifications are, how a program is priced, and which companies have been clients. Ask for names and telephone numbers at those firms who can tell you about results firsthand. If you get wishy-washy answers to questions like these, chances are you'll get that sort of program, too.

## A Word about Women—for Men

Many American male decision makers believe that a female executive, however qualified, is a risky choice to represent the firm in overseas negotiations because of her sex. This myth has two common roots. One is the "Weaker Sex Syndrome," which holds that women are more fragile emotionally than men and are likely to burst into tears under the pressures that international negotiators often face. In addition, without the protection of a male companion, the helpless little ladies will fall easy prey to foreign wolves in negotiators' clothing. The second cause for mistaken concern is a misunderstanding of how male chauvinism operates abroad. Often American men point to Arab countries—where women aren't usually tolerated as negotiators—and proceed to generalize from the Middle East to the rest of the world.

It's true that native women who are corporate or governmental decision makers are exceptional just about everywhere but in the U.S., where nearly 20 percent of managers are female. It's also true that to send a woman as a chief negotiator is generally unwise in the Arab world (although women are sometimes acceptable as subordinate team members). Yet K-Mart Trading Services, with years of international business dealings, broke the rule and did just that. K-Mart sent marketing director Marjorie Alfus to Saudi Arabia—the spiritual leader and most conservative of all Arab nations regarding the status of women—as its chief negotiator. She succeeded in her mission. When it comes to matters cultural, exceptions to conventional wisdom abound.

Elsewhere overseas, if a woman in your firm had the intelligence, ambition, dedication, and guts to get where she is in the corporate hierarchy today—and if she goes abroad cross-culturally aware—you need lose no sleep over the choice simply because of her sex.

In Western Europe, American businesswomen are still considered a bit unorthodox. But if your representative really knows her stuff, this misgiving is quickly dispelled. Frankly, Western Europeans tend to be more put off by the often extreme *youth* of American negotiators, regardless of sex, than they are by female negotiators per se.

As for Latin men making passes, yes, some are bound to try. But it's doubtful that a female executive rose to an important position in your firm by *not* knowing how to handle men. Truth to tell, an American woman who can charm a Latin man may be more effective as a negotiator than a male counterpart with equal qualifications. Latin men appreciate charm; few American men can be called charming.

What about the peoples of East Asia? Female negotiators are still not a common sight in Japan and South Korea today. Not long ago, Japanese and Koreans, for whom after-hours drinking is often an important part of the negotiating process, considered this "baring of souls" in a relaxed, informal setting as a male-only event. That's changed. After decades of studying, living, and working in the U.S., and monitoring American trends from afar, Japanese and Koreans are well aware that many women in our country wield decision-making power. And they have come to accept it. American women who travel to East Asia on business missions often go out drinking with the boys, hold their own quite well, win their colleagues over with their personalities and professionalism, and achieve their goals.

In the People's Republic of China, it's official Communist Party policy that all "comrades," regardless of sex, are equal. Women and men get equal pay for equal work—which isn't always true in the U.S. Make no mistake. China is no bed of roses for our negotiators. But the many problems an American woman will face are the same ones that await American men. They stem from differences in culture and political ideology. The negotiator's sex is irrelevant.

Southeast Asia's Chinese capitalists probably pose the least problems for American women in the region. These savvy businesspeople usually deal comfortably with U.S. executives of either sex, and native industries like fashion and public relations are often dominated by Chinese women, even in top management.

## Going Native

Since this is a book about understanding and adapting to the business and social behavior of other cultures, it's fair to ask: to what extent?

You should know enough about local business and social rules so that the natives can plainly see you've done your homework and are trying to be respectful—something very un-American in the experience of far too many of the world's businesspeoples.

You should know enough about local etiquette so as not to inadvertently insult your native hosts.

You should know enough about native body language, as well as native words and expressions that—even translated into English—may have multiple meanings, in order to choose the correct meaning within the context of the conversation. This is the only way you can truly communicate, not just go through the motions.

Businesspeople the world over may try to use tactical ploys to get the upper hand in negotiations. You should know what the favored ones are and how to counter them.

You should know how local time works. Otherwise, you may make unrealistic scheduling demands, guaranteed to be missed despite what you're promised.

Beyond basic considerations like these, don't try to "go native." Be yourself. That's what businesspeople everywhere expect and desire. If, for instance, you wear a "Mao suit" when dealing in Beijing, you'll seem as clownish as a Chinese visiting your U.S. office wearing an Apache war bonnet.

The more respect for local customs you show, the more you'll be forgiven for the occasional faux pas you're destined to make. If you show no understanding and respect, every little molehill may become a mountain of cultural insult.

A word of warning: If you show a non-American that you know

more about his culture than other Americans have done in the past, he may assume that you have more cultural savvy than you actually do—which can cause misunderstandings during negotiations. Often, when you show that you've done your cultural homework, a native host will pay you a compliment on your politeness, respect, wisdom, or whatever. The appropriate response is one of overtly expressed *humility*. Thank him for his compliment, but assure him that you really know very little about his culture as yet, though you hope to learn a good deal more in the future, hopefully from him. Not only will this be the truth, but your honesty and sincerity will elicit even more of his respect.

## Business Cards

Not every American has his business cards translated into the native tongue on the reverse side, but most do. It's never wrong to have this done; it may be an insult *not* to do it.

This is also true for places like West Germany, Holland, and the Scandinavian countries, where most everyone speaks at least some—often excellent—English in major cities. But as more and more Americans venture into the countryside seeking untapped markets, they find that English fluency dramatically drops. It may be spoken, understood, and read poorly if at all.

Your U.S. corporate title may have a different analog in another language. If you hire a top translator, he'll know how to make the change accurately. Specifically request that it be done.

Don't upgrade your U.S. title to make yourself seem more important to non-Americans than you really are at home. Sooner or later, they'll learn the truth, and when they do, they won't trust you anymore. Nor should they.

In dual-language countries, such as Belgium, have your business cards translated into both languages on the reverse side.

Some international airlines and most major hotel chains will do the translating and printing for you, often at bargain rates compared to the cost of using a top translator and printer in the U.S. Two problems arise from trying to save money this way. You may not get an absolutely accurate translation. And you can *count* on getting a printing job inferior to that on the English side of your card. This mystifies many non-American business sophisticates. "The English side of the card is beautifully printed," they say. "The side with *our* language on it looks rubber stamped. Why do you Americans bother to have your business cards translated as a sign of respect if you are then only going to insult us with such poor quality printing?" Good question.

If your U.S. business cards contain a company slogan—such as "Progress is our most important product"—have both sides reprinted without it. This is something non-Americans often point to as a sign of typical American over-aggressiveness: Even with our business cards we try to sell.

In the U.S., exchanging business cards is an informal gesture; sometimes it isn't even done. Elsewhere in the world, it's usually a formal courtesy, and to overlook it is highly impolite. If you present your business card and don't receive one in return, ask for it. Especially in developing countries, where postal and telephone systems may be less than the best, you wouldn't believe how difficult and time consuming it can be to try to track down a foreign colleague's correct address, telephone number or telex number when you're back in the U.S. Also, peoples' names can be tongue twisters to say and mind benders to remember. Exchanging business cards makes this easier on you both.

International etiquette dictates that dual-language cards be presented native-language side up.

Bring plenty of cards. In much of the world, it's customary to give one to each person to whom you are introduced, even if the introduction is merely a courtesy that has nothing to do with business. In many places, it's polite to give your card to everyone within eyeshot: secretaries, receptionists, clerks, plant foremen, workers—you name it—as well as to each member of the non-American negotiating team. Bring at least fifty to a hundred cards for each week you plan to be abroad. It's better to have some left over than to suddenly find yourself short. This can create a poor first impression. First impressions are hard to change.

If you're dealing with a foreign negotiating *team* rather than a single individual, when seated at a conference table spread out everyone's business cards in front of you in an order corresponding to the seat of each person in the room. Non-American business cards are usually translated into English on the reverse side as well. This way you'll know exactly whom you're addressing and who's talking to you throughout your meetings.

## Business Proposals

The writing skills of many Americans leave something to be desired. If you count yourself among them and your firm employs an advertising or public relations agency, write the first draft of the proposal yourself, then have an agency copywriter polish it up. Copywriters are skilled at writing plain English and control their use of the language to achieve a specific objective, be it selling a product or service, improving a corporate image, or simply communicating clearly.

If the first language of your overseas destination is not English, your business proposal should be translated into the native tongue. However, a translator's job is to keep his translation as close in content and meaning to the English original as he possibly can. If the English text is so poorly written that even another American would have trouble understanding it, it's harder to produce a translation in plain Spanish, Japanese or Arabic that non-Americans can understand.

In the view of foreign readers, American business proposals often sell too hard. They begin with a blunt offer of commercial opportunity to be discussed at length in the document. Instead, the preferred approach is to open your proposal with a soft, low-key statement of what your company is all about: when it was founded, how it has evolved, what products or services it offers (all of them, not merely those concerning the transaction at hand), how it fits into its industry domestically and internationally, and last but not least, what its corporate philosophy is. A corporate philosophy should be the expression of a societal ideal; making money is not such an ideal, even though it may be the truth. "Progress is our most important product"; "Better living through chemistry"; "Reach out and touch someone"—these are corporate philosophies non-Americans can relate to when explained. An old slogan of Braniff Airlines—"If you've got it, flaunt it"—is a turnoff overseas.

Your description of your company should be concise. Keep down use of adjectives, and delete *all* superlative adjectives. Your firm is *not* the biggest and best in the field for international negotiating purposes. Rather, the size of your company is A, and the sizes of your closest competitors are B, C, and D. Be objective, not subjective. Don't draw conclusions for non-Americans as you might when selling here. They resent it. They can put two and two together, and many feel their intelligence has been insulted by Americans who assume they can't.

Never knock the competition in a business proposal or at any other time. That's considered typical American boorishness the world over. Savants take a line or two to actually praise competitors for something meritorious that doesn't conflict with what they're trying to sell. Non-Americans take this as a sign of honesty, sincerity, integrity, and reassuring confidence. These are the pillars of trust.

Keep your business proposal as brief as possible. Foreign decision makers enjoy wading through inch-thick documents about as much as Americans do. An effective business proposal merely needs to whet the appetite of a potential customer. It should not attempt to sign, seal, and deliver the deal. Beyond our borders, a document alone is rarely enough to make a sale, regardless of its completeness.

American business proposals sometimes reveal too much. Some shrewd foreigners may take the oversupply of classified information you generously provide, facts that should have been saved for bargaining points in face-to-face negotiations, and implement the proposed project without you. Never reveal so much information that you're no longer needed, particularly when it comes to technological secrets. That your research and development are protected by U.S. patent or copyright may mean nothing in a foreign court of law.

## Biographical Sketches

Dealing successfully abroad is usually predicated on establishing trust first. Building trust takes time. While it rarely happens overnight, a simple, effective way to speed up the process is to include a brief biography of each member of your negotiating team. These biographies can accompany your business proposal or be separately sent well before your departure date. Points to cover:

• How old are you?

• If you're a woman who calls herself. J.P. Smith, or has a first name that might be a man's, state your sex.

• What universities and graduate schools have you attended? What academic degrees do you hold?

• When did you begin your professional career? Have you changed careers? If so, what else have you done? Which companies have you worked for in the past? What did they do? What were your job responsibilities when you were working there?

• When did you join the firm you now represent? What was your first job title? What is your current title? Where do you fit into the corporate hierarchy? What are your current job responsibilities?

• Are you married? If your spouse works, what does he or she do? Do you have children? If so, what are their sexes and ages? If any now attends college, what is he or she studying to be?

• What are your hobbies, your cultural interests, your favorite sports?

Do you belong to any civic organizations? If so, which ones? What do they do?

• Have you received any awards, citations, commendations, or other form of public recognition? If so, for what?

• Have you ever had anything professionally published? It doesn't matter what it is: a poem, a cookbook, a technical study. If so, mention it. If you wrote a published article, include a photocopy. If you were quoted by name in someone else's article—whether in the *Wall Street Journal* or the *Ladies' Home Journal*—also include a photocopy, with your name highlighted by a yellow marker.

Don't turn this into a resumé; it's a biography. It should consist of sentences and paragraphs, not itemized lists. While short, it should convey the friendly tone of a warm, personal letter. Many non-Americans will begin to compile their own dossiers on you containing just this sort of information well before they meet you. They want to know exactly who they will deal with before the dealing starts. By helping them out, you score points for being smart, sincere, foresightful, and polite.

## Collateral Materials

Collateral materials—technical information, catalogs, price schedules, ads, promotional literature, press releases, etc.—should be translated and printed in the local language as well as in English, even in countries where English is widely spoken but is not the mother tongue.

In dual-language countries, collateral materials should be printed in both languages. Most U.S. company literature is divided into two or three horizontal or vertical columns on each page, with the English text first, and the corresponding translations in other languages second and third. This is wrong. In dual-language countries, for instance, the most widely spoken language should come first, the second native tongue should come next, and the English version should come *last*. Abroad, the language of the land is more important than English, not the other way around.

British, Irish, Australian, and New Zealander English are *not* American English. This goes beyond minor spelling differences like "color" and "colour." That anyone can figure out. But our oft-used idioms—"no way," "bottom line," "in the ball park," "throwing a curve," "piece of cake," "Monday through Friday," "P&L statement," "R&D," "ASAP," etc.—may mean nothing to English-speaking non-Americans. Collateral materials designed for other English-speaking countries usually require translation, too.

Don't use cheap paper. Cheap paper is as much a statement of your firm's reputation, the quality of its wares, and even your personal character as the information conveyed in the literature itself.

Don't use a second-rate printer. Muddy or off-register photographs, illustrations, and type look just like what they are: sloppy. Your production manager—or that of your advertising or public relations agency—should be *at the plant* when the printing is being done to ensure this doesn't happen.

Don't take illustrations selected for foreigners to view for granted. Often they contain hidden insults. Have an expert—a language specialist, an anthropologist at a local university, a cross-cultural trainer, a non-American expatriate living in your area, *someone* who knows what he's looking at—examine them for you. You may be surprised to learn the secret meanings of the most seemingly innocent of pictures.

## Audiovisual Aids

Unless you're negotiating a multimillion-dollar transaction involving large negotiating teams on both sides, audiovisual aids are probably more often a hassle than a help in making your case overseas. Use them only if they serve a purpose for which there is absolutely no substitute. If you can put it in a report, include it on a flipchart, or show it in an illustration, do that instead.

If audiovisual aids are a must, in addition to film reels and slide trays—with superimposed words and voice-over narrations translated into the local language—you'll need the following items from home:

- A slide or film projector
- A spare projector bulb (the one in the machine may burn out)
- An electric current converter
- An outlet adapter
- An extra-long extension cord
- To play it safe, a screen

The hassles don't stop there. The slides or films should be on your lap, under your seat, or in an overhead compartment on the plane. If you check them with your luggage and they get lost or broken, you're stuck. But you'll probably still have to check the rest of the gear needed to put on the show, so it must be specially packed in padded cases or crates to reduce the possibility of breakage en route. Even that's no guarantee it will actually arrive in working order.

Don't assume that even a major firm abroad has such equipment on hand. Many won't, or it won't be compatible with your slide trays or film reels—even in Japan, where much gadgetry available in the U.S. is for export only and has different specifications from that sold locally. Most international hotel chains advertise that their establishments around the world stock the equipment you'll require. But what you may find is that a given hotel has a couple of slide projectors for a thousand guests, and a full schedule of meetings and conventions that have first claim to them. Or the equipment will be out of order when you need it.

## Corporate Giveaways

It's acceptable to give logo gifts in most of the world, but it isn't usually mandatory.

If you want to give logo gifts, bring plenty, enough to distribute to everyone who'll be present at negotiations abroad. If you're a gift or two short, the nonrecipients will feel justifiably slighted.

Your corporate giveaway had better not be a piece of junk. A key ring with a plastic tag, a coffee mug, a tote bag, a tee shirt, or a baseball-like cap are junk. *Any* item made of plastic should be something special if it has your company name on it.

While a logo gift should not *look* cheap, it should not be overly expensive. This smacks of bribery. Bribery will destroy a trust relationship. A gift in the $15 to $50 price range is safe.

The most effective logo gifts somehow symbolize what your company does. One U.S. importer of nails from China gives nail-shaped pens as gifts to the Chinese. *He* knows what he's doing.

Logo gifts should be pragmatic rather than merely decorative. Something handy for an office desk or a business suit pocket is a safe bet. Among cognoscenti, favorite logo gifts include:

- Quality writing implements
- Digital desk clocks with LED displays. These come in every size and shape imaginable, and they can be designed to flash your logo as well as the time
- Address and appointment books. Leather is preferable to vinyl
- Telephone files like those made by Rolodex
- Electric pencil sharpeners
- Pocket calculators, or any of the array of calculatorlike devices now available that do everything from count calories to keep golf scores

- Writing portfolios that hold legal pads
- Executive rulers with built-in calculators, clocks, calendars, thermometers, etc.
- Compartmentalized desk organizers
- Retractable tape measures that come in a variety of classy cases
- Utility knives, like Swiss Army knives, or knives with built-in grooming aids, or "gentlemen's knives" (these are simply fancy pocket knives), or letter openers
- Microcassette recorders for making oral memos

This is but a sampling of possibilities. There are dozens of others. Those which aren't universally acceptable for cultural reasons are noted in the country-specific chapters. One item that's universally *unacceptable* is a wall decoration. Wall decorations are matters of personal taste. Until you get to know an overseas colleague, you can't know what his personal tastes are. Moreover, many offices of the world don't have walls, for reasons to be discussed.

If you'd like to give a logo gift and don't already have one, or feel the one you have won't do, check the Yellow Pages under "Premium Goods." Premium suppliers will send you color catalogs illustrating a sizable selection of corporate giveaways, many of them unsuitable, but you'll usually find some winners mixed in with the rest. When studying a catalog of premium possibilities, remember: If it isn't something that's apt to be in sight when a foreign colleague is sitting at his desk, carried in his pocket, or used by him once or twice in a normal week, it's the wrong gift.

Even a logo gift meeting all these criteria is a poor choice if it's overly ostentatious. It won't look good to the recipient's colleagues. In this context, "overly ostentatious" means too big, too gaudy, too weird-looking—like some paperweights—*too* anything.

Before purchasing a supply of logo gifts from a premium dealer, find out where the items were made. You may end up giving a Japanese colleague something that his firm makes for U.S. export, which doesn't make you seem too smart. Worse, you may end up giving a Korean colleague something made in Japan. As you'll soon discover abroad, many peoples of other nations are less than enamored with their geographical neighbors. It's better to give no gift at all than one the recipient finds offensive. Choose carefully.

## Non-Logo Gifts

Is it appropriate to bring a non-logo gift on your first trip overseas? Yes, if you'd like, but again, you don't have to do it; it isn't expected or required.

With the exception of Arab and other countries with predominately Muslim populations, the most popular non-logo gift the world over is probably Scotch: *good* Scotch. Johnny Walker Black and Chivas Regal are the brands that show you mean business. Don't buy anything more exotic or expensive but not as well-known. A recipient unfamiliar with a costlier but less well publicized brand may mistakenly think you're being cheap. Buy either of the two internationally preferred labels at an airport duty-free shop rather than locally abroad, where a liter will run forty or fifty dollars—precisely why a gift of Scotch is usually well-received.

When meeting a native counterpart for the first time, don't give him the Scotch right away. Save it till the end of your trip to present as a parting gift—a sign you feel that negotiations are off to an auspicious start. If negotiations clearly have *not* gotten off to a good start, don't give him the Scotch. It may be misinterpreted as a bribe. Drink it yourself, or give it to someone at home.

After Scotch, the most popular, safest, and appreciated gift the world over is something that defines where you live in the U.S. Vermont residents, for instance, can give maple syrup in handsome jugs. People from Wisconsin or Oregon can present gift packs of cheese. New Mexicans can bring Navajo crafts. Every state has something inexpensive for which it's well known not just here but abroad, too. As such gifts are conversation pieces, use them in conversation to describe yourself as a unique individual; this discourages non-Americans from stereotyping you as a typical American. Famous homemade items are suitable substitutes for logo gifts and may be more effective as mnemonic devices. It's better to give maple syrup or cheese than a piece of junk with your company name on it.

Often overlooked, yet a really smart gift idea, is a subscription to a monthly consumer magazine like *Reader's Digest* (see "Gifts" in the chapter on China), a business magazine like *Fortune*, or a trade magazine. The price is right, and each month the recipient is reminded of you, which is the reason for giving business gifts in the first place. Many magazines can arrange for foreign delivery. Check the masthead for a telephone number to call for details. Bring a copy of the magazine with a gift card explaining that the issue is only the first of more to come, as new subscriptions take a while to process. Don't give magazines containing controversial news. *Life* and *People* are perfect; *Time* or *Newsweek* aren't.

Another option appreciated the world over is a book about the U.S. Best bets are hardcover, coffee-table volumes illustrated in color. The less text, the better. The book can be about the nation as a whole or your native part of it, but it should not include controversial material.

But on your first trip abroad, don't rack your brain for just the right gift. If you have something that feels natural and right, great. If not, that's okay, too. You don't have to give a gift at the outset of negotiations. Even a perfect gift is no substitute for a sound business offer and a winning personality.

Gifts that are fancier, more personal, intended for the home rather than the office, or for leisure rather than work, or are for a businessman's wife or kids rather than for himself, are out of place until you get to know each other better on future trips. The more you get to know, like, and trust one another, the more important personalized gift giving becomes. Until you reach that stage in your relationship, less is more.

## Telexes

Here's a paraphrasing of an oft-heard story. An American is speaking:

I had spoken with my colleague overseas on the telephone, we had exchanged letters, and I had sent him information about our firm that he'd requested. I figured it was time for us to meet face to face. So I sent him a telex saying that I would be in town from the fourteenth through the twentieth, and if that wasn't convenient, to please let me know by return telex. If the timing *was* convenient, I asked him to book a hotel room for me and to have someone meet me at the airport.

He never sent me an answer so I assumed that everything was set. But when I landed at the airport, no one was there to meet me. I had no hotel reservation and the better places were booked solid. Finally I found a room in a real dive and I was lucky to get that. To make matters worse, I wasn't even expected! The person with whom I had been communicating all along—and who never answered my telex—was surprised to see me. I don't know if he didn't get my message or thought that by ignoring it I wouldn't come. He had to change his whole schedule around to fit me in, and he only did that out of politeness. I had come to be ingratiating; instead I felt like a nuisance. The trip was a disaster, and we haven't communicated since.

Why non-Americans who receive and respond to some telexes apparently don't get or choose to answer others is one of the great unsolved mysteries of international business, but there it is. The practice can be erratic, and the moral of the story is clear: If you've sent a telex overseas, requesting an answer you have yet to receive by return telex, don't assume your telex has reached the proper hands, the answer is yes, and your requests are being fulfilled even though the lack of a response might seem to imply it. Instead, assume that somehow, for some reason, your telex failed to get where it was supposed to go, send another telex, and, if necessary, another, until you get definite verification.

If you receive no reply after the third telex, *that* should tell you something about a non-American's eagerness to do business with you.

## Return Dates

If you're dealing abroad for the first time and your company has no established presence at your destination, it's impossible to set a firm date for returning home with your mission accomplished. This is true the world over, even when each of your appointments has been prearranged and confirmed by telex, mail, or telephone.

Outside the U.S., expect to fit fewer meetings into a day. Each meeting may take longer to conclude, and you still may get less done than you would have in half the time at home. Board your overseas flight with your eyes open and your trip goals realistic. What takes an hour to accomplish here may take a day or more elsewhere. Once you get your feet wet you'll be better able to predict how much time you'll need abroad; until then, it's probably going to be in God's hands. Discuss this likelihood with your superiors to protect yourself from their chagrin; you may have to call long distance after a week to tell them that you've only just begun to talk shop.

## Jet Lag

*Jet Lag and Decision Making*, a report by Brigham Young University, confirms what old hands at international negotiating know only too well:

Studies of people subjected to real and laboratory-created disruptions of the circadian rhythm have revealed that debilities occur in mental alertness, reaction time, short-term memory, and ability to solve simple mathematical problems. Jet lag impairs your abilities just when you need most to be on your toes—during executive negotiating and decision making. This may be so in social gatherings or formal meetings.

More than a hundred bodily functions, from temperature to heartbeat to eating to sleeping, operate on stubbornly change-resistant twenty-four-hour cycles (circadian rhythm) that get knocked out of kilter when several time zones are quickly crossed. If you're going to fly across the Atlantic or Pacific, you're almost certain to suffer some jet lag when you land.

The readjustment process, which can take several days, affects everyone differently, but common symptoms are stomach queasiness, depression, absent-mindedness, and overall fatigue.

While there are a number of jet-lag diets and in-flight exercises intended to reduce its effects, even international travelers who follow them to the letter still get jet lag. As yet, there exists no guaranteed antidote. Given this, what can you do make life abroad easier before and after you land?

If possible, move your arrival date up. Try to be at your overseas destination at least a day or two before your first scheduled appointment. The earlier the better. If you leap from the plane to the hotel and then straight into negotiations, you may blow it; you wouldn't be the first.

If possible, fly first class. Virtually all international airlines have installed sleeper seats in their first-class cabins. These seats enable you to fully recline at an angle of about sixty degrees to the floor, which is almost horizontal. They enable you to sleep comfortably stretched out through much of a ten- or twenty-hour flight.

A few international carriers have converted the upper decks of the first-class cabins in some 747 aircraft into minihotels. These feature private, curtained-off compartments, each enclosing a *real* bed, though it's smaller than a standard twin. Pajamas are part of the package. A bed raises the usual first-class fare by about $100.

Not even sleeper seats or real beds will totally rid you of jet lag, but they do lessen its intensity on many people. Comfortwise, they make trying to get some shuteye in "extra-wide" business-class seats seem like napping in just what they are: plush, wider than coach, somewhat reclinable, but otherwise ordinary chairs that force you to assume a fetal position in order to sleep. Flying first class may seem expensive, but compared to what's usually at stake in international negotiations the price is peanuts.

However, flying first or even business class is not without allures that only make jet lag worse. The less you put into your body a few hours before and during an intercontinental flight, the better. Scientists still working on jet-lag cures strongly urge that you eat light, cut down drastically on cigarettes if you smoke, and say no thanks to the tempting, limitless liquor, wine, and champagne you'll be regularly offered by the flight attendants. One drink at 40,000 feet packs the wallop of *two* on the ground. Drinking alcoholic beverages in flight can significantly prolong jet lag effects when you land.

On boarding the plane, some people set their watches from local to destination time, which they claim gives them a psychological edge; many jet-lag symptoms are thought to be psychosomatic.

Occasionally leave your seat and stroll up and down the aisle during the flight. This stimulates the flow of blood that air pressure at high altitudes causes to coagulate in your feet and possibly your brain.

On landing, stay on a high-protein diet for the first day or so, avoid unfamiliar foods if you're an adventurous eater, and eat *peeled* fresh fruits and vegetables if available.

## Dress

Once necessary to strictly observe, international business dress codes have relaxed considerably. While there are still some culture-specific rules (to be covered later on), here's a set of guidelines for playing it safe:

• Forget about how local businesspeople dress. What you usually wear to the office at home is probably appropriate attire for negotiating abroad.

• Just in case you're atypical, the adjective that describes proper business attire the world over is *conservative*. This applies to both the color and cut of your clothes, regardless of your sex.

• Solid dark colors fit in in more places globally than light colors do. During summer months or in countries where it's usually hot, light colors are generally fine for daytime wear. But in some cultures, dark colors are still mandatory after dark.

• For businessmen, suits are more acceptable in more places than sport jackets and slacks—including navy blazers. Checks and stripes other than pinstripes are out. Vests are up to you. Light blue and yellow dress shirts have become a common sight in business circles everywhere, but the color you'll still see most remains white. Checks and stripes in shirts should also be avoided.

• Ties are *always* a must. Never enter a corporate or government office anywhere with an open-collar shirt. You can be a bit more creative with ties, but the smart money sticks to solids, stripes, or polka dots of conservative hues.

• In foreign climes, lace-up shoes are more businesslike than loafers. Black shoes are more businesslike than brown.

• A Wall Street banker who handles Latin American operations gives his staff this advice: "My people ask: 'Can I wear a checked sport jacket in this or that country? Can I go around without my tie? In Rio, the men wear elegant white suits. Can I wear white, too?' I tell them: 'Absolutely not. You come from Wall Street. You should *look* like Wall Street. Other people *expect* you to look like Wall Street. If you imitate the way they dress, they won't respect you. They will wonder who you're trying to fool. You are employed by a conservative American banking institution. Your clothes should reflect that image in all countries at all times.'" Even if you're not employed by a conservative banking institution, this advice is good advice in Latin America or anyplace else.

• If you're a woman, dresses, skirt-blouse-sweater combinations, and skirt suits are what female executives most often wear to work in other lands. You'll see few pantsuits in cosmopolitan commercial centers. Except in Muslim countries, women usually show their legs up to the knee. You'll *never* see one of the few non-American businesswomen in positions of power in a pair of slacks at the office.

• Don't wear high spiked heels. Foreign businessmen often walk fast. If you can't keep up, you're saying something about your professional abilities, too. And many pavements in other countries are rutted, ripe for ankle twisting. As for boots, some women wear them, but most don't. Those who don't feel quite strongly about it. They feel boots convey too casual an image.

• In most foreign places, businesswomen have a similar look. It's one of classical elegance: tasteful, sophisticated, and well-tailored. It's a look that downplays their femininity yet is not unfeminine or even unisexual. It's a look that makes a statement: "I can do a man's job, but I'm still a woman, and proud of it." Even for evening socializing, if you choose a garment that shows cleavage, you'll pay for it in the conference room the next day.

• Small details are important. Every item on your person—a wristwatch, earrings, a bracelet, a ring, a pen, a pocketbook—should convey an image of professionalism. Don't overdress, particularly concerning jewelry. When in doubt, leave it out. As male colleagues abroad will inevitably judge you by the image conveyed by their own minority of successful businesswomen, it's best to follow their example rather than make a strong statement of individuality. Individualism may be a virtue in the U.S., but elsewhere, it will undermine your credibility in a business world that's still a man's world.

• An effective way to discourage passes from foreign men—particularly Latin men—is to wear an engagement ring with a diamond of impressive size. If you don't own one, try to borrow one. A wedding ring won't work. In the fast lane of global commerce, American women who are married are thought to be beyond love and ripe for sexual adventure, or so many non-American men like to think. An engagement ring indicates that you have a fiancé not a husband, and, by definition, are more in love. A good-size stone says that your fiancé is affluent. Love and money are serious setbacks to men who contemplate making sexual overtures. Foreign men fear rejection no less than Americans.

• Men and women should dress for the plane as they would at the office. Even though the flight may be long and tiring, casual attire worn for comfort is inappropriate. In public, you're always representing your firm. You should always look the part of a professional. You must be "on" all the time. Particularly when you fly in first or business class, the person in an adjacent seat may be a client, a business prospect, or a local banker whose line of credit or nod of approval you may need to seal a deal when you land.

• In addition, your native host may meet you at the airport. When you step off the plane in casual clothes, it doesn't look professional, the situation notwithstanding. Particularly with a person whom you've never met before, first impressions—especially unfavorable ones—may be for life.

## Getting Met at the Airport

Getting met at the airport is a customary courtesy in much of the world. But is it a good idea? Maybe, maybe not. Some people say yes. Having a friendly face awaiting your arrival in a strange land is more than a comfort and a display of good manners: It's a valuable convenience. There may be no English signs to guide you to the bathroom, the baggage-claim area, a taxi stand, a subway station, or a bus stop. At an airport information booth, the informant may speak little or no English. You may be hassled at the customs desk, particularly if you've brought product samples or demonstration equipment—even if you have the right clearances and can produce the documents to prove it.

Ah, but with a *native*—and an important one—at the airport to meet and greet you, to guide you to the bathroom and the baggage claim area, to part the customs officers blocking your exit like Moses parting the Red Sea, to whisk you into a car waiting to speed you to your hotel, life abroad, from the moment you set foot on foreign soil, can be a perfect pleasure.

So says Group One. But other international negotiators disagree. They assert that if you even *suspect* you may be met, do your best to dissuade your host-to-be by mail, telephone or telex before leaving home. In fact, they urge that you *insist* it's entirely unnecessary.

Why? You may arrive on a weekend. Out of cultural mores on politeness, a native host may feel obliged to pick you up whether he really wants to or not. He's no different from you in this respect; his days off are important to him, too. Many foreigners are reluctant to sacrifice personal time for work.

If you arrive on a weekday, you may land at an ungodly hour, or five hours late, leaving your host to cool his heels at the airport until you finally appear. Again, he's no different from you in this respect. If you were stuck at an airport for hours waiting for a guest to land, your mood would probably be something less than chipper.

Also, from an American point of view non-Americans often overdo politeness. There you are, staggering into the airbridge (the telescopic walkway joining aircraft to terminal), or down the mobile passenger steps, bleary with fatigue, stunned by jet lag, clothes looking like you slept in them, which you probably did. The last thing you'll want to do is put on a happy face and be your usual witty, charming self for a couple of hours while your host, himself secretly wishing he was somewhere else, fulfills what he feels is his duty to entertain you for a sufficiently generous period of time.

Lack of English signs? No bathroom? Lost luggage? Customs hassles? Not a taxi in sight? "You'll handle it somehow," say the people of Group Two. "If you can't deal with such relatively simple situations at an overseas airport, how are you going to manage the actual negotiations, a much greater challenge?" Their advice is: Be patient. Be calm. Take charge. Find your luggage and a taxi on your own, take it straight to your hotel, and get some sleep.

These opposing views are neither right nor wrong. Consider both and settle on the one that works for you.

# PART TWO

---

# STRATEGIES

# AND

# TACTICS

# CHAPTER FOUR

---

# Western Europe:
# The Civilization of
# Business

"A person should be allowed to have a few redeeming
vices, but never bad manners."

MARK TWAIN,
*Pudd'nhead Wilson*

Americans are encouraged to think of Europeans as being similar to themselves.

We watch "Americanized" European actors in movies and on television. We easily identify with them. They adapt to our way of life
supremely well. They speak excellent English, though with a trace of
accent that we readily forgive. It's easy to think of them as being Americans, once removed—though it's really the other way around.

From this limited exposure, we tend to generalize: All Europeans
must be like the European actors we feel we know. They're *all* much like
us.

Europe is also perceptively familiar. We study European history in
school. We're bound to Europe by NATO and other treaties; Americans
often consider our European alliances more important than treaties the
U.S. has with other nations. And many Americans have European blood.
Even though their European relatives may be long gone, they are left with
a special kindred feeling for Europeans in the countries where their roots
began.

Furthermore, most Americans who enjoy leisure travel abroad have
vacationed in Europe at least once by now. Often their favorable precon-
ceptions of what Europeans are like are confirmed. Europeans are indeed

courteous, friendly, charming, easy to get to know, speak or understand at least some English, and like the U.S. and us.

To extend this logic within a negotiating context, European business methods, manners, and motivations must also be similar to ours. As such, when in London, Paris, Frankfurt, or Milan, Americans proceed to deal as if they were negotiating with carbon copies of themselves in any major U.S. city.

This is usually when the unsettling truth begins to dawn. The Europeans we admire on stage and screen, or had instantly befriended as tourists, are not the same Europeans now facing us across a conference table. These Europeans are a special breed. They are *businesspeople*. And, while European executives may think and act in ways that more closely resemble ours than those of most other non-Americans, they are not like us.

## Portraits of a Businesspeople

Europe can be viewed in three ways: as a continent of fairly similar business cultures when collectively compared to ours; as a region where two broad business cultures predominate—the Germanic in the north and the Latin in the south; and as a group of thirty-odd countries, each a unique cultural entity.

Old hands at negotiating in Europe—and Europeans themselves— maintain that the last view is most correct, but then, paradoxically, they proceed to offer advice based on one of the first two views. As something valid can be said for each, we'll skip around among all three.

### How Europeans Feel about Americans

Europeans watch the U.S. more than Americans watch Europe, so they know more about us than we generally do about them. But this doesn't mean that we are understood. Europeans see *what* we do, but not *why* we do it, and much of what we do as a nation mystifies them.

Europeans have been forced to recognize their economic interdependence with the world in a way that Americans still resist. Much legislation that's enacted in Washington—a new farm bill, for example—has significant consequences for Europeans and others who import our grain, yet to Americans the matter is purely domestic. Europeans are often confounded that a people as smart and successful as Americans are can concurrently be so naive as to how today's world works.

Adding to ill feelings, Europe has been dependent on the U.S. for four decades now, and many Europeans frankly resent it. They have never forgiven us for entering World War II late—at our convenience—and then winning it for them. They also hold the Marshall Plan against us. We saw it as munificent aid to war-torn economies and the best defense against the spread of Soviet Communism. But many Europeans came to regard it as an underhanded scheme to force U.S. exports down their indebted throats.

Some Europeans managed to console themselves with the idea that we were at least a decent ally, invincible in war and reasonably uncorrupt in government. But after our failure in Vietnam and the subsequent Watergate scandal, our national image was irreparably tarnished. We were still mighty but not immortal. We were still not that bad, but we were not that good, either. This disillusionment persists, and the furor over MX missile installations in West Germany has not helped to make us more lovable.

It's not that Europeans no longer like us. But they don't like us as much as before. They know they need us. But they don't know how far to trust us. Many see the U.S. as a fair-weather friend.

## Trust in European Business

Trust *matters* in Europe. Europeans increasingly use lawyers and contracts, but they don't replace the need for mutual trust between negotiators. Much more business and kinds of business are done on a handshake in Europe than in the U.S., although the practice is dying out. Still, lawyers and contracts may never enter a conversation until trust has been established first. Europeans who distrust you may not deal with you even if they *are* interested in your offer. In Europe, suspicion, if it exists, usually cancels out the desire to make money.

## Civilization and Its Discontents

Americans are informally class conscious. However, Europeans can be quite formal in their sensitivity to class. Professionals are either upper class or upper, middle, or lower bourgeoisie, who attend a university and climb up the corporate or governmental ranks. But whether they are old-family or self-made, Europeans have a clear concept of what civilized behavior is, based on social class. And, though it's rarely verbalized, class-conscious Europeans may not deal with an American who behaves like a boor. It just isn't done.

Deciding if you're sufficiently civilized to be an associate is often the first priority of European executives. Inevitably, you'll be judged against a preconceived stereotype of the "ugly American." A European may want to satisfy himself—reinforced by feedback from colleagues and friends—that you're indeed a discovery, a truly civilized American, before he can begin to take you seriously as a partner, seller, or even buyer.

Social acceptance can make or break a business deal in Europe.

## Conservatism

Even by Wall Street standards, Europeans are highly conservative. They dress tastefully but without colorful flair. They are less aggressive and competitive in selling than Americans. Their expense accounts are less liberal, even at the top. They change jobs less often and less easily. They climb the corporate ladder step by traditional step, rarely skipping rungs—which is why European negotiators tend to be older than their U.S. counterparts, a disparity in ages that disconcerts them. And, as decision makers, they are more cautious, slower to say yes, less willing to take risks, even when enticed with the lure of quick, substantial profits.

## Informality

We think our informality fits in anywhere because being informal is simple; there are few behavioral rules to remember or get upset about if they are inadvertently broken. To deepen our conviction, Europeans who deal in the U.S. often adopt our informal manner because they know it's custom here and they respect that.

However, back home, even Europeans who were casually informal here usually revert to their traditional formality and reserve inside the office and out, which is custom there. Moreover, they expect you to *know* what decorum means in Europe and prove it, which shows them you are serious and sincere in your wish to deal.

American informality is flexible. European formality is not. Rules are not made to be broken in Europe; they are preserved to be observed. For this reason, Europeans may not be quick to forgive faux pas in local etiquette, however innocent, particularly ones that are socially embarrassing. Ignorance in Europe is the *worst* excuse. Good manners may prevent a European from making a public issue of your mistake, but he'll remember it.

## *Enthusiasm*

Americans welcome change. We revere the new. We tirelessly seek what's better in business and in life. The idea that something cannot or should not be improved is alien to us. We're eternal optimists. If the present is bad, tomorrow will be another and better day. We don't dwell on the past. Our eyes are glued to the future and it always seems bright. Every problem can be somehow solved, and we love to compete to find solutions first. We're incurably ambitious. We go to work full of enthusiasm and hope, ready to conquer the world, convinced the world *can* be conquered, confident that with a will there's a way.

Europeans see life differently. Our world has never been conquered. Theirs has, more than once. They have suffered more than Americans as people in history. European nations once controlled vast global empires that are gone for good. As an economic and military force, the whole of Europe is past its prime, and Europeans know it. Only yesterday they ruled the world. Then came World War II, and suddenly their countries were second-class powers. After the U.S. and the U.S.S.R., who matters anymore?

Much of Europe has yet to adjust to the shock of so sudden, dramatic, and permanent a change in the cosmic order of existence. This often makes for skeptical, pessimistic, and somewhat fatalistic businesspeople. Europeans are not necessarily gloomy and sullen. But they are not overly enthusiastic, either. Instead, they tend to be prudent, sober, analytical, philosophical, slow to make commitments, and long-term thinkers who are mindful of the past; they harbor an intense dislike of pressure.

The sheer zest for doing business that Americans unabashedly display runs contrary to the European concept of civilized behavior and the European mind-set, frequently rooted in a glorious past rather than a troubled present and an insecure future. Many Europeans are put off by our zeal to deal. It arouses suspicion. It reminds them of wealth and power that we have and they have lost. It confirms their view of Americans as being naive. Don't we realize how bad things are in the world today? Remarks a Swiss banker, voicing an opinion widely held in Europe: "Whenever I see an American over here, even a tourist, I can't help but think: 'What is he going to try to *sell* me?'"

## European English

Americans commonly assume that English is the universal second language of Europe. Not so. In fact, many Europeans understand English better than they speak it, others speak it better than they understand it, most don't speak it well or at all, and even Europeans who speak English as a first language are baffled by the most ordinary American expressions that we take for granted everybody knows. Arthur South, international marketing manager of Technical Translation International, based in London, explains that idioms like "no way" and "Monday through Friday" mean nothing to a Briton who has not spent time in the U.S.

Hugh McCandless, public information director of Deloitte Haskins + Sells, who has lived and worked in Britain, compiled this glossary of words that divide two nations by a common language:

| American English | British English |
| --- | --- |
| A set of instructions | A brief |
| To check something over | To vet something |
| I was asked to assist Jones | I was seconded to Jones |
| London's financial district | The City |
| Retirement plan | Pension scheme |
| First floor | Ground floor |
| Wake you up in the morning | Knock you up |
| Office boy | General factotum |
| Busy traffic intersection | Circus |
| Less-busy "circus" | Roundabout |
| Exit sign | Way Out |
| Elevator | Lift |
| Sidewalk | Pavement |
| Subway | Underground, or Tube |
| Pedestrian Underpass | Subway |

Americans who negotiate often in Europe usually learn at last one other language out of necessity. Most learn French. Fluency in French is handy because it's the unofficial language of European society. Harriet Mouchly-Weiss, chairman of Ruder Finn & Rotman International Partners, says that when she deals in Europe and the representatives of firms from several countries are present, the language of the meeting is English. But afterward, when everyone can relax, the conversation switches to French, and those who can't speak it miss a lot. When a formal meeting turns informal, that's when the truth tends to be told.

To deal in Paris, you *must* speak some French. Even Frenchmen who are fluent in English may refuse to speak it if you don't first prove you've had French lessons. Paris-born Monique Fong, a conference interpreter who often works at the United Nations, explains that the French are this way because they themselves don't speak foreign languages well. Doing everything well is important to French self-esteem. If you're going to put a Frenchman in the awkward position of forcing him to do something that he can do—but not well—by way of atonement you must speak French badly first. Rest assured, however perfect your French is, there will be something to correct. Every Frenchman is a French teacher at heart. But the ritual is important. It breaks the ice and permits the conversation to proceed in English on terms that both sides can accept.

## Business Customs

Americans often misguidedly breathe a sigh of relief when dealing in Europe. In more exotic places like the Arab world or East Asia, even those of us with no cross-cultural awareness at least are cognizant enough to anticipate that life will be dramatically different. However, because European business customs are comparatively subtler than those of other peoples, U.S. negotiators commonly think that fundamental differences don't exist. In Europe, novices often feel they can relax at last. Compared to dealing in Riyadh or Beijing, executives in Frankfurt or Milan more or less do business in an American way. Still, hidden between the "more" and the "less" are cultural chasms that can be vast.

### Dress

Regardless of your sex, your wardrobe for Europe should be natural in fiber—cotton, wool, silk, etc.—not synthetic. Europeans still joke about the deluge of American tourists in the '50s and '60s in their matching polyester leisure suits. Many see synthetic and think yokel.

### Men

Dark gray, dark blue, and black are the colors European decision makers wear to work. Brown, even dark brown, is considered a bit sporty for office wear, and even at a formal restaurant dark-brown dress may draw stares.

In Latin Europe, white shirts and black lace-up shoes are preferred office attire, and for evening wear they are musts.

Choose striped ties carefully if you're bound for Britain. They may be copies of regimentals, and one doesn't wear an old-school tie when one hasn't attended the old school. It marks you as an unconscionable beast for life.

An English marketer warns about shirt pockets: "American shirt pockets are always bulging with pencils, pens, plastic rulers, packets of cigarettes, and what all. In Britain this is most unsightly."

### Women

While European executive women may be few, they probably outnumber female decision makers elsewhere beyond our borders. Most are sophisticated, moneyed, and genteel. They dress to emphasize these traits and they do it well. This doesn't mean you must necessarily buy new clothes, but your look should be natural, tasteful, carefully tailored, and traditionally elegant—not too trendy, always conservatively understated. Classic lines, good tailoring, quality, and perhaps one carefully selected piece of expensive jewelry—borrowed if necessary—are the keys to an effective sartorial image. Don't wear costume jewelry. Wear the real thing or none at all.

There is probably nowhere in the world where you'll have to look more your best than in Western Europe to gain credibility from European men. And there's no city in Europe where you'll have to look more smashing than in Paris, where acutely taste-conscious Frenchmen will note even the quality of a woman's nylons.

If you weren't born a natural fashion plate, particularly when it comes to applying makeup, seek help from a fashion consultant. They're listed in the Yellow Pages. Or ask at the dress department of a fine store or at a beauty salon.

### Business Cards

Advanced education is greatly admired, particularly among northern Europeans; it carries social as well as professional prestige. If you have an M.B.A. or a Ph.D. relating to your business field, have it printed on your cards. In Europe, it isn't pretentious; it's impressive. It helps establish your credibility.

The Germans, Dutch, and Swiss admire longevity. If your firm is an old one, have its founding date printed on your cards. It makes more of an impression than you'd believe.

In West Germany, you can gauge the importance of the people you meet by the initials preceding their names on business cards and in correspondence. A *ppa*, or *Prokurist*, has registered signing authority; he's a key decision maker, with broad powers to negotiate for management. An *i.V.*, or *Vollmacht*, can also negotiate, but his decision-making authority is limited. If your first contact is with an *i.a.*, *Im Auftrag*, meaning "signing for another," he's not a decision maker, even though he may represent his firm in initial face-to-face meetings.

## Shaking Hands

Most Europeans shake hands both on arrival and departure. Their grip is light, not firm. In Latin Europe, handshakes last about twice as long as ours: five to seven strokes. If you pull your hand away too soon, it creates an impression of rejection. As in many areas of life, the French shake hands in their own special way: one brisk definitive stroke.

Europeans often reshake hands whenever they are apart for more than a few minutes. For example, if you leave a colleague at the office to go to lunch and then return, both on departure and arrival it's polite to shake hands.

When confronted by a group, shake hands with the oldest person or the one of senior rank first, and so on down the line. Whoever has the most rank does the extending; the lesser person does the receiving. It sounds more complicated than it is. Your hosts will probably anticipate that you don't know who comes where in the handshaking protocol and guide you through it.

Shake hands with everyone. Don't stop halfway through even a crowded room with a general wave of greeting to the rest. Neglecting to shake someone's hand is not a neutral act; it's an uncivilized rejection. Even if the people you omit are unimportant, the others see it.

European women shake hands with each other and with men. It's up to the woman to take the initiative with a man, even if he outranks her in age or seniority. If you're a man, let a European woman—such as a male colleague's wife—extend her hand first. If you're a woman, and don't offer your hand to shake when a European man is introduced to you, politeness prevents him from offering his. If you fail to extend your hand to a male executive, you lose credibility.

## Forms of Address

Don't call a European by his first name unless you're invited to. If someone has a title, get it right when you say it. If you don't know whether to call a woman *mademoiselle* or *madame* (or *fräulein* or *frau*, or *senorita* or *señora*), assume she's married and use the latter. To misaddress an unmarried European woman as if she were wed is a mild compliment. To do the reverse is a mild insult.

Latin Europeans may use *two* last names on business cards and in correspondence. For example, if a colleague's name is Juan Garcia Lopez, Garcia is the father's name, Lopez the mother's. The mother's name is not used in conversation. Juan Garcia Lopez becomes Juan Garcia in speech; Lopez is dropped. When writing, though, refer to him as Mr. Garcia Lopez, not Mr. Lopez or Mr. Garcia.

If a European has an academic title printed on his business card, say it as you see it. Fritz Schmidt, Economist, is "Economist Schmidt," not "Dr. Schmidt," "Professor Schmidt," or "Mr. Schmidt." Call him "Economist Schmidt" until he invites you to a beer hall or some other drinkery. After a couple of steins, you can probably call him "Schmidt." You still can't call him "Fritz."

A European may have two titles on his card, common north of the Alps where executives can be especially title conscious. Schmidt's card says he's a company director as well as an economist. Titles that are earned and denote academic distinction are *more* prestigious than conferred titles indicating corporate status. You can either use the academic title alone, or, to play it safe, *both* titles, in which case the academic one comes first. Thus Schmidt becomes "Economist Director Schmidt," not "Director Economist Schmidt."

Don't invite a European to call you by your first name until you become well-acquainted. He probably won't feel comfortable doing it. Most Americans say they can instinctively sense when the time is appropriate to switch to first names—if it ever is. Europeans don't usually feel the need to be as friendly and informal as we do. Younger Europeans may call each other by first names, but they rarely negotiate. European executives may work side by side for years and never get beyond last names.

## The Telephone

It's second nature to Americans to use the telephone to communicate efficiently. To Europeans, it often isn't. Don't arrive in Europe without prior appointments. The telephone doesn't open doors there like it does here. Americans will talk to anyone on the telephone. We often prefer a telephone conversation over meeting a stranger face to face. But Europeans are often shocked by Americans who telephone them from a hotel without advance warning and proceed to sell. In Europe, this is the height of barbarity.

Europeans don't usually conduct business over the telephone with people they have yet to meet personally. Hugh McCandless, while working for the trading-stamp company, Sperry-Hutchinson, was stationed in Barcelona. He placed an order with a local supplier over the telephone. The goods never showed up. His associate, a Spaniard, advised him to meet the supplier personally to break bread, so to speak. McCandless felt this was a waste of time, but he did it, and then everything was fine. He even had to wait outside his house for a half-day to personally introduce himself to his mailman if he wanted to get his mail.

Once a personal meeting has taken place, then you can usually call a European on the telephone. To be polite, ask: "If I have a question, may I call you on the telephone?" Few people will say no.

Europeans mainly use the telephone to arrange future meetings, not to discuss business at length. If something takes more than a few minutes to say, it should probably be said face to face in Europe.

Europeans complain that Americans feel free to call them at any hour of the day or night. In Europe, this is an invasion of privacy. Business hours differ across the Continent, sometimes even in neighboring towns. The Swiss, for example, are usually at their desks by 7:30 or 8:00 A.M., including top executives. Spaniards show up late, around 10:00 A.M., but work late. Find out when the local business day begins, and how it's divided into morning coffee breaks, lunches, afternoon snacks, and quitting times. Those are times *not* to call. In Northern Europe, the morning— around 10:00 or 11:00—is probably the best time to telephone. In Southern Europe, where businesspeople may go home for a siesta from noon till three, the afternoon is best, around four. Even a Latin who is at his desk by 10:00 A.M. may not hit his working stride till the late afternoon.

Even if you have a person's home telephone number and have been assured he won't mind, don't call a European after normal working hours or on a weekend, and never call him at home if you're anything less than old, dear friends. Being a friend of a friend doesn't count.

### Appointments

Be punctual for appointments. North of the Alps, be exactly on time. Don't appear more than a minute or two early. Hang around the building lobby if you must, with your eye on your watch. Never be more than a minute or two late. Merely being five minutes late is frowned upon by many Northern Europeans.

You'll probably stay at a Hilton, Hyatt, or some other chain hotel in Europe. Even at modern hotels, there's usually an old-fashioned concierge whose knowledge of his city is encyclopedic. Ask him how long it takes to get where you have to go, tell him when you must be there, and find out what form of transportation is fastest at the time you plan to use it. A taxi may not be the fastest way to get from a hotel to an office in rush-hour traffic.

In Latin Europe, you may be kept waiting from a few minutes to over an hour in an outer office—even when you show up at a prearranged time. Still, be punctual. It's expected that you sit and suffer. Don't leave and return later. Don't open your attaché case and find busy work to do. Simply sit. You must show a Latin that you respect the opportunity to meet with him so much you'll gladly wait. Latin courtesies are formal and elaborate. Your host may be running late himself, not making you wait merely for its own sake. Nor is waiting necessarily a sign that interest in your offer is only lukewarm. Corporate officers of major U.S. multi-nationals are kept waiting like everyone else. If you lose your temper, as many Americans who are impatient or feel rejected do, you might as well stay home.

In return for having patiently waited, you'll receive as much time as you need with the person you came to see. You won't be rushed in and out. Americans don't keep visitors waiting when appointments have been prearranged, but often we allocate only ten or fifteen minutes for a meeting. A Latin may keep you waiting for an hour, but will give you ample time to speak your piece.

Breakfast meetings are out in Europe, where executives often live in far-flung suburban areas and have long commutes to work. To call a breakfast meeting for 7:00 or 8:00 A.M. may force participants to get up at 4:00 or 5:00 to be on time, disrupting their routine and getting the day off to a bad start.

## Collateral Materials

The businesspeople of Central and Northern Europe are no-nonsense. Collateral materials should reflect this. Their design should be crisp, clean, clear, and classy, but conservative. Northern Europeans in particular hate clutter.

Avoid splashy colors. Keep them stylish but understated. Dark colors are preferred over pastels. Tell your art director to think Wall Street, not Hollywood. If your firm is small and you don't have a big promotional budget, black-and-white literature is fine for the matter-of-fact Germans, Dutch, Swiss, Austrians, and Scandinavians. You don't need to invest in color. The money is better spent on a good copywriter, art director, translator, and printer, and on good paper.

North of the Alps, business proposals, statistical reports, and specification sheets—technical documents—carry more weight than literature with "beauty" shots of scantily clad blondes holding your product. Germans and Dutch may advertise to their own customers this way, but it's not how they want to be sold themselves.

To be shrewd, use index tabs—these can be in color—to subdivide lengthy documents. It makes you seem organized and meticulous about small details. As Germans and Dutch are highly organized and minutely meticulous, it shows them you're on their wavelength.

For illustrations, stick to charts, graphs, and "exploded" diagrams that show your product as component parts—each clearly labeled—and how they fit into the assembled whole. If a photograph or other illustration is purely imagistic but doesn't otherwise contribute to your selling story, leave it out.

Latins like more and livelier colors. You can also use beauty shots sparingly to spice up your selling story. Don't overdo it. Latin business sophisticates know quality when they see it, and they expect to see it in your collateral materials, particularly in cities like Rome, Milan, Turin, Geneva, and Paris where elegance and good taste are near fetishes.

Have as few pieces of translated literature printed as possible. For presentations to them, European executives may think it's fine. But for distribution to their salespeople, clients, or customers, something is bound to be wrong with it. Alan Bain, president of World-Wide Business Centres, recalls a brochure designed in New York for distribution to his affiliates in West Germany. The brochure illustrated a charming Old-World building in which one business center was housed. Bain, from an American point

of view, found this appealing. The Germans begged to differ. They wanted
to stress their modernity, technological sophistication, and efficiency, not
their seventeenth-century charm.

It works the other way around as well, particularly in translation
errors. Bain tells how the name of his firm became "the company with
offices around the world" in a German brochure. "Despite our name," he
says, "we don't have offices around the world."

Initially, collateral materials have only one job to do in Europe: help
you make your case. Don't offer to give a ton of them away with your
wares as an additional incentive for a European to buy. It probably won't
make your products any easier for him to sell. You'll only end up throwing
out a lot of costly paper.


### Small Talk

Americans like to keep small talk down in selling situations. We want
to get to the bottom line fast. In Europe, however, some form of social
chitchat nearly always precedes shop talk. Germanic peoples want to hear
what's on your mind without much to-do. But even they usually like to
chat for a few minutes about the state of your industry in the U.S., how
your firm fits into it, and how you fit into the firm. Then your counterpart
explains how things are in Europe. This exchange of information is short
and sweet. You'll sense the small talk winding down. Then you can segue
into the matter you specifically came to discuss.

After waiting in a Latin anteroom for a long time, you may be
overeager to get down to business. If so, cool it. On being admitted to
the inner sanctum, first you'll probably be invited to an informal lounge
area for something to drink, usually coffee or tea. Even if you don't want
it, take it. If you refuse a drink, politeness prevents your host from
drinking. Without drinks, you have no excuse to exchange views on the
world, on people, art, politics, sports, nature, and other civilized matters.
If you want to deal later, you must exchange such views first. It isn't
optional. It's mandatory to build trust.

Having coffee with a Latin is a relaxed, casual affair, part of the
payoff for having patiently waited. Enjoy it. There's no need to rush.
Civilized people are in no particular hurry. Your colleague will want to
hear about some of your nonbusiness interests and to tell you about his.
To talk shop at such a time marks you as a boor.

Across the Atlantic, small talk isn't something that precedes negotiations. It's the start of the process. The decision to do business—or not

to do it—is often made in a twinkling over coffee, before the details are even discussed. In Europe, you must learn to talk small before you start talking big.

## Presentation Style

North of the Alps be direct, factual, detailed, and thorough—almost academic in approach—but concise. Don't use superlative adjectives. Dispassionate objectivity will do more to convince Germanic, Nordic, and British peoples than Madison Avenue–style hype. Hard sell is distasteful. It arouses suspicion. Europeans often wonder what's wrong with a proposal that it must be sold so aggressively rather than being allowed to stand on its own merits. Selling hard in Europe not only slows down the decision to say yes, it can also get you a quick no.

Be logical. Make the benefits of your proposition apparent, but don't spell them out or draw conclusions. "In Europe," says Belgian-born Henri Alster, an international real-estate developer, "the purpose of a presentation is not to sell; it is to *clarify*." By way of clarification, he offers this analogy: "You are confronted by a jungle. An American will take you by the hand and lead you through it to the other side. A European will remove the shrubbery so that a path to the other side is clear, and then let you decide whether to take it or not."

In Southern Europe's major commercial centers, like Milan, the same presentation guidelines apply. But as you move farther south, you may have to slow down a bit. English may be less widely spoken or understood, so speak slowly, pause after each important point to let it sink in, and practice making the same point in different ways before leaving home. In Portugal, Spain, southern France, southern Italy, and Greece, patience is a virtue. Never be condescending, something Latins are acutely sensitive about. That a Latin colleague may not speak good English is as much a reflection of his intelligence as your ability to speak *his* language.

Throughout Europe, be conscious of American idioms—"bottom line," "no way," "ASAP," "downtown," "I need it yesterday," etc.—and avoid them. They won't be understood, and few Europeans will come right out and say "I don't understand." This is especially true of Europe's best second-language English speakers—Germans, Dutch, and Scandinavians—who pride themselves on their mastery of textbook English, not idiomatic American English. Remember that even where English is the mother tongue—the United Kingdom countries and Ireland—*their* English isn't always the same as ours.

Don't tell jokes. Most Europeans won't understand them; the rest won't like them. Even small talk is serious in Europe, not a time for levity.

Never knock the competition. It's extremely gauche. A European will think: "One day he'll say that about me."

Don't share local industry gossip. Europeans are private people. They don't want to know about their competitors' dirty laundry. If you repeat yesterday's lunch conversation with person A to person B today, he'll know you can't be trusted.

Don't talk too loud or too fast. Avoid coming on too strong. Europeans complain that we overwhelm them with our crackling psychic energy. Many find us too intense for their taste. Most Europeans in business and government probably see themselves as urbane scholar-professionals. They're calm and objective. They may act more like U.S. college professors attending a seminar than like U.S. executives attending a meeting. They respond best to logic, and prefer to deal in situations where emotions—including zesty salesmanship and facial expressions that reveal anger, frustration, incredulity, amazement, arrogance, and superiority—are kept controlled.

## Negotiating Notes

A department store manager in Munich tells of an American wholesaler who wanted him to carry a line of shoes. The American had done some homework and knew his shoes were better than what the German now sold, and their wholesale price was less. How could the Munich manager refuse? The American produced a contract and uncapped a pen.

But the German did say no. The reason was that his current supplier had been his friend for ten years. When there was a problem, the supplier took care of it. They were drinking buddies. Their wives knew each other. Their kids played together. Frankly, he admits, he might have been persuaded to stock two similar lines of shoes. But the American attacked the situation as if it was either/or and simply a matter of money. The German had no intention of cutting out an old friend just to make a buck. Their lives were intertwined. He was not about to change all that.

Was the American given an explanation? The Munich manager shrugs. "What was there to explain? One doesn't talk about such things in Europe. They're obvious. Besides, it was none of his business." Meanwhile, the

American walked off scratching his head, and probably still doesn't know why he failed to make the sale.

Here are other not so obvious insights.

### France

When an American speaks of the French, he usually means the Parisian French, and the Parisian French pose more negotiating problems for Americans than anyone else in Western Europe. As these Frenchmen see it, they set the taste standards of the Western world in all things aesthetic, including their language, the beauty of which—when properly spoken, which only another Parisian can do—is beyond compare. Arrogance is usually a secret sign of inferiority, and with France's economic woes Parisian arrogance may be highly developed today. The French prefer to live in their rich past, not in their troubled present and uncertain future. To Americans, who live in the here and now and look optimistically ahead, Parisians seem to have an "attitude." They're critical of everything that's not French. They consider us philistines. And they want us to deal with them in ways that go against the American grain.

To most Frenchmen (including those outside of Paris), negotiating sessions are opportunities to argue and philosophize. We may thank the French philosopher René Descartes for this propensity. Cartesian logic is taught in French schools, and it's the logic of conference rooms throughout the nation. One circles around an issue, examining it from all sides— from pragmatism to metaphysics—until reason points the way to a solution. This is precisely the opposite of our negotiating logic. Americans want the solution first, because if we don't like the bottom line, there's no point wasting time discussing details that are irrelevant. And nobody in Corporate America gives a fig about metaphysics.

Parisians are also easily insulted by anyone—their geopolitical neighbors on all sides as well as us—who fails to appreciate their standards of good taste and follow them to the letter. Even an attempt to conform— like taking French lessons—is unappreciated, merely another sign of the world's hopeless barbarism. Cranky, finicky, critical, hypersensitive, and highly ethnocentric, the French rub many people the wrong way. But then so do we, which is why, when Frenchmen and Americans try to negotiate, both often come away older but not wiser.

Because the French consider themselves philosophers they may argue simply for argument's sake. While they get down to business quickly, it can take forever to conclude, with negotiations getting mired down in moral debates.

Adding to frustration, France is now a Socialist country. In 1982, President François Mitterand approved a plan for the public-sector takeover of five industrial groups, thirty-nine banks, and two financial organizations, "so that we will be able to wage a coherent fight against unemployment and implement a coherent policy of industrial restructuring." The industries now under government control range from electronics to steel to petrochemicals.

The problem is that what the French consider coherent is often incoherent to us, putting many U.S. firms at an unfair negotiating disadvantage. Says an American manufacturer of pharmaceuticals in France:

> French companies in many nationalized industries have become governmental regulatory agencies. Yet they still continue to compete for business in the private sector. While this is contradictory and a conflict of interest, the French, despite their intellectualism, see nothing wrong with it. If you try to enter the country to register products that compete with those of a nationalized firm, lots of luck.

Given all this, many U.S. multinationals have pulled out of France. Those remaining or seeking successful market entry have learned that to be effective a presentation must show that one has the best interests of the French people at heart, what French Socialism claims to be about. Stress how your proposal will benefit the nation by putting unemployed Frenchmen back to work and downplay profits, evident though they may be. If a factory must be built, as a show of good faith be ready to build it in France, whether or not it's the best location. For all the French love of argument, this point may be non-negotiable. Expect plenty of red tape, unexpected delays, and unrealistic demands when you deal in France, particularly with the government. Profits tend to come slowly, after endless patience and perseverance.

### Britain

Americans have it both easier and tougher in Britain than they usually expect. While British society is highly stratified, we can move easily from class to class and be accepted by all. To noblemen and working-class Britons, we are, as John le Carré describes us in his spy novels, "the cousins."

But we're not entirely likable cousins. We're rich and powerful and Britain isn't anymore; even Hong Kong, its most important colony, goes back to China in 1997. Somehow we always seem to manage to rub it in.

Many Britons consider us condescending and smug. We don't ask them what they think; we tell them what to do. To retaliate, they often subvert our efforts.

We can talk shop for hours and Britons are often forced to let us, for in their culture to interrupt is impolite. They squirm and stare and the light goes out of their eyes, but we fail to take the hint. Accustomed to being told when to stop, we go on and on.

We demand answers Britons aren't prepared to give bluntly. They respond with nasal mumblings that drive Americans mad. As tourists, we think they're quaint and charming because they're so formal and polite, but as businesspeople it only gets in the way. And we underestimate the British because they *are* polite. We think them incapable of the same cunning and ruthlessness as everyone else; some Americans learn too late that they aren't above it.

Most mystifying of all is the British lack of ambition. We expect Britons to work long hours to meet our deadlines, and they won't. The upper class considers work uncivilized, and hard work out of the question. The lower class thinks hard work is futile; they can't improve their lot so why work overtime? Caught in between, the middle class combines these attitudes, producing managers who are often capable yet curiously inefficient from an American point of view.

### West Germany and Holland

Most Americans consider the Germans and Dutch Europe's most sophisticated businesspeople because their business methods are similar to ours. They differ more in degree than in kind. Both peoples are highly disciplined, cautious, conservative, concerned about small details, and fussily exact. They like their accounting ledgers neat and tidy. They prefer long-term relationships to one-shot deals. As a whole, they are tireless, methodical, dependable workers rather than dynamic individualists and innovators who put challenge before risk. However, such traits have also built West Germany's economy into the strongest in Europe.

While a German or Dutch executive may want to get better acquainted with you personally before saying yes, this mainly happens in the evening, over drinks, dinner, or cultural entertainment. In the office, they're all business; with only a few preliminaries, they're ready to talk shop.

However, once you leave the major commercial centers of either country, it's like moving back in time. Negotiations are slower and more old-fashioned, and people are initially more intersted in who you are than in why you've come; trust begun, dealing can proceed.

### Belgium

You'll deal either with the Belgian Flammands in the north, or with the Belgian French in the south. As most Americans are bound for Brussels, they usually deal with the Belgian French. While the Belgian French may seem to take their cultural cues from Paris, they are easier to negotiate with than their French neighbors. For example, if you make an attempt to speak some French in Belgium, it will be appreciated. You'll generally find the Belgian French to be more polite, less argumentative, less critical, and less philosophical about business principles. Because their country is small and new—Belgium became a nation in the nineteenth century— and not well endowed with natural resources, Belgians are more pragmatic than the French, and more open to compromise in bargaining sessions. Also, because the country is a constitutional monarchy rather than being Socialist ruled, much of the bureaucratic red tape you may find yourself entangled with in Paris is not a problem here.

### Austria

In major commercial centers, like Vienna, Austrians resemble their German neighbors, and what holds true of negotiating in Germany generally applies to Austria as well.

### Switzerland

Switzerland is a tripartite country, with German language and culture prevading in the north, Italian in the south, and French in between, each modified into something uniquely Swiss. Take your negotiating cues from the country each region emulates. Most Americans deal in Zurich or Berne, and should negotiate as they would in Frankfurt or Hamburg.

### Scandinavia

While Norway has a fairly formal business culture, Denmark, Sweden, and Finland are probably the least formal in Europe. This does not mean you can dispense with wearing a tie. Americans probably have the most negotiating problems in Sweden. Many claim the Swedes don't negotiate at all. Instead, they quote a price and you can take it or leave it, regardless of the size of the order. While the Swedes are meticulously punctual on social occasions, in business matters they often are not. Your letters and telexes may go unanswered and your deadlines may be missed with no explanation as to why. These observations should not be taken too literally. While they're based on repeated experience, their validity still varies with the individual. It's no more accurate to lump all Swedes into a stereotype than it is to do so with Americans.

A good example of this discrepancy is the Scandinavian personality traits of coolness and aloofness. Often Scandinavians seem a passionless, emotionless people. Not so. As you'll find with the Japanese in a different cultural context, Scandinavians keep their emotions hidden until you go out for a drink, have an elaborate smorgasbord buffet, or otherwise socialize. Give them a chance, try to get to know them better, and you'll probably find them as warm and friendly as anyone else. Scandinavians have won foreign contracts over U.S. competitors by being patient and taking time to socialize, rather than rushing to close a deal.

### Mediterranean Europe

Spaniards, Portuguese, southern Frenchmen, and southern Italians are among Europe's most formal, traditional businesspeoples. Go slow, stress your humanity before your professionalism, and observe local courtesies at all times. Personal loyalties to family and friends take precedence over profit. The fact that you have a better product at a lower price is no guarantee that you'll make a sale. If you take the time to learn who is connected to whom, and how, you'll considerably improve your chances of negotiating success.

### Northern Italy

Don't underestimate northern Italians. People in industrial centers like Milan and Turin are quite different from their southern countrymen. Far from the stereotypical image of the siesta-loving Latin, they are among the cream of Europe's business sophisticates. As such, treat them as you would northern Swiss or Germans rather than Neopolitans. Be on time. Expect appointments to be kept punctually and social talk to be minimal. State your case concisely and objectively. And know your facts cold.

### Greece

Like other Mediterranean peoples, Greeks dislike directness. To bluntly state your business purpose shows a lack of class. Often you'll be invited to a taverna to sip ouzo, retsina, or coffee while discussing world—not business—affairs.

In the office, explain the general principles of your proposal with tactful indirection. Don't quickly sum up key points. Greeks love to talk. The principles governing a transaction should emerge or evolve during a conversation, and be muted at the edges, rather than quickly and succinctly summed up with knife-sharp clarity.

Greeks typically move from general principles to specific details within the confines of the same meeting. As a result, a meeting in Greece can last a long time, often hours. If your destination is Athens with no stopovers in between, you'll take one of the longest U.S. to Europe flights. You may suffer jet lag even *more* intensely here than elsewhere. If you don't give yourself at least a day of rest, you'll have a tough time making it through an exhaustive Greek bargaining session.

Americans, particularly those representing large firms, tend to be generalists who delegate details to subordinate specialists. Delegating details behind the scenes back home wins no points in Greece. To establish trust, Greeks want *everything* discussed openly where it can be heard by all. If you're unprepared to play by their rules, it may arouse suspicion. Often the feeling is: "What's this American trying to *hide* that he's *afraid* to talk about something in front of us?" Explaining that you simply don't know all the answers is no excuse; it marks you as insincere and incompetent. Negotiating in Greece can be an intellectual endurance contest, whether you're an individual or a member of a team.

## The Decision-Making Process

While decisions are often made in Europe faster than in other parts of the world, they nearly always take longer to make than they do in the U.S. Why?

### Centralization

Most European management systems have assumed the feudal structure of medieval fiefdoms from which they evolved. While there are occasional examples of industrial democracy, particularly as one travels farther north, most European firms are highly centralized, with top management—or the chief executive alone—making even minor decisions. As a result, European executives are often overburdened with responsibilities. Compared to us, it may take them longer to reach a verdict on a given transaction.

### Autocracy

In the top tiers of centralized European management, executives tend to jealously guard their power. Many dislike delegating responsibilities to subordinates, even those with more detailed expertise on specific issues than superiors. European executives don't usually exchange views with underlings; they give orders, and the orders are obeyed without question. As to the big picture, subordinates are kept in the dark. In many centralized firms, this prevents different departments from coordinating their efforts to most efficiently achieve common goals, as only corporate higher-ups know what the goals are. Working in a vacuum makes the job of middle management difficult, and it helps to slow the decision-making process.

### Red Tape
Bureaucratic hassles from European governments can bog down decision making. This is particularly true in France today. Says an American manufacturer seeking to deal in the country:

> We spent an eternity complying with one governmental roadblock after another that was thrown in front of us. We had to build a laboratory so that once our products arrived in France, they could undergo a complete quality-control process that had already been done in the U.S.—with a French pharmacist personally certifying that our goods met every requirement and specification the French impose. When we built the laboratory, we thought things would ease up. They didn't. We had to go through an inspection. Lots of nitpicking details weren't quite right, or a new piece of equipment was needed, or something was wrong with the qualifications of our pharmacist. It went on and on. It was really a non-tariff barrier to entry. Finally we were forced to appeal to the office of Senator Percy, chairman of the Senate Foreign Relations Committee. We appealed to the German and Dutch ambassadors, because we manufacture our products in Germany and Holland as well. Eventually the business ended up on François Mitterand's desk before things began to start moving. Even then, we had to go back through the whole bureaucratic process to get the products registered so that manufacturing could proceed. This has been dragging on now for three years.

### Trade Barriers
Looking at an atlas map of Europe with all the countries neatly nestled together, Europeans of different nationalities may seem like one big happy family. Unfortunately, this is anything but true. If your firm is established in one country and now seeks to expand into a neighboring land, or if you hope to trade for the first time in several adjacent nations at once, you're apt to find that Berlin isn't the only place in Europe divided by a wall.

In *The Europeans*, Luigi Barzini cites the French in this regard:

In the Common Market they are reluctant to give and take. They like
to see everybody buy vast quantities of French produce and goods but
are unwilling to open their borders to other peoples. They refuse to allow
the free importation of Italian wines and of Italian oysters (cultivated in
controlled, clean waters), British turkeys and lambs, German pigs, and
many other products from partner countries. At the same time they
complain bitterly about the Germans regulations involving the quality
of beer, which prevents the sale of Alsatian beers across the Rhine.
(Simon and Schuster, New York, 1983).

Tariff and non-tariff barriers to trade exist throughout Europe and
should be anticipated.

## Lawyers and Contracts

Do you need a lawyer to negotiate in Europe? Lawyers, of course,
usually say yes. But the opinions of businesspeople vary widely, and many
feel the answer is not nearly as obvious as it is in the U.S. A European
CEO offers this advice:

One of the worst things that can be done—and it happens—is to meet
with a European, work out an agreement, and then say: "Okay, now I'm
sending you my lawyer." That just about kills the deal. Now *he* needs
a lawyer. And suddenly doing business becomes complicated. Many
Europeans will back out at that point.

Even with a well-established relationship underway, lawyers may be
out of place in future European negotiations. Says a native of Zurich,
who now works on Wall Street:

I had a situation with a bank in Europe not long ago. I had to resolve
some problems and called the manager for a meeting on his home ground.
He said: "All right. I'll sit down with you. But I want you to know I
am not going to have a lawyer with me, and I expect you not to come
with a lawyer."
    Frankly, I *would* have come with a lawyer. But I didn't, against
the advice of my lawyer here. And we settled the case between ourselves.
Had I gone with my American lawyer, we would *never* have settled the
case. For *he* would then have needed a lawyer, and it would have been
a different ball game.

However, doing business on a handshake is dying out in Europe, as
Europeans increasingly adopt our practice of crossing every *t* and dotting

every *i* in a formal agreement. Yet voluminous legal documents are still not standard across the Atlantic. Among the comments of international attorneys:

> We have to explain American contracts to our European clients. They simply aren't used to the long, detailed instruments common over here. This is often true of the Germans, the English and the French.

> In France, there's constant analysis and emphasis on the use of language. It's part of the education of the French businessman. He also has the French Civil Code to refer to if he wants. It's as available to him as it is to his lawyer. He may not understand it, but he often thinks he does. He feels self-confident. And most Frenchmen can *write* better French than Americans can write English. They take more pride in their language, and strive to better master it. As such, a Frenchman is often induced to write documents that are in the nature of agreements without consulting a lawyer. It keeps the negotiating atmosphere much lighter.

> We had an American client who wanted to acquire a rather substantial French concern. He prepared a standard U.S. acquisition agreement. It was fifty pages long and full of representations and warranties. We sent it to a very good French lawyer who was representing the seller. He took one look at it and said: "No Frenchman is going to sign this." He cut it drastically before showing it to the owner of the French firm.

With short, incomplete contracts or none at all, many Americans wonder what happens if you have to go to court. The fact is, it's not so easy to take someone to court in Europe. What makes it hard are European cultural mores. Suing someone isn't civilized. A U.S. corporate officer explains:

> If you have a contractual disagreement with a European firm, the dispute is more likely to be settled out of court by an arbitrator than in court by a judge. In the U.S., arbitrators are mainly used for labor-management disputes, not disputes between managements. But in Europe, the reverse is true. However, even arbitration is not usual for Europeans to seek out. Normally, the disputing parties just sit down and work things out between themselves. It's a kind of honor system, and in Europe, it works, which is why it persists.

Even if you do manage to take a European company to a European court for breach of contract, *winning* the case is another matter. Says the president of a New York-based multinational firm:

Don't think that if something goes wrong with your agreement that you can easily sue. You can't. There's no such thing as huge penalties in a case—even if you're in the right. You won't collect triple damages in Europe as you might in the U.S.

## The Name Game

Americans can be careless about national, political, and other terms of reference, and Europeans may be insulted if you get theirs wrong. Some oft-repeated blunders:

### Britain
The term *Britain* refers to England, Scotland, and Wales. It's equally correct to call the people of these countries Englishmen, Scotsmen, and Welshmen, or simply Britons.

The people of Scotland are never "Scotch." Whisky, salmon, tomatoes, beef, broth, and tape are "Scotch." Scotland natives are either Scots, Scotsmen, or Britons.

It's best not to refer to Britons as "Europeans," even though it's technically what they are. The typical Briton regards himself as a culturally and geographically separate entity from his neighbors across the Channel. To call a Briton a "European" isn't an insult. But it's confusing and often disorienting. It makes Britons pause and ponder before they finally decide, somewhat resignedly, that you're right. But it won't endear you to them.

Northern Ireland is part of the United Kingdom, not Britain. The United Kingdom or U.K. is the term most often used in British business discussions by way of general reference.

### West Germany
The official name of the country is the Federal Republic of Germany. Despite the fact that its government is Socialist, the official name of East Germany is the German Democratic Republic or GDR. Don't mix them up in correspondence. In conversation, you can call the Federal Republic of Germany "West Germany" or simply "Germany"; it's assumed in West Germany that "West" is implied, in the same sense that "America" implies the U.S.A., not other countries in North, Central, or South America.

### Scandinavia
In Norway, Denmark, and Sweden, Finland isn't considered part of Scandinavia. The reason is mainly linguistic. Finnish has Estonian and

Hungarian roots, not Germanic. Finland's strong commercial ties to the Soviet Union intensifies feelings of separateness among other Scandinavians.

The people of Finland can be called "Finns" or "Finnish." However, Finns *do* consider themselves Scandinavians, linguistic differences and U.S.S.R. trade notwithstanding. About 10 percent of Finland's population is Swedish, and public signs in major cities are dual-language. Be careful whom you call "Scandinavian" in mixed company.

### Belgium

The people of northern Belgium are either "Flemish" or "Flamands." They are never "Flems." The natives of southern Belgium, including Brussels, may be linguistic and cultural relatives of the French but they aren't French, they're Belgian.

### Greece

Most Americans negotiating in Greece end up in a café or taverna sooner or later, where they chat with their hosts over small cups of strong bitter coffee. Some Americans call it "Greek" coffee, others "Turkish." But in Greece, coffee is always "Greek" to a Greek, and any other reference may become a major insult.

### Turkey

Turkey is part of Europe, not the Middle East, to most Turkish businesspeople and government officials.

### Body Language

Europeans may have different concepts of *space* from each other and from Americans. To Germanic peoples, if you can be seen outside an office doorway, you're felt to have *entered* the office by entering the occupant's field of vision, which is rather rude before being formally invited inside.

In France and Mediterranean Europe, executives may not have walled offices. Their desks are in the middle of an open departmental area, enabling the person in charge to keep an eye on his subordinates, a sign of power. In the U.S., having a walled office is a status symbol. In Latin Europe, it isolates and thus confines managerial authority—a reason to limit presentation aids to those that fit on a desk top.

Latin Europeans usually stand or sit closely together in conversation, often only several inches away. Americans comfortable conversing at about arms' length may feel their personal space has been invaded by the Latin need to be close. However, don't back off. To a Latin, retreat implies insincerity and rejection.

Latins may also finger your lapel, tap your chest, or squeeze your upper arm or shoulder as they talk. This also tends to make Americans uncomfortable. But it's merely a cultural style of expression and has no sexual implications. If you flinch, you reject.

North of the Alps and in Britain, businesspeople don't talk much with their hands. If your hands are continually in motion when you converse at home, practice making a presentation with them in your pockets or behind your back to reduce unconscious movement, which may be distracting or thought rude. But never actually speak to a European with hands in your pockets, or, if you smoke, with a cigarette in your mouth. Doing either is bad manners.

Latin Europeans behave charmingly to American women. They may kiss your hand in greeting or pay small compliments on your outfit, a piece of jewelry, or how becomingly you wear your hair. American women sometimes mistake such attentions for a pass, but there's usually nothing sexual implied when they come from Europe's managerial elite. Misinterpretations like these arise when female executives fail to accept that they aren't dealing with American men in Europe. Most American men are not instinctively charming. When an American man is charming, it's often a conscious effort that may well be a prelude to a pass. Enjoy the little attentions you'll probably receive in Latin Europe. Back home among American men, compliments may be few and far between. Says Harriet Mouchly-Weiss, chairman of Ruder Finn & Rotman International Partners, if her European colleagues ever dreamed their charming manners were being misconstrued as flirtation, they would be deeply embarrassed.

## Social Customs

The negotiating process doesn't end when you leave a European office; it has only just begun.

### Conversation

Listen to the loudness of the voices around you; if necessary, readjust yours to a lower volume to match the others. As a nation, Americans talk louder than Europeans do, and Europeans consider it obnoxious.

Don't brag about your personal accomplishments. It's best not to mention them unless specifically asked. Replies should be humble, not seem like you're being self-congratulatory.

Don't discuss money: not how much you earn, your company's net worth, etc. If you're a woman, and complimented by a European on your dress, never reveal what a "steal" it was, what it cost, or where similar bargains can be found in the U.S. To European cosmopolites, this is the height of vulgarity.

Don't ask a European family man about his wife and children until you're well-acquainted. Europeans usually consider any discussion of family to be an intimate subject. As a stranger, it's none of your business. Let them ask about your family first.

Innocent American questions like "How's business?" are shockingly indiscreet in Europe, like asking someone what his salary is, how much cash is in his wallet, or how much he pays in taxes.

Don't ask the national of one country how he feels about his geo-political neighbors. In dual-language countries, don't ask someone who speaks Language A how he feels about his countrymen who speak Language B. This may plunge you into local embroilments faster and deeper than you had in mind.

What can you safely discuss? Read European publications like *The Economist*, the *Financial Times of London*, the European edition of the *Wall Street Journal*, and the *International Herald Tribune* at least a couple of weeks before leaving home. You'll find them at a growing number of newsstands and in many libraries. They're chock full of conversational topics currently in vogue—business, politics, art, music, other cultural events, sports, and more.

It's okay to talk about business in general in social situations, but avoid discussing the business you're in Europe to specifically propose. That's best limited to the office.

Discussing politics can be tricky but may be unavoidable; Europeans love to talk about it. Savants learn just enough to ask intelligent questions and then let their hosts dominate the inevitable debate that ensues. One executive says he's amazed at how often he asks a political question, merely grunts and nods from then on, and afterwards reaps praise for his astute insights! And while he's listening, he often learns a lot that news-papers omit.

Cultural prides are always safe to praise and discuss. Every European country has its great painters, poets, performing artists, historical periods, athletes, craftsmen, foods, and drinks. Do research. Know what you're talking about. If you can't field questions that may be asked, your lack of sincerity may do more harm than good.

Give some thought to how you might answer questions about the U.S. Often we fail to anticipate them, and then find ourselves tongue-tied trying to sum up how 235 million Americans feel about inflation, nuclear disarmament, or the World Series. When discussing U.S. politics, whether or not you agree with government policy never knock our country. Even Europeans who aren't particularly fond of us are stunned when Americans speak disparagingly of the U.S. If you show no loyalty to your own nation, how much loyalty can Europeans expect from you? In Europe, you're not merely an individual American. You represent us all.

### Drinking

Everyplace in Europe has a favorite toast. The British say, "To the Queen"; the French, "à votre santé"; the Germans, "Prost" or "Prosit"; the Finns, "Kippis." There may also be a formal toasting etiquette. In Sweden, the traditional drink is snaps (akvavit), downed in one fiery gulp and followed by a beer chaser. Hold the shot glass up to your toastee, look him straight in the eyes, declare "Skäll," and empty your glass without breaking eye contact. The concierge at your hotel will know which toast to use and how it's delivered.

Americans drink more hard liquor than most Europeans. This is even more true of American women than men. In Europe, a woman who orders Scotch is pretty unusual. Executive women or the wives of male hosts normally prefer a lighter glass of wine, beer, or an aperitif. Ordering something more potent may make a poor impression on male colleagues.

Ask your hotel concierge what's locally drunk and drink it, or follow your host's lead. In Britain, the preferred drinks are beer, ale, gin and tonic, or perhaps a glass of sherry before dinner. The French generally sip aperitifs, the Greeks retsina or ouzo, the Spanish their own sherry, the Germans their own wines and beers. Of course, many Europeans do drink hard liquor, with Scotch (called "whisky" in Europe) most popular among men.

"On the rocks" is an American idiom Europeans may not understand. If you want ice, ask for ice. However, once you leave the local Hilton, ice may not be available. Traditionally, Europeans drink liquor without ice. Excepting white wine and champagne—but not excepting beer—refrigerated drinks aren't common. Don't frown if you can't get what you want cold or with ice. You'll embarrass your host.

If you order a martini, you may get Martini & Rossi sweet vermouth. Specifically request gin or vodka with a touch of *dry* vermouth.

If you drink bourbon, buy a bottle at an airport duty-free shop. Bourbon is hard to find in European watering spots, and at modern hotels you pay cognac prices for it.

With few exceptions, mixed drinks aren't popular in Europe. Trying to explain how to mix a drink is usually an exercise in futility, and may embarrass your host. Few Europeans have heard of white wine spritzers, tequila sunrises, or Singapore slings.

Sometimes it's okay to talk shop over drinks, sometimes not. It depends on the individual more than on the culture. The wise let their hosts broach the subject first, or mention a brief reminder as they go their separate ways.

When it comes to hard liquor, most Americans can probably drink most Europeans under the table. Particularly if the conversation is going well, American men who drink regularly at home can sip for hours. Europeans have usually had it after a couple of drinks. Pace yourself by their example.

In Scandinavia, car renters must know local drunk-driving laws, which are strict. If you're stopped by a policeman and fail to pass a "breathalizer test," you can be fined, jailed, or forced to attend alcoholic rehabilitation meetings. Three beers may be enough to flunk the test.

While we may outclass Europeans as hard-liquor drinkers, the reverse is often true with other types of alcohol. At a formal business luncheon in Europe, you may begin with aperitifs, proceed to white wine, then to red wine, with brandy or port served at the end of the meal. Sip slowly or you may not be able to stand. If you can't—or don't want to—consume that much alcohol, accept it anyway and don't drink it, pretending to take an occasional sip. If you refuse, it puts your hosts in an awkward position. They want to drink. But decorum dictates that they defer to the guest's wishes, particularly if the guest is a woman among men. If you don't drink, Europeans may feel they must abstain as well, spoiling the meal.

Most Americans should consider European wine lists hot potatoes. If you're hosting a meal and the sommelier hands you the wine list, invite your colleague to do the ordering, or let the wine steward choose. In all Europe's wine-producing countries the natives are immensely proud of national wines and enjoy showing off the refinement of their palates. Let them have center stage and be a good audience.

Even if your knowledge of wine is nil, don't reveal it. If you're totally untutored in wines, how can you appreciate a colleague's choice?

Admitting you have no education in wines may be honest, but telling a European that you can't appreciate *his* education is uncivilized.

Whether or not you're an oenophile, if you do the ordering choose a local label, even in places like Austria, Switzerland, and Greece where the local product may not be favored by those in the know. As for Europe's major wine-producing countries, if you order a French wine in Germany or Italy, or vice versa, it may cause an international incident.

## Entertaining

You may be a guest or host on your first business trip to Europe, but it isn't written in the stars. In German-speaking countries, there may be a company cafeteria where employees—executives included—eat lunch. It won't be fancy, but it will still run rings around U.S. cafeterias, and the cost is modest. Few Europeans have expense accounts as lavish as ours, and even those few are less liberal in using them.

To be polite, a European may invite you to a restaurant dinner even when he'd rather not. When an experienced negotiator senses this, he gives the reluctant host an easy out. This is particularly true of American women, whom European men often feel obliged to entertain. Says one businesswoman: "Europeans value their evenings as much as we do. I always explain: 'I know you've had a long day and would like to relax at home with your family. Frankly, I'm bushed, too. Please don't feel you have to entertain me. I'll be fine, really.'"

However, a *married* European man may not even invite an American woman out for an innocent lunch let alone dinner, for fear his colleagues will talk. And it won't melt any ice at home. On the other hand, if a European *insists* on hosting a meal and the invitation is to a restaurant, accept or refuse as you see fit. It's not insulting to politely decline. But a houseguest invitation is an honor and shouldn't be turned down; you probably won't get one on your first trip. Not being invited home to dinner isn't a bad sign, but receiving such an invitation is auspicious.

### Playing Host

Lunch isn't the business opportunity in Europe that it is here. If you're still talking shop when it's time for lunch, it's polite to ask: "Would you like to continue our discussion over lunch?" If the answer is yes, you're tacitly the host as the suggestion was yours and you're obliged to pay the check. Even if a European agrees to join you for lunch, don't dwell on business from appetizers through dessert. Lunch is more often a respite from work rather than an extension of it. Mealtimes should be mostly used to learn more about your colleague as a person, and to tell him something of your personal interests. Lunch over, there may be a battle for the bill. Because you're a foreign guest, a European may feel honor-bound to pay the tab, even if the meal invitation was yours. Be this as it may, the check always ultimately belongs to the host, stranger or not.

On your first trip, don't invite a European to a restaurant dinner until you're certain that negotiations have gotten off to a good start. If they haven't, don't use dinner as a tactic to improve the situation. It won't.

In Germanic Europe, if you do the inviting *you* must pick the place. To ask a guest where he'd like to eat may be practical from an American point of view, but it's bad manners to force a European to make a choice; it shows a lack of foresight, and costs professional as well as social points. Ask your colleague's secretary or assistant where he generally likes to eat.

Even if you have a huge expense account, or are entertaining a top executive of a major European concern, don't take him to a gastronomic landmark. Europe's great restaurants cost a fortune—at minimum over $100 per person before you get to wines—and frivolously spending that much money is in poor taste, even if you can afford it. Europe's culinary legends are reserved for special occasions, not business luncheons and dinners. Remarks a Swedish shipping magnate about the American host of one such repast: "What was he trying to do? Impress me?" He *was* impressed. By the gaucherie of it all.

If you're a host*ess*, don't invite only *one* European man to a restaurant meal. Everyone's ears within a hundred yards will perk up. Ask at least a couple of male guests.

An American woman who does the inviting should pay the check, but *never* in front of European men. If the check is brought to the table, the men will feel compelled to fight over it to spare themselves the humiliation of *not* fighting over it. This is one ramification of European civility. When you telephone to make a restaurant reservation, which you should always do at the better eateries, arrange with the maitre d' to pay for the meal in advance. Slip him your credit card as you're shown to your table, and pick it up on the way out as you pause to sign the receipt.

At the end of the meal, should a male guest inquire about the check, reply that *it* has already been paid. Don't say: "*I* paid it."

Regardless of your sex, if a male colleague is married and you invite him to dinner, extend the invitation to his wife as well, and let him decide whether or not he wants her along. If he's also a father, don't include the kids. European children kick and squirm in restaurants just like American children do.


## Table Manners

Europeans say that American table manners are fine in Europe, and then proceed to contradict themselves and criticize our eating habits. Here's what they notice most:

• European restaurants are places of quiet murmurs, where the clinking of utensils on plates is the loudest sound. Says a Viennese CEO: "Whenever I enter a restaurant and hear a loud voice, I know an American is in the room."

• If you're invited to a home-cooked meal, be on time. Europeans don't say "sevenish," they say "seven" and they mean it. North of the Alps, people are the most punctilious. When *they* say "seven," if you arrive at 7:06, you're late! In England, says an American who has lived in London, a 7:00 invitation means that cocktails will be served from 7:00 till 7:30, at which time dinner punctually begins. If you're just wandering in around then, you've got some explaining to do.

• Northern Europeans are fond of toasting each other at formal dinners, whether at restaurants or at homes, and to show you're civilized, you should participate. However, don't toast a guest older or of higher rank than you are, or the host or hostess, unless he or she initiates it first.

• You'll probably find more utensils on a European dinner table than you're used to at home. Forks are to the left of the plate, knives and spoons are to the right. Begin at the outside and work your way in, using a new set of utensils for each course. If there's a knife above your plate, it's for butter. If there's a spoon, it's for soup.

• Europeans say we *saw* our meat like lumberjacks. We *stab* the pieces with our forks like Zulu tribesmen. And we *snap* the morsels with our teeth like starving wolves. If you're a sawer, stabber, or wolfer, try to use your knife and fork more delicately, cut smaller pieces, and chew more slowly. This is practical, too. Meals that last two or three hours are common in Europe, and there may be a long wait between courses. Europeans rarely rush a meal, so take your time.

• Americans are known in Europe as "fork switchers." We hold our forks in the left hand to cut our meat, then switch it to the right hand to spear and eat it. Europeans consider this inelegant; it involves a clumsy extra movement. To eat like a proper European, the fork is always held in the left hand—tines *down*, not up as we hold them—with the knife in the right hand, and no switching.

• While we consider it bad form to use the knife to push or load food onto a fork, Europeans use the knife to load as well as cut.

• When not holding utensils, empty hands—never elbows—should be on the table, not in your lap.

• When you're done with a course, lay your knife and fork side by side on your plate. If you do this before you're done, your plate may be taken away as this is a sign that you're through. If you just want to put down your utensils for a moment, place them on your plate in an inverted V. Don't bridge your knife on the table against the edge of the plate; this is only one step removed from eating raw meat with your hands. Europeans usually hold their utensils in their hands till they're done eating. Their hands are empty between courses, but not in mid-course.

### Britain
The traditional British meats are roast beef and roast lamb. At a restaurant, if you like meat rare, request it "bloody." In Britain, "medium" and "rare" are synonyms for "well done." But think twice before you ask for bloody meat. The face of your waiter, and possibly that of your host, may turn green.

### French-speaking Regions
Everyone in Europe whose first language is French considers cooking among the highest forms of human endeavor. Each dish is seasoned for you just so, or so the cooks insist, and if you don't take their word for it, it can cause a scene. Richard Smith, vice-president of American Steel Export, was invited to a dinner at a French home. As is his custom in the U.S., he salted his meat without tasting it first. The hostess had a fit and chewed him out on the spot.

But be wary of seasoning your meat even *after* you taste it. You'll never get a Frenchman's wife on your side that way—and her husband may seek her approval before he tells you yes.

If you're served a fish dish, don't use a meat knife. If a special fish knife is not provided, pick around the bones with your fork.

French table bread is usually a *baguette*, a long slender loaf. Tear off pieces with your hands. Don't slice them with a knife.

A round of cheese may be served for dessert. Slice it as you would a piece of pie. Don't lop off a corner at the outer edge. The shape of the round should be preserved.

### German-speaking Regions

North of the Alps, potatoes are cut with a fork, not a knife. German peoples eat bread in big thick slabs, heavily buttered. Don't tear or cut them up; you just gnaw on the slice.

### Scandinavia

Except for Norway, where it's a late breakfast, smorgasbord is the traditional luncheon buffet of Scandinavian peoples. They don't eat smorgasbord every day. It's usually reserved for special occasions or a weekend meal. But a business luncheon with an American guest may be special to Danes, Swedes, and Finns. Even on your first trip to the region, you may be treated to this repast.

A smorgasbord table is long and may be laden with forty or more hot and cold dishes. Take a plate—there will be a stack of them on the table—and start with the cold platters: fish dishes first, then salads and meats. Afterwards, sample the hot dishes in any order you wish. You can go back for seconds or even thirds of any course category, but once you move from cold fish to cold meat, or from cold to hot dishes, you don't backtrack. Never bring a used plate back to the buffet. Leave it at your dining table, where a waiter will remove it. Take a clean plate from the stack each time you return to the buffet. The feast can last the better part of an afternoon; pace yourself or they'll have to carry you out. Scandinavians often talk shop while they eat.

If you're invited to a Scandinavian home for dinner and are seated to the left of the hostess, you're the guest of honor and must make a short speech at the end of the meal, preceded by the comment *"tak for maten"* ("thanks for the do"). A knife tapped against a glass by the hostess is your signal to rise.

### Spain and Portugal

Here dinner begins late, often after 10:00 P.M. Many restaurants don't get going till midnight, as businesspeople arrive and work late. To keep stomachs from growling between lunch and dinner, everyone snacks. The traditional snackery is a tasca, or tapas bar, which abound in major cities. Each has a long counter laden with dozens of finger foods (tapas) that you wash down with a local wine or sherry. Tasca etiquette is simple: Oyster shells, toothpicks, napkins—everything inedible—is thrown on the floor. If you don't do it, the barman or your colleague will. It's great fun, but don't overeat or drink heavily. It's easy to lose track of time and get stuffed or inebriated, and the subsequent dinner may be a six course meal with several wines.

Among other universal rules: If you smoke, don't light up before, during, or after a meal, unless the host or hostess does so first or you ask permission. If another guest lights up, this doesn't mean you may do likewise; *he* may be out of line. If no one is smoking at any time, and you don't see ashtrays anywhere in sight, don't bother to ask if you can smoke; you know the answer.

Always send a handwritten note—delivered by messenger rather than by mail—the next day. This may be to express thanks for a restaurant meal, evening entertainment, special favors done for you, or courtesies shown, and *especially* for a home-cooked meal. Never telephone to say thank you in Europe; it's crass. For a European colleague's wife who has played hostess the previous evening, your note might read:

Dear Madame————,
    I want to thank you again for a most enjoyable evening last night and a delightful dinner. You are an excellent cook and hostess. I had a marvelous time.
Sincerely,

You need be no more effusive than that.

## Houseguest Gifts

If you're invited to a European home for cocktails or dinner, you'll need a gift for the hostess. Business gifts may be optional; hostess gifts are not. Your gift can be messenger-delivered early on the day of the event, carried by you to the door as you punctually arrive, or messenger-delivered the next day, with your mandatory thank-you note (the least preferable course). As an American, it's important to establish credibility as soon as possible at all times and in all ways—including your good manners—rather than putting it off for even a day and leaving your hostess to wonder whether you're civilized or not.

A popular hostess gift is flowers. But some flowers have symbolic meanings in Europe, so be careful. Red roses are for lovers, not hostesses; you'll embarrass everyone by giving them. White flowers are for funerals.

In France, Belgium, and French-speaking Switzerland, chrysanthemums are for All Soul's or All Saint's days, and they are inappropriate to give at more festive times.

Don't bring twelve flowers. "Cheaper by the dozen" is one American idiom Europeans know only too well.

Don't bring thirteen flowers. It's bad luck.

Don't bring a lot of flowers. Five, seven or nine will do. Explain the nature of the occasion to a local florist and let him arrange a proper bouquet; he'll know what's right.

Do bring an odd number of flowers. Flowers are part of nature and nature's beauty is asymmetric. As Europeans see it, an even number of flowers is unaesthetic and in bad taste.

In Germanic regions, unless the flowers are wrapped in transparent cellophane, remove the wrapping before handing them to the hostess. Flowers should be presented in their natural state with artifice removed.

On any pleasant occasion when flowers are appropriate, chocolates are a suitable substitute. Most Europeans favor pralines. Buy the best, but don't bring a big box. It's the thought that counts, not the quantity. In Europe, giving too much of anything is gauche, and Americans are known for overdoing it.

An alternative to flowers or chocolates is a liter of good Scotch or cognac. Johnny Walker Black, Chivas Regal, Rémy Martin, and Courvoisier are guaranteed to light European eyes throughout the Continent. As these are more prestigious (though no more acceptable) gifts than flowers or chocolates, give the bottle to your hostess discreetly. Don't make a big to-do before other guests. Some may not have brought gifts or given ones as generous as yours. And if the bottle is publicly presented, the hostess may feel obliged to serve it at once—or risk being thought miserly—while secretly preferring to save it for another time.

If you don't wait till the next day to have your gift delivered along with your mandatory thank-you note, you'll need another note to accompany your gift. For example:

Dear Madame_____,

Here is a small token of my appreciation for being invited to your home. I am looking forward to an enjoyable evening.

Sincerely,

Some Americans say they give wine as a hostess gift. Unless you're convinced it will be appreciated, wine is ill-advised. Europeans can be highly touchy about wines. Some may see in your gift an implication that you don't care for their taste in wines. Or perhaps you think there won't be *enough* wine without your contribution. And if it turns out that you bring a really good bottle—better than what the hostess has to serve—the situation can turn tense. Most Americans should not give wine. Even oenophiles who know wines may step on someone's toes.

Don't give perfume. Perfume is too intimate a gift for an American man to give to a European's wife, something like giving her lingerie. Even an American woman won't know what a European woman's taste is in perfume before meeting her, maybe not even then.

During the evening, observe the house. Look for clues as to what you might give as a more personal gift on a future trip, should further negotiations be warranted. What books are on display? What's the furniture style? What about wall decorations? Objets d'art? If there are children, how old are they? How grown up do they act? Get a general feeling for the decor of the house as it expresses the personalities of its occupants. Savants make notes back at their hotels. When a future trip calls for a more personal gift, the more you match it to the recipient, the more appreciated it will be.

# CHAPTER FIVE

---

# A Thousand and One Arabian Nights

"God obligeth no man to more than he hath given
him ability to perform."

*The Koran*

If your image of the Arab world is a lingering one from period films like
*Lawrence of Arabia* and *Lion of the Desert*—in which the Arabs were
portrayed as bedouin nomads—you may have some updating to do. In
Arab world destinations where most Americans are bound—particularly
those of the Arab Gulf—major commercial centers and infrastructural
development have been greatly modernized since oil was discovered in
Saudi Arabia in 1938.

Saudi Arabia is a case in point. In the decades since World War II,
the Saudis have invested billions of dollars in building new roads, schools,
hospitals, and airports. A national telephone system has recently been
installed by Canadian Bell. Large cities like Jubail, Yenbo, and Khamis
Mushayt are being built. By the year 2000, each is expected to have a
population of tens of thousands of people. In ancient trading centers like
Jidda, buildings of concrete and steel are edging out those of mud brick.
Today, there are modern international hotels, television stations, air conditioning, and telex machines.

Even what many Americans envision as typical Arabs—bedouin
nomads—increasingly roam the desert in Jeeps, Toyotas, even Mercedeses.
Camels are now mainly used as sources of meat and milk, not transportation.

## Portraits of a Businesspeople

Today the Arab world is in a state of cultural flux. In some countries, sophisticates in business and government—the Saudi Government is said to have more Ph.D.s than any in the world—continue to behave in traditional ways. But as more Arabs are attending universities in the U.S. and Europe, they return home seeking a cultural compromise by which their people can enjoy the fruits of progress while still maintaining their age-old identities as Arabs.

### What Is an Arab?

An Arab is a person who speaks Arabic and *thinks* of himself as an Arab. A Muslim, however, is not necessarily an Arab. He practices Islam, the world's largest form of worship. Islam is practiced in some ninety countries.

People who speak Arabic form the majority of Middle-Eastern peoples. But not all non-Jews indigenous to the region are Arabs. For example, Turks speak Turkish and Iranians Farsi (Persian), not Arabic, although they are similar to Arabs culturally.

Not all Arabs practice Islam, but most do. Christian Arabs and other minority religious groups are sprinkled throughout the Middle East. The fighting between different religious factions in Lebanon, and the persecution of the Baha'is in Iran, are testimony to how poorly Muslims get along with non-Muslim neighbors and with Muslims of different sects. About 90 percent of Middle-Eastern peoples are Muslim.

Just as every Arab is not a Muslim, so every Muslim is not an Arab. In the Middle East and North Africa, where most Arabs live, they number nearly 120 million people, most of whom are Muslim. But Islam is also practiced in such farflung places as Indonesia and China. An Indonesian or a Chinese who is Muslim is still Indonesian or Chinese by blood, language, and culture.

### The Arab Gulf

The Arab Gulf is often labeled the "Persian Gulf" in atlases, which is the traditional British reference. However, in the Middle East today, the term Persian Gulf is used only in Iran, a Muslim but non-Arab country. In Iraq, Saudi Arabia, Kuwait, Bahrain, Qatar, and the United Arab

Emirates, the body of water they border is known as the Arab or Arabian Gulf. The Arab Gulf is the term used throughout this chapter.


## Arab Oil

Americans often speak of Arab oil as if every Middle-Eastern country was oil-rich. In fact, only a handful are. Most border the Arab Gulf. In order of 1982 production size, Saudi Arabia, Iran, the United Arab Emirates, Iraq, Kuwait, and Qatar have the most oil. The only Arab members of OPEC with substantial oil production and reserves beyond the Arab Gulf area are Libya and Algeria.


## Modernization Versus Westernization

"Modernization," "Westernization" and "Americanization" are not synonyms. Most Arabs have not been Western-educated and are as rooted in the past as their forefathers were. Those who have attended universities in the U.S. and Europe usually accept the need for modernizing. But in the process of trying to effect change, a new, concurrent problem has arisen: cultural pollution. Many religious, government, and industry leaders in the Arab world are trapped in a dilemma with no simple solution. On one hand, they want and need Western technology. On the other, implementing Western technology requires Western experts who bring with them contagious, culturally corrupting Western ideas, many of which run contrary to traditional Muslim and Arab values.

Arab intellectuals fear Americans and Europeans may take advantage of and use them, which has historical precedent; Arabs have been consistently exploited by Westerners until only recently. They despise the technological advancement of the West because it makes them feel inferior as a people, yet they desire its benefits in order to progress.


## Types of Arab Negotiators

Complicating matters, royal-born and nouveau-riche Arabs, as well as a growing number of those of lesser rank who receive academic scholarships are being educated in the U.S. and Europe. Many return after years of living in the West acting less traditionally Arab than before. Out of this cultural flux, several types of Arab negotiators emerge.

### Bedouins

Bedouins, the first Arabs, were the original nomads and they remain the role model for most of the modern Arab world. Yet their numbers are on the wane. About 90 percent of today's Arabs are sedentary rather than being perpetual wanderers in the desert.

Still, the bedouin heritage exerts a powerful influence on settled Arabs as a source of deep ancestral pride. And the bedouin values of hospitality, generosity, courage, honor, and self respect remain ethical ideals for most people of the region.

While most Arab negotiators are not bedouins, a few may be. Those who are often have considerable power, authority, and financial resources. Because bedouins are usually strict traditionalists, you may be driven into the desert to convene in a tent, the customary meeting place. Bedouins may not have university education, Western or otherwise, and may not speak English. Yet bedouins have been master traders for centuries and many show a remarkable gift for—and willingness to—learn foreign languages to more effectively negotiate. The English of some may be excellent.

Bedouins are the purest of all Arabs in preserving the age-old customs. Because the influence of bedouin heritage on more modern Arabs varies with the individual, Americans who want to play it safe should understand and respect bedouin business and social conduct; it's the starting point of trust in the Arab world.

While the bedouin life style may be spartan and seem primitive, don't underestimate a bedouin's intelligence. When it comes to hard bargaining, he can be as skilled as negotiators elsewhere on the globe.

### Middle-Class Arabs

Fellahin, peasants and agricultural laborers living on the outskirts of oases, who are unskilled or semiskilled, compose the majority of all Arabs. They are migrating in ever greater numbers from impoverished desert areas to comparatively wealthy commercial centers to seek their fortunes, where some succeed as small merchants or skilled laborers—receptionists, clerks, lab technicians, computer operators, etc. Others become professional people—doctors, lawyers, accountants, teachers, middle managers, and low-level government personnel. They may also serve as professional agents—third-party representatives between foreign firms and local public or private sectors. In the latter case, it may be mandatory for the individual to be a native of the country in which he operates. For example, it's unlawful

for an Egyptian expatriate in Kuwait to serve as an international intermediary in commercial transactions; he must be a Kuwaiti. Keep this in
mind when seeking local representation.

At the top of the middle class are nouveau-riche Arabs who may
own large concerns or occupy important government posts. They, too,
may serve as professional agents.

A middle-class Arab may or may not speak English or be Western-
educated. Yet even those with little or no fluency in English may be
familiar with Americans and how we deal.

While middle-class Arabs may be more tolerant of American faux
pas than nomadic bedouins, meet them at least halfway in adapting to
local customs, as a sign of respect. And know which Arab rules must not
be broken, regardless of the individual. In upcoming pages, they will be
stressed.

### Nobility and Upper-Class Arabs

The Arab elite may be royal-born or members of the middle class who
have reached the top echelons of industry, government, or the military.
Their blood relations—regardless of individual authority and wealth—
are also upper class by affiliation. Among this group, English is commonly
spoken and Western education has become the norm for younger generations, many of whom are now middle-aged. While the Middle East was
once one of the few remaining refuges from international homogeneity
on the commercial map, this is changing. Even in Saudi Arabia, spiritual
leader of the Muslim world, Saudi cosmopolites in Jidda often attend
international social functions wearing the latest fashions from Paris or
New York.

### Internationalized Arabs

What confuses many Americans is the remarkable, often contradictory,
cross-cultural adaptability of Arabs they have met in the U.S. Arab visitors
to our country may shed their traditional robes and wear Pierre Cardin
suits when dealing in New York, Chicago, Washington, or, for that matter,
London or Paris. They may drink hard liquor, an Islamic taboo. They
may make passes at women who are not their wives; at home this could
well result in death by assassination or execution.

Novices who have met internationalized Arabs in the U.S. or Europe
may expect to find them in the same Cardin suits, drinking the same
Scotch, and making the same passes at native women back in the Middle
East. What they often find instead is the Arab they thought they knew so

well once again wearing traditional robes, offering them floor cushions instead of chairs, shunning alcohol, and treating native women with utmost respect. Yet the same individual and his wife may appear at an evening social function in a cosmopolitan Arab city in Western clothes.

How do you treat such an Arab? Like a Bedouin nomad, by traditional custom? Like a fellow American, as you may have done in the U.S.? Or somewhere in between?

The answer is usually somewhere in between. This is why it is essential to first understand what Bedouins expect from you by way of decorous behavior, and then modify it to match the personal preferences of your native host. It requires sensitivity on your part. Some Arabs well-versed in American ways won't feel insulted if you pass a document to them with your left hand or expose the soles of your shoes, because they realize no insult is intended, having spent years being handed documents with left hands and seeing shoe soles exposed in the U.S., Europe, and other parts of the world. Others, however—even with Harvard M.B.A.s and world-travel experience—may view such behavior as offensive when *they* are the hosts and *you* are the guest.

Observe common rules of etiquette in the Arab world. Don't try to "go Arab"—the attempt will be futile and considered patronizing—but show that you've done some cross-cultural homework. Many Arabs who expect and even want you to behave as Americans normally do will simply tell you so in a direct American way. Arabs are not people who take pains to hide their emotions. If an Arab feels complimented or insulted, it will usually be clearly written on his face.

Try to appear natural in your demonstrations of Arab etiquette. With an internationalized Arab, if you make it painfully apparent that you're bending over backwards to pass him documents with the right hand only, he may misinterpret your attempt at politeness as condescension. After all, or so his thinking may go, *he* knows that you're not an Arab. *He* has lived here or visited the U.S. and understands American customs. Why are you insulting him by treating him as if he was not an international business sophisticate? Practice basic Arab mannerisms that you may find initially awkward before leaving home so that you don't draw attention to what may otherwise seem comical, absurd, or boorish efforts to an Arab host.

### Instant Islam

"Allah is not unaware of what ye do."
*The Koran*

Arab loyalties assume the following order of importance:

• Nuclear family—fast becoming the rule in urban centers, where housing is in short supply, although extended-family ties remain close
• Extended family—which may be elaborate, including second cousins of in-laws
• Muslim Arab friends
• The Arab Islamic community as a whole
• Their country
• Non-Arab Muslims

To most Arabs, religion is among the paramount matters of life. Theoretically if not always in actual fact, a Chinese or an Indonesian Muslim commands the natural loyalty of a Muslim Arab even before a fellow Arab and countryman whose religion isn't Islam.

Islam is less a religion in the Western sense than it is a way of life and a reason for human existence. Its adherents don't worship for an hour or two once a week. Proper practice is daily and day-long. Islam influences most areas of Arab life: business hours, personal conduct, social relations, the treatment of women by men, the contents of national constitutions, and the structure of legal systems.

As most Americans are neither Arab nor Muslim, we may come last on a Muslim Arab's list of people priorities. Knowing a little about Islam may help to improve your rank, avoid unintended insults, and demonstrate your sincerity to do business. Without even rudimentary knowledge, your chances of success in the Middle East are not good. You don't have to struggle through the Koran itself; only a scholar is likely to appreciate the subtle implications of the text. There are many short, easy-to-understand volumes *about* the Koran in bookstores and libraries that clarify the meanings of important passages.

Here's a basic Islamic vocabulary:

*Allah*
The Islamic name for God.

*Muhammad*
Allah's greatest prophet. Noah, Abraham, Moses, and Jesus are also Islamic prophets. But even though they antedate Muhammad, they are

considered less important than he. Despite Muhammad's prominent stature in Islam, don't confuse *prophet* with *deity*. Christians consider Jesus to be God. But Muhammad is not the Arab counterpart of the Christian Jesus; he is not *He*.

### Muslim

One who worships Allah or God and believes in the teachings of Islam. The fundamental Islamic creed is "There is no god but Allah and Muhammad is his prophet." Muhammad, not being a deity, is revered but not worshipped.

### The Koran

The Islamic holy book. Conceptually, the Koran is holier to Muslims than the Old and New Testaments are to Christians. The Koran represents the *direct word* of Allah, unlike the Bible which Christians and Jews consider to have been written under God's *guidance* rather than directly by Him. As a concept worthy of reverence, the Koran outranks even Muhammad. More than a book of worship, it's an ethical and civil code as well as the standard reference for classical Arabic as a written and spoken language.

### The Five Pillars of Faith

These five rules, stated in the Koran, are prescribed duties for all devout Muslims: professing faith—repeating the Muslim creed; praying five times daily; giving alms; fasting; and making a pilgrimage to Mecca—Muhammad's birthplace—at least once in a lifetime, if able.

### Mosque

An Islamic house of worship. When possible, Muslims congregate in mosques at sunrise, noon, mid-afternoon, sunset, and in the evening each day to enact ritual prayers. Friday is the Muslim day of rest.

### Ramadan

The ninth month of the Islamic calendar, a time for fasting. From dawn till dusk of each day during the month of Ramadan, Muslims are forbidden food, drink, cigarette smoking, and other necessities and pleasures.

During Ramadan, even U.S. multinationals with Middle-Eastern operations cut back on work, and Arab office hours may be rearranged, reduced, or even cancelled. As the month wears on, the pace of business continually slows, often coming to a stop. Even top government officials may be at work for only a short time each day, from 11:00 A.M. to 1:00 P.M., and may not be eager to see American business travelers then.

Because Ramadan is a fasting month, Arabs tend to become crankier as the holiday progresses. Nerves get frayed. Tempers wear thin. And you have to watch what you do in public. If you eat, drink, or smoke in front of a fasting Arab, you may get angry looks or loud rebukes.

As the Islamic calendar is based on lunar rather than solar cycles— as Western calendars are—the date of Ramadan changes yearly, although it usually occurs in the summer, signaled by the thin crescent of a new moon.

### 'Id al-Fitr

The Feast of the Breaking of the Fast. This four-day holiday begins *Shawwal*, the month after Ramadan. 'Id al-Fitr can last from three to five days or longer. Many Arab offices close two days before it begins, and a week or more can lapse before business returns to normal.

### Hajj

The twelfth month of the Islamic calendar, when those Muslims making the holy pilgrimage journey to Mecca during a given year. An average 2.5 million Muslims throughout the Arab world make the sojourn during Hajj, flocking to Mecca via Jidda, the nearest major city, clogging roads and airports. If you must be in an Arab country, particularly Saudi Arabia, during Hajj, arrange your schedule so that you arrive when Arab pilgrims are leaving Mecca, or return when they are about to depart from the holy city of Muhammad's birth. Otherwise, business travel will be arduous at this time.

## Arab Time

> "Arab clocks have no hands."
> *U.S. oil company executive*

George Daher, former communications advisor to the Saudi Arabia's Ministry of Defense, tells this anecdote:

> An Arab and a Mexican are discussing time. The Mexican says: "I understand that in Arabic there is an expression very similar to our *mañana*." "Yes," replies the Arab. "The word is *bukra*. Like *mañana*,

it means 'tomorrow.' But *bukra* does not imply the same sense of *urgency!*"

The Arab concept of time is not the minutely divisible concept that's the norm in the U.S. Arabs don't view nature or human events as being controllable by man through advance planning, clock watching, and discipline. Such matters are determined by Allah alone, whose will is unknowable and unforeseeable.

Arabs traditionally view time as a continuous flow of events in which past, present, and future blur together rather than being separate and well-defined. An American expatriate in Riyadh recalled inviting a Saudi couple to his home for dinner on a Wednesday evening two weeks hence. The couple appeared at his front door on the proper day—but a week early. From the American's point of view this was a mix-up. From the Saudis' point of view it was not. By Arab standards of temporal flexibility, they were "on time." In business, unfortunately, it usually works the other way around. Arabs are more apt to be late than early—yet still, as they see it, on time.

If unanticipated events prevent an Arab from doing something he would have liked to do on time—like meeting deadlines on agreed-upon dates—it's the immutable will of Allah. Therefore, it's inevitable, beyond human control. This logic is the most difficult for Americans to accept, yet to not accept it will give you ulcers before it will get a job done any faster.

You'll hear the word *inshallah*—"If God is willing"—liberally used in Arab conversation, even English conversation. Inshallah implies uncertainty: God may *not* be willing to have your deadlines punctually met as promised. Americans believe that where there's a will there's a way, and of course the will is human, not divine. God's will has nothing to do with meeting our deadlines and is an unacceptable excuse. Arabs believe just the opposite: God's will determines what gets done, despite an individual's sincere intentions.

Arabs neither view time as money nor put business before family, friends, or religion. The week before a promised deadline is due, your colleague may have to mediate a family dispute, attend to the illness of a friend, or observe a religious event that he simply didn't take into account during early negotiations. Meanwhile, during the final critical week, nothing gets done. He may not even go to the office. How could he know that a squabble or illness would occur in advance? He can't, but the possibility always exists in his mind, and such unforeseeable events are

covered by implication with the interlarding of "inshallahs" in every conversation involving any kind of commitment.

Even English-speaking Arabs with Western M.B.A.s may not be
punctual for appointments, or may miss deadlines with what Americans
typically misinterpret as an infuriatingly nonchalant air, due to the inevitable interference of Allah's unpredictable and mercurial will. This is not
what U.S. stockholders want to hear.

What can you do to change the concept of Arab time? Not much.
But not nothing, either. Keep scheduling flexible. Show an Arab tangible
signs of respect to cement a trust relationship. The more an Arab trusts
you, the more he'll try to listen to American "reason" in speeding up
delays. Otherwise, Allah's will may have an increasing tendency to slow
things down.


### Privacy

The Arab concept of privacy is different from ours. In public, Americans try not to touch each other. But public touching doesn't bother Arabs
a bit. They bump, brush, nudge, and jostle each other on the street; finger,
pat, and squeeze each other during conversations, and may appear out of
nowhere to "steal" a taxi for which you've been waiting. Such behavior
is natural, not rude, in the Arab world. Everyone does it with no psychic
spatial transgressions intended or perceived. Be prepared for it.

Also be prepared for what you're likely to find on your first meeting
in an Arab office: unwanted company. Many American novices eager to
discuss classified company business enter an Arab office and are stunned
to find their host surrounded by friends, relatives, and professional associates, none of whom make a move to leave. All are equal in Allah's
eyes, according to the Koran. By extension, guests of the same host are
viewed as one, without entitlement to special privileges like privacy. (An
upcoming section discusses what this seemingly compromising situation
is really about, and how to deal with it.)

What *do* Arabs consider private? Their personal lives. Their homes.
Their families, *particularly* their women. Family honor is among the most
important of Arab values. The greatest threat to it is the loss of chastity
of a female member out of wedlock, or a married female relative caught
in an extramarital affair.

As pillars of family honor, Arab women are what most Americans
would consider overrevered. Not only are they vulnerable to the carnal
thoughts of men but also to their own latent promiscuous desires. As such,

they're a perpetual source of anxiety and trauma to their male relations, who see sexual temptation lurking in every shadow.

In the past, women were rarely permitted to leave the house. This was less a matter of restraint than of protection. Today women have become a common sight on streets in major cities. But most continue to appear veiled and fully cloaked in *abayas*—long, voluminous black robes hiding arms as well as legs—when in public. Morever, even though Arab women, particularly those of Arab Gulf countries, are entering local workforces, and some who have been Western-educated are wearing modest Western dress to the office, they remain a sensitive subject best avoided in conversation.

## Hospitality

There are few places globally where generosity matters more than in the Arab world, where a charge of stinginess is a serious insult. To ancient bedouins, from whom modern Arabs take many cultural cues, the purpose of hospitality was to strengthen group ties, vital to security in a tenuous nomadic existence in the harsh desert. Today, Arab hospitality is still a two-way street—a show of mutual respect, reciprocity, and delicately balanced obligations between host and guest who will then, in a future situation, become guest and host.

Not only is an Arab obligated by cultural values to give a guest—even a stranger—food and protection, but for a guest to *refuse* such generosity is an insult, a rejection of bonding to the group with which his host is aligned. When the situation is reversed, the former guest must now play the host with equal, but not greater, hospitality, so as not to create an imbalance in the relationship resulting in the former host's loss of face.

When you're offered something by an Arab colleague—coffee, tea, a soft drink, nuts or dates, an invitation to dinner, a gift—in the office or out, politeness dictates that you should accept it. Whether or not you want it is irrelevant. It's the *symbolic meaning* of an offer and its acceptance that matters, not the content of the offer or your desire to receive it.

However, it's impolite to be too quick to say yes. Initially you must enact a ritual refusal, which may be prompted by as simple a matter as accepting a cup of coffee. In conversation, an offer, refusal, and acceptance work like this:

"I will serve you some coffee."

"Thank you. But I don't want to put you to any trouble."

"Please. Have some coffee."

"Really, I don't want to be a bother."

"It is no bother. The pleasure is mine. I insist."

"In that case, yes, I would like coffee. Thank you."

Notice that even the initial refusals are tentative ones, not definite nos. After one or two halfhearted refusals, you finally give in and say yes, which is what your host expects. Enacting this ritual is particularly important if hospitality is offered to you in the presence of others, as is apt to happen. The strangers you meet in the company of your host may have more to say about your private dealings than you think.

## Arabic

Arabic is among the world's most widely spoken languages, the mother tongue of nearly 120 million people in the Middle East and North Africa. It's written and read from right to left in a twenty-eight-character script with the same ancestry as the Roman alphabet. The Arab's love of his language rivals that of the French. It's a rhythmic, musical tongue, full of color, variety, and nuance of sound. But it's also a language that encourages hyperbole and elaborate verbal rhetoric spoken with great flourish. *How* something is said may matter as much as or more than its actual content. In Arabic, the medium often *becomes* the message. Observes one scholar: "It is characteristic of the Arab mind to be swayed more by words than by ideas, and more by ideas than by facts."

Simple statements of yes or no may require constant reemphasis on your part or an Arab colleague's for them to mean other than merely "maybe." This is another reason why promised deadlines so often get missed in the Arab world. When an American says yes, it's taken for granted that the answer is definite. It also implies that he can do whatever it is he is agreeing to do by a certain date. Even Western-educated Arabs who speak excellent English may still *think* in Arabic. This may also be true of Arab interpreters.

For many Arabs, merely expressing an intention to meet a given deadline may have the same psychological effect as actually having met it. No immediate thought is given to how and when the promised deed is actually going to be done. This is why even those events which are *not* unpredictable—be they upcoming religious events, lack of local labor (often an endemic problem), or congested ports (which may nearly always be congested)—might not be considered in a simple answer of yes.

The way pros handle this predicament is to take the Arab tack of constant reemphasis. "Do you really mean yes?" "Are you certain?" "Are you absolutely, positively 100 percent sure?" "You are sure you're sure beyond a shadow of a doubt?" Many Americans cite a list of potential problems, seeking reassurance that none will pose a foreseeable obstacle, or if one will, what the roadblock will be, how it can be surmounted, and how long the solution is likely to take.

But even when you've taken extra care to establish that an Arab yes truly does mean yes, somewhere in the conversation the term "inshallah" will probably be used. This lets even an Arab who has told you absolutely positively yes off the hook if he should in fact fail to deliver on time.

Journey to the Arab world knowing that quick profits are rarely made, and that a guaranteed yes is rarer still. Make sure your superiors understand this before you leave the U.S. to protect yourself from being the brunt of blame if deadlines are missed. The profit potential of your mission should warrant tolerating probable delays. If anticipated profits can only be justified within short, precise time frames, you're heading for the wrong part of the world to do business.

## U.S. Executive Women in the Arab World

Most American women in Arab countries are the wives of managerial expatriates; they're not permitted to hold local jobs themselves. U.S. business travelers who are women are rare, and most who have tried to deal in the region fail to open Arab doors because of their sex. But slowly this is starting to change. When K-Mart Trading Services sent Marjorie K. Alfus to Saudi Arabia as a chief negotiator, she became one of the few female successes. But this probably had more to do with her offer, in which the Saudis were highly interested—an instance where desire for modernization overrode cultural mores—than with Alfus's skill as a negotiator and the persuasiveness of her personality. She recalls:

> I went with another gentleman of our company who has a lesser position than I do. We met with a group of Saudis who epitomized the feelings of men in that country toward women. We were in the office of the chairman of the Saudi firm, and for the first hour he continually addressed my associate, ignoring me, because he would not accept my presence as a woman. Finally I turned to him and said: "Mr. X, you are directing your questions and answers to my associate. If you are seriously interested in doing business with our company, I suggest you direct them to me, because it is me with whom you will have to negotiate." I was very

direct because I sensed that he was being direct. But I think he respected my approach. I didn't feel indignant or slighted as a woman. It was a matter of who it is that a person wants to seek out. I had no problems after that.

Still, most American women who have lived in the region for years as the wives of male managerial expatriates maintain that a female representative is a poor choice for dealing in the region, and will only complicate commercial transactions which are already complex enough. Harriet Mouchly-Weiss has lived and worked in Israel as a public relations manager for Hilton International, traveled widely throughout the Arab world, and numbers many Arabs—men as well as women—among her friends. She speaks for most Americans, regardless of sex, who know the region well:

> A woman is a poor choice to represent your firm in the Arab world because it violates Arab cultural mores. It makes Arabs *uncomfortable*. This is a sign of disrespect and a weak basis for building trust.

## Business Customs

Inexperienced Americans often learn too late that Arab business customs are a far cry from their own. And yet, despite significant differences, many contracts are lost because U.S. negotiators fail to take basic selling steps they wouldn't dream of ignoring at home.

### Pre-Trip Research

According to Yousif Al-Hamdan, Deputy Minister of Commerce for Saudi Arabia, a major reason why Americans fail in his country is that "they do not take the Saudi market seriously enough to do the thorough investigation that success in the market demands."

What is meant by "thorough investigation"? Business International Corporation, a market research and publishing firm based in New York, offers a detailed report—*The Middle East Forecasting Study*—that discusses factors affecting medium-term business opportunities in Algeria, Egypt, Iran, Libya, Morocco, Saudi Arabia, and Turkey. The current edition advises, "Your ability to hedge losses and capitalize on opportunities will very much depend on how you 'read the signs' of these changes and plan for them" in the Middle East between 1983 and 1987:

• Basic political goals of the country in question

• Likely political developments over the next one to three years

• Socioeconomic and political forces at work—military, bureaucrats, approved political parties, banned political groupings, religious leaders, religious extremists, middle class, unions, urban poor, farmers, youth, etc.

• Short-medium-term prospects—GDP growth, inflation, budget, reserves, foreign debt and servicing, trade and balance of trade prospects, balance of payments, currency

• Government role in business—socialist, capitalist, mixed—and its likely evolution over the forecast period

• Incentives to invest and outlook—tax relief, capital and dividends, profits, remittance conditions, import duty guarantees, import protection, labor availability and restrictions, etc.

• Countervailing demands—required transfer of technology, local content use, export requirements, investment approval hurdles, harmonization of projects with development priorities, attitudes toward accessibility to foreign exchange, etc.

• Business conditions affecting profitability—labor policy and wage trends, taxes, import duties and conditions experienced by U.S. firms in the Middle East, access to foreign exchange, price controls, remittance experience of U.S. firms, competition with state-run companies benefiting from subsidized inputs, borrowing from the local market, etc.

## Visa Requirements

In many Arab countries, including those of the Arab Gulf, business travelers are issued visas by invitation only. The invitation must come from a government official, a local executive, or a professional agent empowered to act as a middleman in negotiations and to represent your firm in daily relations with an Arab prospect once you return to the U.S. To secure an invitation from an appropriate Arab, check the New York Consumer Yellow Pages under "Governments—Foreign Representatives," where the current addresses and telephone numbers of most Arab consulates and/or United Nations missions are listed. Our own Foreign Trade Administration, based in Washington, D.C., may also be helpful. In addition, a growing number of reputable Arab firms have opened branch offices in either London or the U.S.—mainly New York and Washington— to oversee their affairs locally. Such places can often supply the name and telephone number of an appropriate contact here, or the name and telex number of a professional agent in the Middle East.

Once you receive a formal letter of invitation to visit an Arab country on business, you can usually get a visa in about two weeks.

It can be extremely difficult for a woman unaccompanied by a man to secure a visa. Don't try to fool an Arab by defeminizing your name. You may end up traveling thousands of miles for nothing. Arabs who are eager to deal with certain U.S. firms are slowly starting to grant visas to American businesswomen, but such instances remain rare. Be prepared for rejection.

### Dress

Except for Iraq, where Western dress has become the norm, expect your Arab counterparts—particularly in Gulf countries—to be wearing national costumes in the office, the local equivalent of a pinstripe suit. Such three-piece outfits include a long loose robe called a *dishdasha* or *thobe* and a headpiece, a white cloth *kaffiya* banded by a black *egal* to secure it.

Arabs neither expect nor want you to imitate their style of dress. As many Arab countries are hot for a good part of the year, clothing should be lightweight for comfort and conservative, preferably dark-colored— although lighter hues are acceptable for the hottest months—and mono- chromatic rather than patterned. White shirts and black lace-up shoes are universally approved American dress.

If you're a subordinate female member of a negotiating team bound for the Arab world, take your clothing cues from the dress guidelines for men. In addition, floor-length dresses that cover your ankles are univer- sally approved. Arms should be covered from shoulder to wrist. Dresses and blouses should be loose fitting to hide body contours and the swell of breasts. Don't wear gossamer fabrics that reveal undergarments or flesh. Don't wear slacks or pantsuits—which show off legs, however indirectly. American women often wear babushkas, pareos, shawls, or scarves to hide their hair in public, the showing of which may also be an indiscretion.

Regardless of your sex, don't underestimate an Arab's ability to appraise the quality of Western dress. Your attire conveys your personal image and that of your firm. Wear good-quality, well-tailored clothes— even though women's clothes should not fit them like gloves—put on your Sunday watch, and use your major-contract-signing pen. Fountain pens are classier than ballpoints. Dress for success; it will be noted.

If you normally wear jewelry with religious significance—a crucifix, a St. Christopher or other saintly medal, a Star of David or other Jewish ornament—that can be publicly seen, leave it home. It will cause offense and in some countries it's against the law to wear Western religious objects.

## Appointments

You can usually obtain an Arab calendar from the sources listed in the previous section on visas. It's handy for scheduling trip dates. Western peoples use the Gregorian calendar. Arabs don't. Our calendar begins with the birth of Christ. Theirs starts with the flight of Muhammad from Mecca to Medina in 662 A.D., called the Hegira. Arabic calendars use the acronym A.H. (*Anno Hegirae*—"Year of the Hegira") instead of the Christian A.D. (*Anno Domini*).

The Hegira or Arabic calendar rotates on a thirty-year cycle, including nineteen years with 354 days and eleven years with 355. One Hegira year overlaps two Gregorian years. Since the Hegira calendar is based on lunar rather than solar cycles, as the Gregorian calendar is, there are only 29.5 days in an Arab month, and an Arab year is shorter than a Western year by eleven days. This may affect the dates on which annual holidays occur. For example, the holy month of Ramadan takes place about eleven days earlier each ensuing year.

Arab calendars are often printed with Gregorian as well as Hegira dates in parallel columns. Most Arab correspondence—particularly government letters and telexes—will bear the Hegira, not the Gregorian, date. For example, October 18, 1982 to October 6, 1983 A.D. corresponds to the year 1403 A.H.

Use an Arab calendar to ask questions about the practical timing of your trip. When are the hottest months of the country you plan to visit? Temperatures in the Middle East can climb to over 120 degrees Fahrenheit, and while some Arab offices are air conditioned, others are not. Arabs usually save their vacations for the summertime to escape the brutal heat. Decision makers may adjourn to London or the Riveria. In Saudi Arabia, government officials often relocate to the resort city of Taif, the summer capital in a cool mountain setting. Appointments can be hard to make, and even if prearranged, they may not be kept during summer months.

Even with your appointments carefully scheduled don't expect them to be punctually kept. It may still take you several days or a week after a prearranged meeting date to make initial contact with a local company or government agency. Meetings invariably take longer than novices predict, less gets done at each, and subsequent meetings can be hard to schedule. Keep your return date open.

Richard Smith, group vice-president of American Steel Export, an old hand at Arab-world negotiations, describes the Kafkaesque business of trying to make appointments in the Middle East:

When I return to the U.S., my colleagues ask: "What have you accomplished in four days?" I reply: "I spoke to two people." They're astonished. *"Two* people in *four* days!" So I tell them how it is in the Middle East. I telephone an Arab contact. It turns out he's busy. But he says that he'll call me back to make an appointment. Meanwhile, I'm stuck in my hotel room waiting for his call. I can't call someone else I need to see who may be available for a meeting tomorrow, because that's when the first person I called may want to meet. Often I have to wait in my hotel for two days before Arab One calls me back.

Persistently retelephoning Arab One is generally futile. Few Americans in the Arab world can change Allah's will. You must be patient and prepared to be available at your counterpart's convenience.

Arab and American business hours are not the same. Working hours vary from place to place in the Middle East, but as a rule:

• Arabs usually work a five- or a five-and-a-half-day week. The Arab weekend is Thursday and Friday, not Saturday and Sunday. Friday is the Muslim day of rest. The half-day of work, where it applies, is Thursday morning, a bad time to make appointments.

• Banks are usually open from 8:00 A.M. till noon, plus one afternoon per week.

• Professional people like lawyers and accountants, as well as service organizations, usually work from 9:00 A.M. till 1:00 P.M. and from 2:00 till 5:00 P.M., typical U.S. business hours.

• Shops are open from 8:00 A.M. till 1:00 P.M., and from 4:00 till 7:00 P.M. These are also corporate and governmental working hours. From 1:00 till 3:00 or 4:00 P.M. is siesta time, when the midafternoon heat is most intense. Don't try to contact an Arab during his rest period.

• Many Arabs, including top executives, work later than 7:00 P.M. Serious work is often done between 8:00 P.M. and midnight, when it's comfortably cool. But these are not normal working hours. Don't telephone during this time.

• Old hands feel the best time to make appointments is late in the morning, around 10:30 or 11:00, when Arabs are usually fully involved in their daily agendas and before the saunalike afternoon heat.

• Devout Muslims pray five times daily, but no one knows how many Muslims are devout. Some are more religious than others. Those apt to

be *least* devout are Western-educated and speak English. Americans, however, should get to know individuals, not jump to conclusions that may
be wrong.

• Work abruptly ceases for devout Muslims during prayer times. If
you're in a restaurant, bank or other public place of business at such times,
leave the premises. The prayer ritual usually takes from fifteen to thirty
minutes, possibly longer if an individual goes to a mosque to worship.
But many religious Arabs excuse themselves from meetings and pray
privately at the office.

• Most U.S. multinationals with Arab-world operations follow the
Arab custom of giving employees Friday off instead of Sunday out of
respect for Islam and convenience, but the other weekend day is usually
Saturday, not Thursday, as it is for Arabs.

• You'll get little done on the Arab weekend, but experienced negotiators often arrive at that time to give themselves at least a day or two
to recoup from jet lag. Most Americans are bound for Arab Gulf countries.
The long exhausting flight and thick heat frequently encountered on landing retards recovery time. You'll welcome a rest before your first meeting.

## Business Cards

Business cards should be translated on the reverse side before you
leave home, and the printing on *both* sides should be of equally high
quality.

If your firm is not internationally known, the English side of your
cards should contain a phonetic transliteration of your company name.
Otherwise, many Arabs whose English is imperfect may have trouble
pronouncing it. Even if your firm is world renowned, *your* name should
be transliterated phonetically if it's hard to pronounce, but your company
name need not be. Its logo or logotype will usually have immediate visual
recognition.

Present your card promptly after shaking hands, Arabic side up.
During your meeting, your host will keep the card before him and probably
refer to it often.

You may or may not receive a business card in return. If not, ask
for one. It will genreally be translated on the reverse side into English.
Arab business cards may contain unlisted telephone numbers and addresses
that you might need and are difficult to find by indirect means.

## Collateral Materials

Technical and promotional literature should be translated. Particularly for Arabic it pays to hire the best translator available. Give a translation bureau as much lead time as possible to find precisely the right person for the job. Whatever you predict the translation will cost, it will probably be higher. Expect it, pay the price, and write off the expense at tax time. A bargain-priced, second-rate translation can have fatal consequences metaphorically and literally. A Kuwaiti was killed by a crane because his poorly translated operating manual instructed him to turn a lever to the left instead of right.

If there's interest in your offer, you may deal with two types of people: decision makers first, then technical personnel. Arab decision makers are strategists, not tacticians. They want the big picture in broad brush strokes, not elaborate technical details. The shorter a business proposal is, the better. A ten-page document can be more persuasive than a fifty-page tome. Save detailed technical reports for subordinate specialists who want to see them and are trained to know what they mean.

If you're representing a service company selling an intangible, like market research, be forewarned that many Arabs aren't used to paying for raw knowledge or statistical data. For this reason, many service and think-tank outfits align themselves with manufacturers of tangible goods. Arabs may not relate to products they are unable to physically *touch*, and a set of neatly bound pages falls into this category. Product samples, demonstration equipment, and working models that turn abstract services like market research, advertising, public relations, or consulting expertise into something that can be seen, handled, and admired as a concrete physical entity will often have greater impact. If what you're selling is only images or information on paper, your business proposal should spell this out in no uncertain terms up front, the point should be reemphasized during your oral presentation, the cost should be explicitly defined, and the logic of its justification should be patiently, carefully, and completely explained.

Arab legal documents should be translated into English and interpreted for you by an attorney knowledgeable in *Shari'a*—Islamic legal code. In all legal transactions, the Arab document, with its countless unstated implications and interpretations, is the final authority.

Ironically, a common error in collateral materials is using the *wrong* language or not *enough* languages in translation. Oil-rich Arab nations are rife with foreign work forces, which may form the majority of consumers of your products. For example, in Dubai, part of the federation of the United Arab Emirates, only about 10 percent of the population speaks Arabic. Most residents are Pakistanis, Indians, Iranians, Indonesians, South Koreans, and other foreign nationals, who speak and read only their native tongues.

A subtler but potentially more counterproductive problem is the improper use of illustrations. Arabic is read from right to left, and pictorial sequences are also viewed from right to left. One U.S. marketer of laundry detergent, unaware of this, designed ads for Arab countries showing a series of three illustrations as Americans would view it—with soiled clothes on the left, the product in the middle, and clean clothes on the right. To Arabs, who viewed the sequence in reverse, the detergent took clean clothes and left them soiled.

"Beauty shots" of sexy models displaying your product can seriously offend the Arab sense of female propriety. Muslims are hypersensitive to female flesh publicly shown in any form; even bare arms and legs are an Islamic taboo. A Detroit auto maker found himself in trouble in Abu Dhabi when he presented ads featuring curvaceous women clad in outfits that, while acceptable by U.S. standards, outraged his Muslim customers.

An international airline, unaware of the strict Islamic taboo on drinking alcoholic beverages, nearly lost its Saudi Arabian routing when it ran ads in local newspapers that showed flight attendants serving liquor to passengers.

Illustration problems can be subtler still. To the untrained eye, Arabs in national costumes—thobes, kaffiyas, and egals—dress alike. But differences in national attire do exist from one country to the next, and Arabs can tell at a glance when they are looking at a picture of a countryman or of an Arab neighbor, for whom they often harbor intense dislike. To illustrate your product with a Syrian and show it to a Yemenite can be bad enough. To show a non-Arab like an Iranian or a Turk, who also wear seemingly similar dress, to a Saudi can seriously impede negotiations.

On February 13, 1983, *Time* magazine reported an instance of how images of the wrong Arabs can become grievous insults:

> It was intended by its U.S. producers to be a tribute to the late Egyptian President, but when the TV film *Sadat* was screened recently for a censorship committee that included Egyptian Minister of Culture Muhammad Radwan, something had obviously been lost in the translation. . . . Radwan banned from his country not only *Sadat* but all films produced or distributed by Columbia Pictures. Egyptian objections to

the four-hour movie are not so much that Anwar Sadat is played by a black actor [Louis Gossett, Jr.], as some reports have suggested, but that accents are often Pakistani rather than Egyptian; some of the garb worn is found in Morocco, not Egypt; Nasser is shown kissing Sadat's wife, an abominated Westernism.

Illustrations designed to sell effectively in Arab markets should use no creative license. Arabs are intensely nationalistic and may have profound misgivings about their geopolitical neighbors. There exists no all-purpose photograph of an Arab. Collateral materials that include illustrations of Arabs should be of the *right* Arabs—Saudis for the Saudi market, Kuwaitis for the Kuwaiti market—or they'll do more harm than good.

## Business Gifts

Don't feel you must bring a business gift on your first trip to the Arab world. Your host won't expect one. Too lavish a gift may put an Arab in a compromising position in which he must reciprocate or lose face.

If you meet with an Arab several times during the same trip, as a gesture of friendship and goodwill you can give a small gift. Don't give logo gifts, particularly to the Arab elite; logo gifts are considered distasteful hard sell. Don't give a gift that's too cheap or too expensive; the latter may be perceived as a bribe. Government officials in particular take a dim view of extravagant gifts.

Don't give any alcoholic beverage as a gift, no matter what you may have seen an Arab drink in the U.S. In the Middle East it's an Islamic taboo. It's also best not to bring food as a gift, which may offend an Arab's sense of hospitality, in which an abundance of food as a show of generosity is stressed; presenting an edible item may imply to an Arab host that you think him miserly and that he won't have enough food without your contribution.

For gift suggestions, check Chapter Three. Most logo items you'll find listed make suitable gifts—without the logo.

## Shaking Hands

You may shake hands with an Arab several times in one day, each time you're apart for a while and remeet. Exchange greetings as you shake hands, and continue shaking until greetings are done, which may take several minutes. Arabs rarely say anything concisely. A simple "hello" is too abrupt in the elaborately flowery Arabic style of expression; it lacks sincerity and warmth. A typical greeting might begin:

> Good morning. How are you? Things are fine with me. I'm in good health. Are you? I hope so. Yes? Ah, that's good. It's a pleasure to meet you [or see you again]. The weather's hot today, isn't it? Does it bother you? I don't find it that uncomfortable. I was at my hotel, and now I'm on my way to...

It goes on and on. You shake hands all the while.

Americans have an aggressive handshake. We grip firmly and shake for three or four strokes. The Arab handshake is gentle and limp. Don't squeeze too hard. Hold an Arab's hand loosely. The actual shaking is light, with only a slight up-and-down movement, never a pump.

Arabs are conscious of rank and expect their protocols to be observed. Shake hands with the most important person in an office first. You'll spot him easily, as he'll be sitting in the middle of the room, surrounded by other guests who pay him visible obeisance. If you're accompanied by a local interpreter or agent, he'll point out the person of highest rank.

Regardless of your sex, it's the duty of the guest to extend his hand to the host.

If the room is crowded, no matter. After shaking hands with the host, you must greet and shake hands with each guest in turn. A general nod to the others in the room is rude. Pros work the room in sections, taking care not to leave anyone out, even though the guests may have nothing to do with business and you may not know who they are.

As you shake hands and convey a greeting, maintain eye contact throughout. Eye contact is a sign of sincerity.

Everyone rises when a new guest enters the room, waits for him to shake hands with and greet the host, and then prepares to be greeted and shaken hands with in turn. Rising is a sign of respect. If other guests arrive after you, and those in the room stand up as they enter, so should you.

You may see some Arabs use both hands to shake hands, with the four hands gently clasped into a ball. This gesture is usually used with old friends, not new acquaintances. But follow your host's lead. If he clasps your right hand with both of his, cover them with your left hand.

## Forms of Address

Don't call an Arab by his first name unless you're invited to. Until he does, don't invite him to call you by yours. Probably most Arabs with whom you'll deal will introduce themselves, or be introduced, with first and last names, as in Hassan Ammar. Call him "Mr. Ammar."

Other than members of royal families, ministers, and high-ranking military officers, Arabs aren't fond of titles. Gulf Arabs in particular disdain pretention and display, titles included.

The term shaikh or sheik can be confusing. It's normally used to address someone deserving special respect: a wise teacher, an elder, a religious leader, a member of a royal house. When you call a person "Shaikh" who's a *real* shaikh in power, prestige or wisdom, he may modestly protest his worthiness for so august a title. But continue to address him as "Shaikh" unless he specifically requests that you do otherwise.

However, some Arabs who call themselves shaikhs are not true shaikhs. Often they're only nouveau riche, and wealth alone doesn't make an Arab a shaikh. Such a person may be trying to impress with the title, particularly impressionable Americans. But you'll probably learn quickly who are real shaikhs and who are shams. Other Arabs, resentful of this misuse of a revered title, may tell you. Still, even if a shaikh is a sham, call him what he wishes to be called.

Shaikh is also a proper name, so you can't assume anything about an Arab simply because he's called Shaikh. Overt signs of deference from those of lesser rank marks a shaikh by title from a shaikh by name.

In the Arab Gulf, rulers—often called amir or emir in general reference—are personally addressed as "Shaikh," followed by their first names, as in Shaikh Hassan.

While modern Arabs may use first and last names, traditionalists may be formally named Moktar ibn Abdullah ibn Mohammad ibn Hassan. *Ibn* means "son of." You don't have to recite an Arab's entire family tree in conversation. While other Arabs may refer to him simply as "Moktar," begin by calling him "Mr. Moktar" even though Moktar is a first, not a last, name. If Moktar wants the "Mister" dropped, you'll be told.

## Presentation Style

Appear punctually for appointments, but expect to be kept waiting for a few minutes or an hour. Arabs know Western standards of punctuality and expect you to abide by them, even though in their culture being late isn't rude.

Present your business card to the receptionist, who'll probably be male. When you ask if your host is in, he may simply indicate an office doorway. If your host isn't inside, don't enter. Take a seat in the reception area. Don't pester the receptionist by asking every ten minutes when the boss will show up. Relax.

While you're waiting, don't read, write, open your attaché case and shuffle through papers, or do anything else. Simply sit.

Don't glance at your watch every other minute. Showing impatience is impolite.

Don't daydream. Keep alert, but don't seem to listen in on conversations that occur nearby. When your host appears, promptly rise and shake his hand—as the guest you must initiate the act—and prepare for an elaborate greeting.

Government offices are usually modern, with desks and chairs. Company offices may or may not be. If not, you'll sit on floor cushions instead of chairs.

You may or may not be the sole guest in the office. If not, shake hands with everyone before you sit.

In a group situation, people may be coming and going constantly. Guests already present don't rise and reshake hands when someone in the room leaves and then returns, only when a new guest arrives.

Whether your seat is a chair or a floor cushion, don't expose the soles of your shoes. The feet are the lowest part of the body. They touch the dirty ground. It's offensive to make a public display of them.

Once you're seated, refreshments will be offered—coffee, tea, perhaps fruit juice or a soft drink. Currently popular is "Saudi Champagne"—Perrier and apple juice. Coffee is usually flavored with cardamom; it's strong, thick, and bitter. Tea is very sweet but weak. Both are served in small handleless cups. If you're offered a choice of drinks, take what you want, but take something, whether you're thirsty or not, and refuse two or three times before you accept, a show of courtesy. When a subordinate appears with your beverage choice, take it with your *right* hand. The left hand is reserved for using toilet paper, nothing else. It's an insult to accept, offer or hold *anything*—food, drink, cigarettes, documents, even pens—with the left hand. If you're a southpaw and must write in the presence of an Arab, apologize for being forced to use your left hand so that he knows no insult is intended.

If the beverage is coffee, pass the cup under your nose to savor its aroma, which shows you aren't a philistine.

As the coffee cup is only about the size of a shot glass, you can sip your coffee or gulp it down, but pace yourself. Many Americans don't like Arab coffee, and you'll probably drink more than your fair share before you leave the Middle East.

You don't need to slurp, but if you do, that's fine. A slurping guest is a happy guest to an Arab host.

When your cup is empty, someone will appear to refill it. Whatever you drink, have one cup and ask for at least one refill, which you must taste but don't have to finish. This demonstrates that you've adequately sampled Arab hospitality.

After you've had your mandatory one-and-a-half cups of coffee or tea, if you don't want any more hold the cup in your right hand and shake it gently from side to side when the server reappears. You can also put your right hand over the cup. Or simply say in English that you've had enough. It's usually understood. The Arabic word for "enough" is *buss*.

Once you permit your cup to be refilled, you're obliged to take at least one sip. Each small offer of hospitality you accept you must make at least a token effort to enjoy.

Such matters of etiquette may seemingly have little to do with presentation style, but during your initial meeting with an Arab you must sell yourself before you sell your company or its wares. Making a good first impression is essential. Your host will engage in small talk as you partake of refreshment. How was your flight? Is your hotel okay? Have you seen the local sights? If not, you must. If so, what did you think? Is there anything you need to make your stay more comfortable? And so on. An Arab will try to relax you at your first get-together, but at the same time he's sizing you up. Don't introduce business subjects when drinking coffee and chatting about nonprofessional matters. Be patient. Building trust in this way lays the groundwork for negotiations.

An Arab office can be a flurry of sounds and movements. A host may hold several conversations at once. The telephone will continually ring. Guests will come and go constantly. Once your host has chatted with you for a few minutes, rather than permitting you to proceed with your presentation he'll probably turn to another guest and begin a new conversation, or pick up where one in mid-progress left off. Often he'll move from one person to another "sampling" conversations. Eventually, he'll return to you.

As such, prepare your presentation in short self-contained segments for Arab traditionalists, each about ten minutes long and devoid of technicalities. However, when dealing with a Western-educated Arab, he may prefer an American approach. Learn the preferences of the Arabs with whom you'll deal before leaving the U.S. They are not hard to find out if you ask around. It's crucial to effective presentation design.

Arab traditionalists view business presentations as entertainment rather than serious discussions about making money. Attention spans may be short. Americans dealing with old-fashioned Arabs often use cartoons or comic strip storyboards created by their ad agencies to clarify abstract concepts and convey selling points entertainingly, simply, and quickly. Says one old hand: "Don't expect an Arab to concentrate for long periods of time or think deeply about what you're saying. If your presentation is too technical, you'll lose him in a few minutes."

Once you've lost an Arab by talking too long, boring or confusing him with technicalities, or having him turn his attention to another guest, use the time before he returns to you to make small talk with other people in the room. Ask about each person's health, etc. Mixing with the group rather than remaining aloof from it creates a good first impression, and your host may ask other guests what they thought of you after you've left.

At initial meetings audiovisual aids are usually inappropriate. It's best to simply give your host a short business proposal that he can read at his convenience. If there's further interest, he'll let you know, usually in a couple of days—which is why return dates should be kept open and your superiors informed of this likelihood by you.

After your third cup of Arab coffee, the service will be removed. After an interval it will be returned. The length of time between coffee servings is the length of your meeting. It signals that your host has heard all he cares to hear for now, whether or not you have more to say. After repeating the drinking ritual previously described, say good-bye without waiting to be asked. If your host wants you to stay, he'll repeatedly urge you to remain.

## *Negotiating Notes*

Once an Arab has read your proposal, he'll pass it on to subordinates who are technically expert in the matter. They'll advise him as to whether or not the offer is interesting. If it is, you'll be told. If it isn't, you may or may not be informed. Telephoning an Arab who doesn't want to speak to you is useless. Most Americans without feedback wait around as long as they can, then fly home and try to reopen communication from the U.S.

If there *is* interest from the Arab side, a second meeting will be scheduled, in which Arab specialists, often with American Ph.D.s, will preside. The decision maker you had initially met may not be present. Now's the time for technical data and for audiovisual aids if you've brought them. While the traditional Arab who ultimately decides may have enjoyed looking at cartoons, they are inappropriate for the second team. Arab engineers, architects, and M.B.A.s are as professional and sophisticated as their counterparts elsewhere. They know their business and expect you to know yours.

Even Western-educated Arabs prefer a quiet, logical, friendly-persuasion approach rather than hard sell. While at times Arabs can be aggressive, their emotions are usually tempered by conservatism and reserve. Says one veteran of Arab negotiations: "When dealing with younger-generation experts, be direct. Spell out what it is you propose and why you think they should have it. But then back off and give them room to breathe."

If a woman is part of the negotiating team, she should play a subordinate role in discussions. When she has information to contribute, it should be offered indirectly. The male team leader does the cross-cultural communicating. When input from a female expert is required, he addresses her, she answers *him*, and he relays what she has said to the Arab side, even though her reply may have been clearly overheard by all.

Don't give an Arab the feeling that your business with him is merely one item on a detailed agenda, and that you must be out of Riyadh on Tuesday to be in Abu Dhabi on Wednesday in order to make Cairo by Saturday. Haste will get you nowhere fast in the Arab world. Regardless of the truth, seem patient and calm. You may be working on an ulcer because you're way behind schedule, but outwardly appear to have all the time in the world. If you make an Arab think you're crowding him into your busy schedule, you may find him crowding you out of his.

Iraq is an exception. If an Iraqi ministry is interested in your offer, you may receive an invitation to visit Baghdad to discuss it further. Gulf courtesies don't normally apply in Iraq. Local ideology holds that government officials remain anonymous so as to better focus on their functions rather than on their personalities. This usually makes business brisk and efficient to conduct, with little time spent on small talk and other rituals of courtesy.

## Decision Making

Arab decision making seems to take place at the top, but more often middle managers advise superiors and their counsel is heeded. This is one aspect of Arab elitism. Arab company presidents and government ministers tend to view themselves as master overseers and grand strategists above handling routine paperwork and bothersome details. They may not have the expertise to deal with technical matters. Unlike Americans, Germans or Japanese, who generally work their way up corporate hierarchies and often have in-depth knowledge of overall operations, a wealthy Arab may have simply purchased his decision-making status—or achieved his position not by ability but through family connections—and know little about his organization and how it functions.

In Gulf countries, particularly underpopulated Saudi Arabia, the true decision makers may not even be natives. There, Palestinians, Pakistanis, Egyptians, Yemenites, even Britons and Germans are employed to counsel ministers and executives.

At least several trips are usually required before productive relationships can be established in the Arab world. Trust takes time to build, and Arabs are often slow to say yes. An Arab will consider your proposal while you're in town. Once you leave, he may attend to other matters until you next return.

Once a project is underway, usually trips can be reduced. But periodically reestablishing good interpersonal rapport remains the key to success throughout the Middle East. It's the best assurance that your schedules will be met within reasonable proximity to your deadlines and with a minimum of Allah's divine interference.

## The Name Game

Don't call a Muslim a Muhammadan, implying that he worships the prophet Muhammad, not God. In Islam, this is blasphemy.

Be careful of who you refer to as a Muslim, an Arab, or even a Saudi if you happen to be in Saudi Arabia. You may be dealing with a non-Muslim Arab, a non-Arab Muslim, or an Arab Muslim expatriate whose native home is elsewhere. People can be highly sensitive about improper reference. Don't make assumptions. Learn an individual's background before you label him.

Never call a Turk or an Iranian an Arab. Neither speak Arabic nor think of themselves as Arabs. Turks are Turks, Iranians Iranians.

Culturally, Turkey may be part of the Middle East, but politically it's allied to Western Europe and thus considered part of it. From a Turk's point of view, not only is he not an Arab, technically he's a European.

## Conversation

If you know your host is a family man, don't inquire about the health or anything else concerning his wife and children until you have personally met them.

However, Arabs who are familiar with American custom may inquire about *your* wife and children, or ask if you're married and have a family. This *still* is not a sign to reciprocate.

If you're invited to an Arab home for dinner, and are introduced to the wife and kids, on subsequent trips you can ask after their health. If you're introduced to an Arab wife, simply say "hello." If you compliment her on her appearance, her husband's face may freeze.

Even mild American expletives are shocking to Arabs. Words like *damn*, *hell*, or even *darn* should be avoided. If you use God's name in *any* expletive, however innocent, like *God-awful* let alone *God damn*, that may be the end of that.

Don't raise your voice to an Arab. Don't shout, yell, or talk too loud. Never criticize or scold someone in public. If some rebuke is called for, take the person aside and quietly explain how you would like things done rather than calling him stupid or saying the way he did something was inept. *He* doesn't lose face, *you* do! If you lose face negotiations may grind to a halt. If you lose face midway through an already ongoing venture, Allah's unknowable will may become increasingly extravagant in its bottlenecking whimsy as your deadline draws near.

*Do* ask after an Arab man's health, and do it sincerely. Bring it up in conversation on a daily basis.

You may be asked about your professional achievements and avocational interests. Be modest in discussing them. Never boast, which Arabs find vulgar.

In talking shop, particularly when discussing the nature of the business relationship you have in mind, Arabs usually think long-term and are less interested in one-shot deals. Be this as it may, keep talk of the future to a minimum. As Arabs see it, the future is Allah's domain, not man's, and too much talk about tomorrow may make them uncomfortable, testy or impatient with its absurdity, as no mortal can second-guess what Allah will do next.

Don't jump the gun and announce the "near agreement" on a major deal between your U.S. firm and that of an Arab concern. To many Arabs this is a breach of confidential trust and disrespect for God, in whose hands final agreement inevitably rests. Let your Arab colleagues make the announcement first, and temper the enthusiasm of your own public relations people by the tone of the Arabic text.

Avoid talk about local or inter-Arab politics. Unless you're an Islamic scholar, discussion of religion is also unwise.

One subject that's always safe is Arab "football" (soccer). Try to familiarize yourself with local teams and let your colleague dominate the conversation.

Also fairly safe is praise for a productive local industry, like Egyptian cotton; a technological achievement, like the building of the cities Jubail, Yenbo, and Khamis Mushayt in Saudi Arabia, or the Medjerda River irrigation project in Tunisia; scientific accomplishments, like the invention of mathematics, records of which date back to the second and third millennia B.C. in Egypt and Mesopotamia; or important historical figures, like Al-Khowarizmi, a ninth-century resident of Baghdad who wrote a seminal work on algebra. Be careful, though. Expressed admiration for Saudi oil reserves wins no converstional points. Compliments on certain historical figures, like Cleopatra, are outright insults; Egyptians consider her a whore.

When talking shop, Arabs may be reluctant to say no out of local mores on politeness. If you're in a position of authority, this is especially true. If an Arab tells you "maybe" or "perhaps," chances are good that you're receiving a courteous but definite no. "Yes, Allah willing," means "maybe" in the Middle East.

## Body Language

While some types of nonverbal communication have previously been noted—conversational distance, touching, use of the left hand, eye contact, exposing the soles of the shoes—there are other forms of body language you should know as well.

Arabs normally stand closer than Americans do in conversation. But as a discussion becomes more animated they may move closer still. This blocks the listener's peripheral vision and ensures his undivided attention. Also, unlike Westerners, Arabs have a keen sense of smell and may use a person's body odor as a trait by which to identify and personalize his character. The closer two people stand, the easier it becomes to recognize the other's characteristic scent.

You may see Arab men walking hand in hand, arm in arm, or with hands on shoulders in public. This is merely an expression of platonic friendship.

Arabs consider direct, consistent eye contact in conversation a sign of sincerity, but don't stare. Eye contact is a searching or attempt to look "behind a person's eyes" to gauge the inner qualities of the individual. For this reason, Arabs neither converse nor greet each other publicly with sidelong glances, as Americans often do. Rather, they stop, turn, and face each other squarely in order to chat eye to eye.

Don't turn your back on an Arab. It's impolite.

Don't point your finger at an Arab to emphasize a point.

Don't beckon to an Arab with your hand or finger; this is how dogs are summoned.

Don't pat an Arab on the back in a friendly American way, or refer to him by nicknames like *pal*, *buddy*, *man*, or *Charlie* as in "sorry, Charlie." Don't refer to an Arab as "your friend" as in "look here, my friend," unless he really *is* your friend.

If you consciously or unconsciously but continually glance at your watch, take it off and put it in your pocket. Some Americans habitually glance at their watches from time to time; to an Arab, this indicates rejection of his companionship: obviously you'd rather be with someone else.

Don't let your eyes drift idly around the room, as if you're bored. An Arab neither wants nor expects your eyes to be glued to his. But in conversation, your fields of vision should always overlap *directly* not peripherally. It shows you're paying attention and it's a sign of respect.

No is said nonverbally in the Middle East by a haughty, backwards jerk of the head, a sudden raising of the eyebrows, or a clicking of the tongue. The most common body language for no in the U.S. is a sideways shake of the head. In the Arab world this means yes.

In the midst of negotiations, there may be long periods of silence on the Arab side. Novices are quick to misinterpret silence as a sign of displeasure. Some make needless concessions to resolve a perceptibly bad situation that in fact doesn't exist. Extensive silences in bargaining sessions are normal and frequent in the Middle East. It's how Arabs digest what's been said and decide how to respond. Accept silence. Don't try to fill it.

Many Americans catch cold in the Middle East by moving out of air-conditioned buildings into sweltering heat. Be discreet about sneezing and blowing your nose in public, particularly if you do it loudly at home. To Arabs, public display of such bodily functions is the height of vulgarity.

Never walk in front of an Arab who's praying in a public place; it's highly disrespectful.

You aren't likely to be invited to visit a mosque and it's best not to request an invitation; you're a business traveler not a tourist. Still, some Americans are taken to mosques by their Arab hosts. If you're among them, on entering remove your shoes, avoid stepping on the prayer rug, and behave with the same respectful quiet as you would in a house of worship in the U.S.

Despite your best efforts to conform to Arab preferences, expect to make an occasional faux pas. Even the most traditional Arab will tolerate an innocent error made once or twice. Be sensitive to facial expressions; you can usually tell when you've inadvertently erred by a momentary tightening of a colleague's facial muscles, a sudden hardening of his eyes, or a fleeting look of discomfort or embarrassment. Don't be afraid to ask if you did something wrong so that you don't make the same mistake twice. By repeating the same blunder, you may create an indelibly bad impression. As long as you aren't condescending or arrogant, and are able to laugh at your own errors, a quiet apology will make amends for most faux pas.

## Social Customs

Socializing is a way for Arabs to judge your suitability as a business associate in purely human terms, an evaluation separate from—but no less important than—the offer itself.

Newcomers to the region are usually asked out to a restaurant meal, often at a modern international hotel if one exists at the destination. But it's possible that you may be invited home for dinner. The better known your firm is internationally, and the more prominent your position in it, the more likely you are to be a houseguest. If such an invitation is extended, it's bad manners to refuse.

## Entertaining

Because devout Muslims pray at sunset, and unpunctuality is not considered rude in Arab culture, home-cooked meals may take place well into the evening. While Arabs themselves may not be punctual house-guests—often showing up an hour late—Americans are expected to adhere to their own standards of punctuality and be on time.

Cosmopolitan women of the Arab elite are increasingly attending social functions that were formerly male-only affairs. But it's more often true in the Middle East for men and women to lead separate social lives. Particularly if your host is an orthodox Muslim, expect the dinner party to be stag.

If your wife has accompanied you on your trip, you may ask if the invitation extends to her as well. If an English-speaking, Western-educated Arab says yes, chances are that his wife and perhaps the wives of other male guests will be included, and the company will remain mixed for the duration of the affair.

However, if a traditional Arab says yes, your wife will probably fraternize with the Arab women of the house and possibly the wives of other male guests in separate rooms. You may not see her again until it's time to leave. The wives of older, orthodox Arabs may speak no English and are usually busy cooking, serving, and cleaning up after the meal for the men. If your wife is really keen on sampling a non-American culture literally behind the scenes, she may enjoy the experience. Otherwise, she'll be better off remaining at the hotel.

On entering a traditional Arab home, remove your shoes. You'll find the house is flexibly compartmentalized, designed so that any room can be opened to or sealed off from others by opening and closing doors. This permits the women of the house to go about their hostess tasks unseen by male guests. For example, dining-room doors may be shut to block the view of male guests conversing in an adjacent room while the women prepare the table for dinner. Then they leave through another exit, closing the door behind them, and once the room is empty the men enter through another door to enjoy the repast. The meal over, the men adjourn to another room with the same opening and closing of doors. With the dining room once again empty, the women return to clear off the table, still sight unseen.

But in major commercial centers your host may live in a modern apartment building, a private contemporary house, or—in the case of

high-ranking government officials and Arab nouveau riche—a palatial
mansion. In such places you may not have to remove your shoes. If you're
unsure of what to do, ask.

## Table Manners

Whether the meal you're served is traditional or modern, it will
usually have three parts: coffee, the meal itself, then more coffee. Coffee
rituals in the home are the same as those described earlier for the office,
and the time between coffee servings is the duration of the evening. The
first serving, offered shortly after you arrive, is often accompanied by
dates, figs or nuts. It's a time for cocktail conversation. After the final
serving, express your thanks and make your good-byes.

As most Americans deal in comparatively cosmopolitan centers of
the Arab world, the dinner may be Western style, eaten at a dining table
with the guests sitting on chairs rather than floor cushions, and with
Western utensils and plateware. In this event, American table manners
are usually accepted and expected, including holding the fork in the left
hand. To be sure, ask your local representative, an interpreter, another
guest, or your host beforehand. You still should pass or accept food and
drink with the right hand. The menu is apt to include roast lamb, sauces,
rice mixed with raisins and nuts, and fruit.

If you're invited to a traditional feast, traditional courtesies concerning the use of hands and hiding of feet soles apply. Americans may keep
their left hands behind them or tucked under their belts at the small of
the back to avoid inadvertent use. There are no utensils at an old-fashioned
repast; eat with your right hand. Depending on the number of guests, a
sheep, a goat, or a small camel may be the main course. Roasted or
broiled, the flesh is tender and easily torn off with the fingers. Dip the
pieces into a variety of relishes before eating. There will also be heaping
mounds of steaming buttered rice served on copper or brass trays. Shape
the rice into little balls with your right hand, dunk them into the relishes,
and consume.

As with coffee, when anything is offered to you at a traditional Arab
meal it's bad manners to accept at once. Two or three lukewarm ritual
refusals should precede eventual acceptance. As generosity is a Muslim
virtue, plenty of food will usually be served. Taking seconds is not only
acceptable but desired. The more hospitality you accept the better Arabs
like it.

The same holds true when *you* are playing host, whether in the Middle

East or in the U.S. If you invite an Arab guest to a meal or a cocktail party at home a few hors d'oeuvres is an insufficient offering of food. To avoid being marked as a miser, there should be more to eat than can be consumed.

If an older, orthodox Arab is the host, he may remain standing throughout the meal and eat nothing himself. His only concern is to attend to the needs of his guests.

At the end of a traditional repast, Arabs customarily burp as a sign of pleasure. You don't have to follow their example. At a Western-style meal hosted by an Arab, belching is as indecorous as it is in the U.S.

Don't smoke at an Arab dinner table or while seated on the floor around a traditional meal unless other guests have already lit up. Probably they won't. Cut down on *all* public smoking—whether at a dinner party or in the street—as much as possible.

At the end of a restaurant meal a ritualistic fight over who pays the check takes place. But whoever did the inviting is the host and everyone understands that he's the one who finally pays. Still, even if you're the guest, make two or three attempts to pay the bill yourself before you acquiesce. If you're the host, your Arab guest will do the same.

## Houseguest Gifts

On this subject experts are divided. Some say it's best *not* to bring a gift. It's not expected, and it may embarrass the host, putting him in a position where he feels he must reciprocate.

Others say it's appropriate to bring a small gift or send one the following day with a handwritten thank-you note. But even Group Two adds that gift giving isn't mandatory, merely a nice gesture. An illustrated book about the U.S., a carton of American cigarettes if the host smokes, or a box of good cigars are the right sort of gifts to bring. While some Americans give chocolates, it's safest not to bring gifts of food or drink, which may imply your host is miserly and be taken as a tacit criticism of his hospitality.

Whether or not you choose to give a gift, a messenger-delivered note of gratitude addressed to the *host* is in order. For example:

My Dear Ahmed,
    Thank you for an enjoyable evening last night. Your hos-

pitality and generosity were appreciated. You were an excellent host. I had a wonderful time.

Sincerely,

You may have heard that if you innocently admire an object in an Arab home, it will be promptly forced upon you as a gift, whether it's an item of little value or a Picasso oil. This may have once been true but times have changed. However, to avoid potentially awkward situations, compliment the decor of a home in general rather than a specific item in it. Or admire something specific within the general context of the room. For example: "I like the way you've arranged that chair, plant, and statue in the corner." Don't say: "That's really a great statue."

If you inadvertently admire the statue alone, and your host suddenly insists that it's yours, don't abruptly refuse. Arab hospitality is based on mutual reciprocity. A refused gift is a rejection of the giver and an insult. If the statue seems valuable, explain that it would only look as magnificient if left where it was due to the decorator's skill. If removed, the beauty of the arrangement would be spoiled. If the statue seems inexpensive, accept it graciously. To balance obligations, you now must bring something suitably reciprocal on your next trip. Still, rumors of Arabs cavalierly giving away priceless objects that are admired is highly exaggerated.

# CHAPTER SIX

---

# Getting Oriented

"We do not dislike everything that shines, but we
prefer a pensive shadow to a thin transparence."

TANIZAKI JUNICHIRO,
*In Praise of Shadows*

Too often the adjective *inscrutable* is incorrectly used to describe the
Orient. To many Americans it implies not that Oriental peoples are difficult
to understand—they certainly can be—but that they are beyond comprehension. This is patently false. However, particularly with East Asians,
it's true that they are "pensively shadowed" rather than "thinly transparent"
as we typically prefer. In this chapter, we'll shed light on the shadows
that commonly confound U.S. negotiators, as well as contrast the business
cultures of Japan, the People's Republic of China, and South Korea, three
countries that share Confucian roots yet are as different from each other
as night and day. Even the terms used to refer to the region can be
confusing. Let's begin by defining what they mean.

## The Orient

The term Orient was originally used to contrast the Occident, the
East versus the West, or more specifically, Asia (and sometimes North
Africa) as opposed to Europe. This is still the main meaning. Arabs,
Afghanis, Indians, and most Russians are as "Oriental" as Chinese,
Japanese, and Koreans. But, over time, the Orient has taken on a more
specific secondary meaning: the countries of the Far East or East Asia.

## The Far East

Historically, the Far East denoted those portions of the Asian continent and archipelagoes farthest from the nineteenth-century European maritime powers: China, Japan, Korea (then undivided), Mongolia, and the easternmost part of Soviet Siberia. Taiwan, then called Formosa, was not an independent nation. Depending on the period, it either belonged to mainland China or was annexed by Japan. The meaning of the Far East has also been extended to secondarily include the nations of Southeast Asia.

## Southeast Asia

Traditionally, this region includes the Philippines, North and South Vietnam (formerly Indochina), Kampuchea (formerly Cambodia), Laos, Thailand (formerly Siam), Malaysia, Singapore, Burma, Indonesia, Hong Kong, and Macau. Depending on the reference book, Taiwan may be part of the Far East, East Asia, Southeast Asia, or simply omitted from the countries listed under each term as if it didn't exist.

## East Asia

To simplify matters, this is the *only* general term used in the text from now on. It includes the one fully industralized country of the region, Japan, and the newly industrializing countries of China, South Korea, Taiwan, Hong Kong, and Singapore. The last four have been nicknamed the "New" or "Little Japans" due to their rapid modernization, often rivaling that of the "Japanese miracle."

In fact, the peoples of East Asia are the most rapidly modernizing of all non-Western peoples, and modernization requires trade. In the past decade Americans have done more annual business with the Japanese, South Koreans, and Chinese than with the combined peoples of Western Europe.

Two or three decades ago, East Asians were almost fanatical in their zeal to export while curbing imports. Today, the situation is changing. Rapid industrial growth, shifts from low- and medium- to high-technology industries and from light to heavy industries, lack of natural resources and often of technological know-how, as well as growing economic, political, and military ties with the West have forced most countries to increasingly import consumer items, capital goods, and raw materials in order to progress and to achieve better balances of trade demanded by their Western partners.

Still, many potential Western partners have been slow to understand and accept how business is conducted in the region. Americans often conclude that because East Asians, regardless of country, look alike in contrast to themselves, and may act in superficially similar ways, they are the products of a single cultural mind set.

This erroneous assumption probably causes more commercial transactions to fail than any other misunderstanding. Older-generation decision makers of different East Asian nations are heirs to unique cultural heritages. However, their sons or grandsons, many of whom are now middle-aged and have taken over as decision makers in their own right, are often Western-educated and fairly internationalized, increasingly taking their business-cultural cues from the West, mainly the U.S.

## Portraits of a Businesspeople

While East Asian cultures are significantly different from each other, their differences have grown more pronounced over time, and in key ways their origins are similar. What makes them unique now can best be understood by first going back in history to examine the common roots from which they evolved.

### Confucianism

The wellspring of most East Asian cultural similarities today was the widespread influence of Confucianism over 2,000 years ago. Unlike Buddhism, Islam, Taoism, Shintoism, and Christianity, religions practiced in modern East Asia, Confucianism is not a system of belief or worship. Instead, it's an ethical and civil code that originated in China and exerted a powerful impact on neighboring societies, coexisting with native religions. While few East Asians currently consider themselves Confucian in a conscious, formal sense, the effects of Confucianism on human interrelations have survived the centuries, and continue to be felt in today's business meetings from Seoul to Singapore.

Prior to the third century B.C., when Confucius lived, tyranny and warfare wracked China. The pervasive, wholesale slaughter of human life inspired Confucius to conceive a set of moral precepts for the civilized running of society. These precepts also gained acceptance beyond China's borders as an antidote to despotism and human bloodshed and an effective way to ensure the harmony, stability, and self-perpetuation of social order.

Confucius saw the basic unit of society not as the individual, as we do in the U.S., but as the *family*. The concept of the family could be extended to any larger societal group—a community, a corporation, a government, a nation—much like bricks are building blocks layered to form a wall that's larger than its component parts, yet dependent on each of them for its stability.

For society as a whole to remain stable, its component families had to be stable. To ensure stability, each family needed one set of universally accepted rules governing how its members should interpersonally relate. To keep family relationships unstrained, Confucius advocated many rituals, customs, and codes of etiquette by which harmonious behavior could be expressed between individuals. These rules were inflexible. Regardless of unique or extenuating circumstances, the violator was automatically in the wrong.

Confucius defined the key societal relationships as those between ruler and subject, parent and child, older and younger brother, husband and wife, and friend and friend. While the friend-friend relationship may seemingly concern U.S. negotiators the most, ruler-subject, parent-child, and older/younger-brother relationships may also play a symbolic role in bargaining sessions.

Such relationships could be expressed by demonstrating the cardinal virtues Confucius propounded: filial piety, kindness, righteousness, propriety, intelligence, and faithfulness. Of these virtues, filial piety remains paramount today, even for East Asians who have had no formal training in Confucian ethics at home or in school. Tae-wan Yu, former director of the Korean Cultural Service in New York, speaking of his countrymen, might well be speaking for East Asians of other nations when he says:

> We instill loyalty to family in our children from birth, next loyalty to community and nation. Which is the reason, I think, we have done as much as we have in the past thirty years.

Confucian relationships are *reciprocal*. For example, parents are just as obligated to provide for their children as children are obligated to obey and respect their parents, and, by extension, their surrogate parents: teachers, employers, government leaders, and other authority figures.

To establish good rapport between negotiators, the virtues extolled by Confucius must be mutually demonstrated. Today, however, the behaviors by which these virtues are expressed have been considerably modernized. Be this as it may, the success of commercial transactions may depend on how sincerely Americans abide by modern ethical ideals with Confucian roots.

## Modernization

Americans who have visited East Asia twenty years ago and haven't returned until recently are often struck by the incredible modernization that's taken place since. Those who still think first of the Korean War when South Korea comes to mind may be amazed to find the blasted landscape depicted in *M\*A\*S\*H* no longer exists. As late as 1960, Seoul was a drab, gloomy, shell-pocked cluster of low-rise buildings. Today it's a neon-bright, billboard-painted, skyscraper-filled city of nine million people, whose hectic rush-hour pace suggests New York rather than what has traditionally been called the "Land of the Morning Calm."

Similarly, only two decades ago Tun Hua Road, now one of Taipei's most fashionable streets—lined with new twenty-story buildings and glittering boutiques with marbled floors, mirrored walls, and French names— was merely a bicycle path bordered by rice paddies. Japanese *Hikari* "bullet trains," rocketing at speeds of over 125 mph, slash the formerly lengthy trip from Tokyo to Kyoto to under three hours. A new, punctual, spotless subway system runs beneath Victoria Harbor, connecting the New Territories and Kowloon with Hong Kong Island—a wonder of modern engineering. Singapore, only yesterday East Asia's "black hole of Calcutta," may now be the world's cleanest city, where throwing a cigarette on the street can get you fined.

China, where business and tourist travel were scant prior to 1978, is erecting swanky skyscraper hotels with indoor gardens and revolving penthouse restaurants with previously unheard of speed. While China's infrastructural development lags behind its hotel boom, it's not standing still by any means. A modern six-lane expressway, due to be completed in 1985 or 1986, will link Canton with Hong Kong and Macau, easing interdestination travel.

How such rapid modernization was possible to achieve almost overnight is mainly due to the extraordinary cooperation of the public and private sectors of East Asian countries. One trait of East Asian governments is their *stability*. Stability enables them to undertake long-term policies of dramatic economic change that U.S. presidential administrations, with only four-year terms and no longer guarantees of continuity, cannot. Underlying such stability is the willingness of East Asian citizens to be governed, a willingness only possible with strongly inculcated feelings of group solidarity and national loyalty. These are legacies of Confucius.

## Westernization

If rapid modernity suggests an embracing of Western thought and practice in modified forms, it's often true, particularly in the New Japans. In Japan itself, with the most homogeneous and tradition-bound of the region's people, many children and even adults prefer Western tableware to awkward chopsticks. Japanese teenagers, imitating youngsters in the U.S., are forsaking revered customs like respect for authority; one result is growing urban violence. Younger generations in Japan are becoming more individualistic and less enthusiastic about the prospect of lifetime employment than were their fathers. And among their fathers—managers in middle age—psychiatrists report depression and suicide are on the rise, often stemming from traumas caused by Japan's lifetime employment and seniority systems.

Being Communist, one might think the People's Republic of China would vehemently oppose Western ideas. But despite government criticism of "cultural pollution," residents of major cities are demanding more out of life. In 1983, per capita annual income reached $295 in Beijing, nearly 30 percent more than in 1979. Fast-food restaurants selling hot dogs and hamburgers are now popular. Western-style suits and dresses are selling out in factories as fast as Chinese clothing designers can furnish new stock. Over 30,000 live-in maids are employed in the capital and its suburbs. Exercise classes and hairdressing salons are the rage among Beijing women. Even more astonishing is the growing demand for cosmetic surgery that would have been unthinkable during the bleak years of enforced proletarianism under Mao Zedong. Beijing plastic surgeons charge about $20 to create a Caucasian look by slitting and retucking the eyelids, and the cost of a Western-style nose job is about $25.

Americans new to East Asia may read such news and assume it reflects trends that are taking universal hold, and that their negotiating counterparts can now be treated as if they were fully Westernized. This is not usually the case.

Despite the headlines it makes, Western influence affects only a minority of East Asians. Mainly they are young and rarely hold positions of negotiating authority. Your business colleagues in Japan are more apt to be the success stories of that country's lifetime employment and seniority systems, not managers who see psychiatrists because they feel depressed.

Negotiators in Beijing still wear baggy "Mao" suits rather than Western clothes, and none will have unnaturally Caucasian eyes and noses reshaped by plastic surgery. Even in South Korea, Taiwan, Hong Kong, and Singapore, where Western influence is most pronounced, you'll find this is only true compared to other East Asian countries; Koreans and Chinese capitalists have not become Americans once removed.

## Foreign Devils

It may seem paradoxical that many younger East Asians are enthusiastically embracing Western customs while traditionalists not only shun —but may actually *fear*—personal contact with Americans, but such contradictions do coexist.

A flaw of Confucian-based societies is their rigidity. For Confucianism to work, its tenets must be universally approved and practiced without exception. Historically, this meant outside cultural influence had to be curbed or totally curtailed, which is why Korea has been dubbed the "Hermit Kingdom," and why Japan remained closed to international traders until 1854, when an American naval officer, Matthew C. Perry, forced the country's opening of trade with the West.

Fear of foreigners still lingers in East Asia. It's why Chinese Communist Party leaders decry cultural pollution, why Chinese capitalists refer to Americans and Europeans as *kweilos* (foreign devils), and why Japanese call even Japanese Americans *gaijin* (outsider). Recalls Sol Sanders, International Outlook editor of *Business Week*, who has lived and worked in Japan:

> I've known officials in the Japanese Government—in the Ministry of Finance—powerful people, who constantly deal with Americans and who have a terrible time. I've known Japanese ministers who get diarrhea when they have to negotiate with Americans, they get so nervous.

Confucian-style group solidarity may read well on paper, but its lasting effects on East Asians today may breed mistrust even of fellow countrymen who don't belong to a particular social group. Japanese firms may profess to be working for the betterment of society at large, yet they are as fiercely competitive as U.S. companies, with elaborate intelligence systems to conduct domestic and international industry surveillance. Were they strict adherents of Confucian tenets, such information would be openly shared for the betterment of all. Similarly, China's ministries may function more like mutually exclusive organizations rather than different arms of the same government working toward a common good. Often officials of Ministry A must learn what their counterparts at Ministry B are up to from Americans, Europeans, or Japanese who must deal with both in order to trade!

As a cultural outsider in East Asia, at the outset of negotiations, expect to be instinctively mistrusted by native colleagues. East Asians with interest in your proposal will strive to establish trust bonds with you mandatory for them to deal. You must know how this will be done in order to properly reciprocate. If you inadvertently fuel their innate sense of threat by behaving in ways that violate local customs, you'll probably join the extensive and growing ranks of Americans who fail in the region, regardless of the attractiveness of your offer. Profits alone are not the sole incentive for an East Asian to do business.

## Historical Consciousness

Establishing a trust relationship begins by understanding and respecting East Asian pride in national history—ancient as well as modern—something that for many Americans is easier said than done. Probably for most of us, *meaningful* history—events to which we can personally relate as individuals—roughly coincides with our lifespans to date. American history that antedates our lives is often something separate to which we who live in the present and look ahead rather than behind feel disconnected or only remotely related. Appreciation of American history is the business of scholars more often than it is of businesspeople. It's a subject for the classroom, not the living room, much less the conference room.

However, while our society may stress self-control of personal destiny and individual initiative, East Asian societies—which are not 200 years old but several thousand—emphasize family and larger group cohesion, loyalty, conformity, and national pride. The conditioning process by which these traits are instilled in individuals begins almost at birth, and includes a highly developed personal identification with national histories and cultural achievements. Such pride far exceeds the appreciation American parents and teachers usually succeed in instilling in their youngsters.

As a result, the East Asian perception of an historical event, even one that occurred well before an individual was born, is often so vivid as to seem almost personally experienced. For example, the nineteenth-century Meiji Restoration may be as "living" a memory—over a hundred years later—for Japanese today as more recent events such as World War II or the Korean War are for Americans. Put another way, if you were raised with an East Asian sense of historical consciousness, you might remember the American Civil War as vividly as you do the war in Vietnam!

East Asians are invariably impressed and complimented by Americans who take time to acquire some knowledge of their history, and there will be ample opportunity to introduce it as a subject of social or even professional conversation. Those with extensive experience dealing in the region are of one mind in maintaining that the more you know about a nation's history, the better able you'll be to understand your colleagues as products of cultures vastly different from ours. The deeper your understanding, the more you'll improve your chances of business success.

## The New Japans

Americans usually consider Taiwan, Hong Kong, and Singapore the easiest of East Asian places in which to deal. While South Korea is also dubbed a "New Japan" and poses fewer negotiating problems than are predictably encountered in Japan or China, its business culture is more complex than those of the smaller island nations and is separately discussed.

What makes Taiwan—also known as the Republic of China, ROC or Free China—easier to do business in than Japan or China is also generally true of Hong Kong and Singapore. It's a free-market economy in which entrepreneurial spirit is high. When the Nationalists retreated to Taiwan in 1949, per capita income was $45 a year. Since then, the gross national product has climbed by an average of 9 percent annually, one of the best records in the world. Today the per capita income stands at $2,474, almost ten times higher than that of Communist China, making the Taiwanese among the wealthiest of East Asia's peoples. Most homes have color televisions, refrigerators, and washing machines. Motorcycles have largely replaced bicycles for transportation (bicycles remain the norm in the People's Republic of China), and even motorcycles are increasingly being supplanted by cars, many of which are now built in Taiwan. Public facilities are highly developed. Health care is excellent. Labor insurance is being expanded to cover more workers and unemployment, by most standards, is minuscule. While skilled labor is no longer the bargain it once was, it still offers good value. As Taiwan's annual imports and exports roughly equal its gross national product, the country is heavily dependent on international commerce. With a burgeoning number of firms seeking foreign trade densely clustered within a small geographical area, competition for business is keen, creating an auspicious negotiating environment for U.S. traders who do their professional and cross-cultural homework.

Taiwan is also similar to Hong Kong and Singapore in its gradual blending of traditional and modern management philosophies over the past fifteen years to twenty years to catalyze spectacular economic growth. Older-generation business leaders were autocratic. Despite often limited knowledge of company operations, their word, as authority figures in the Confucian sense, was law. Predictably, many professional decisions were less than best, although some old-guard executives had—and have—brilliant business minds.

However, economic growth expanded the ranks of the middle class, whose buying power went well beyond the acquisition of daily necessities. Discretionary income enabled younger-generation Taiwanese to go abroad to study. Western-educated, English-speaking, bicultural, well traveled, and well attuned to the ways and means of global commerce, many returned home with greater technological expertise than their predecessors, and greater business vision. They introduced new options, flexibilities, and modes of thinking to meet more sophisticated and ambitious corporate goals—such as moving out of cheap-labor industries into high-tech fields like computers and semiconductors, a process that continues today. With the greater pool of specialized brainpower among middle-management personnel, decision making is becoming more decentralized in many firms with younger CEOs. Among the new guard, there is an increasing willingness to take risks and participate in new, unfamiliar ventures.

If this sounds close to the American style of doing business, it is. Fredric M. Kaplan, president of Eurasia Press, explains: "In Taiwan, Hong Kong, and Singapore, you're mainly dealing with Chinese capitalists. As a rule, they are fairly familiar creatures, people who usually have the same instincts and motivations for doing business as the typical American. Still, they are *not* Americans, and there are some differences: a greater veneer of courtesy and formality, more attention paid to matters of face, and varying attitudes toward the use of lawyers and the form of contracts."

Such differences can be significant. They often have Confucian roots and may affect negotiations in China, Japan, and South Korea as well. What are these universal themes?

## Hierarchy and Rank

Of the five societal relationships defined by Confucius, only that between friends was of equals. The others were superior–subordinate relationships based on authority, age or sex, resulting in highly stratified, class-conscious societies that persist in East Asia today. It's still important to know a person's rank within a given hierarchy so that one can give the respect due a superior, receive the respect owed by a subordinate, or know that two individuals are equal in status and can be so treated.

Sometimes this is easier said than done. A stranger's rank might not be known, or, perplexingly, the respect and allegiance due person A may mutually exclude one's obligations to person B—a dilemma to which Confucianism provided no solution.

Japanese samurai movies often address this predicament: people with a highly developed sense of honor confronted with two sets of mandatory but mutually exclusive obligations that are beyond their human capacity to meet at the same time. The dilemma may stem from the fact that duty owed to one's family precludes that owed to one's lord, or family versus country, or family versus teacher. Inevitably, the consequences are extreme and tragic, which is why so many samurai depicted on film commit hara-kiri (ritual suicide), an act that to the Japanese mind of the period wiped out the shame of failure, even though extenuating circumstances beyond human control made shame and failure impossible to avoid.

While East Asians don't expect Americans to master perfectly the subtleties of respect for hierarchy and rank, they do expect some show of minimal awareness. Without it, establishing trust—which *is* a must to do business—will be difficult.

### Business Cards

Nowhere is exchanging business cards more important than in East Asia. Why? Because your card contains your company title, indicating your rank in the corporate hierarchy. For most East Asians, particularly Japanese, knowing how to treat you is a major concern. To do so disrespectfully may result in loss of face. Whether or not you actually take offense or are even aware of any subtle slight has nothing to do with it. East Asians will go to great lengths to preserve face for themselves and others. Try to help them as much as possible.

### Seniority

There are two common instances when you should show respect to an East Asian: when you know he's higher than you in professional rank, and when he's older—particularly when he's old. Veneration of age, another legacy of Confucius, is extremely important in the region today; to ignore it is the height of rudeness. For example, when a colleague who is your senior appears at a doorway at the same time as you, he should be permitted to enter or leave first. You don't merely linger behind. You make a visible show of obeisance by pausing, extending your hand, bowing slightly, and saying "Please, after you." Your politeness may be appreciated by an older or higher-ranking individual but graciously refused. No matter. You still gently insist. You may be refused again. If so, insist again. Eventually, though, your colleague will acquiesce to your good manners and pass through the doorway first.

Similarly, a senior person should be allowed to sit down first, whether in a home or office. Never interrupt when he's talking. If you're dealing with a negotiating team and communicating through interpreters, the senior representative on the East Asian side should be directly addressed from time to time, another sign of respect, even if he doesn't understand a word of English. Americans often confine their remarks only to interpreters or East Asian colleagues who speak English; they may be the *least* important people at a meeting. Showing respect for seniority or age is what East Asians expect from Americans by way of basic awareness.

### The Age of a U.S. Negotiator

The older your company representative is, the better. Even if he or she is not a corporate officer, a person in his fifties, sixties or older is automatically accorded the most respect by East Asians because they believe age breeds wisdom that youth, however brilliant, can't replace. Even in the most internationalized of the region's business environments—South Korea, Taiwan, Hong Kong, and Singapore—veneration of age, regardless of an individual's native culture, is keen. Throughout East Asia, it's the obligation of the son to care for his elderly father and mother, who may live under the same roof with his wife and children, and in family or business matters the counsel of the old and wise is sought and heeded. This reverence extends to negotiators as well. Age may speed the trust-building process; youth may hamper it.

### The Rank of a U.S. Negotiator

The preferred rank of a U.S. emissary differs from place to place in East Asia. In Taiwan, Hong Kong, and Singapore, whether or not your representative is a corporate officer matters less than his knowledge of overall company operations. However, the Chinese Communists often expect a high-ranking individual, preferably a chief executive, to personally open negotiations, which has pitfalls to be discussed. On the other hand, American decision makers typically undervalue the importance of middle management in Japanese firms. Unless a business proposition is so consequential that senior Japanese executives must be present at negotiations at the outset, initial meetings are apt to be conducted by middle managers. The president of a large U.S. concern who far outranks them in corporate status may cause embarrassment, impede the forming of trust bonds at the first crucial level of decision making, or force a top Japanese executive to attend at a presumptuous time merely to balance the lines of power and preserve face, getting negotiations off to an awkward start. This may also be true in South Korean firms that operate on a modified Japanese model. To clear up such confusions, ask the East Asian side or a third-party intermediary the hierarchical level of the individual or team you should send to get discussions smoothly underway.

## Face

While Americans have some concept of "face," the East Asian implications of the term are more subtle, complex, and serious. Preserving face for oneself and others is essential to maintaining harmony within the group, be it a family or a corporation. This is particularly true in East Asia, which is densely overpopulated. Add to this the region-wide migrations of rural poor to comparatively wealthy commercial centers, where housing is in short supply (it's said that in Japan, houses come in two sizes: small and very small), and the situation is ripe for disharmony if gaining, keeping, saving, and restoring face were not so deeply ingrained in the East Asian consciousness.

For East Asians, face is such a delicate, important, omnipresent concern for self-status and the status of others that it can be extremely fragile and easily broken. Once you cause an East Asian to lose face, particularly in public, your prospects of business success may be seriously jeopardized.

Even among old friends, uninhibited conversation can be dangerous due to this intense preoccupation with one's public image. T. O. Beidleman, an anthropologist at New York University who teaches a course in Japanese business culture, tells this story:

> I consider myself pretty skilled when it comes to relating to Japanese whom I don't know. But once you get to know them, you start to develop this erroneous illusion that the Japanese are not really so different from us after all. That can be fatal. I have a Japanese friend, an author, who visited me with his wife in New York. His latest book had just been published, but after several days of socializing together he still hadn't

mentioned it. Finally he said: "Here's my new book. Read it and tell
me what you think." So I read it and gave him some honest, objective
criticism, with his wife kicking me under the table all the while. Midway
through the conversation, it began to dawn on me that he didn't want
the truth at all. I was causing him to lose face. We hadn't known each
other long enough for that kind of frankness. We had only been friends
for twenty years.

After-hours socializing—which often includes heavy drinking—is
an essential part of negotiations in much of the region, and usually occurs
early on in the bargaining process. While the forms it takes and appropriate
etiquette for the occasion vary from one country to another, the purpose
is the same: to let the liberal consumption of alcohol begin to erode the
otherwise impermeable mental walls behind which personal feelings are
confined, and would cause loss of face if allowed to escape in formal
business situations. So strong are the constraints against stating a blunt
truth that East Asians may literally have to get drunk for it to be permissible
to speak with *some* semblance of frankness.

Note that *some* is italicized. In East Asia, even being drunk does not
mean you can say *anything* that comes to mind, true or not. As such, it's
important to know how to preserve face for yourself and others to avoid
causing offense that may destroy the possibility of trust.

Avoid making direct, blunt declarations of fact—a virtue in the U.S.
but anathema in East Asia—to which not even courteous but circumlocutious rebuttal is possible. *Always* give East Asians a way out rather than
trying to pin them down.

Try not to ask forthright questions that require yes or no answers.
While businesspeople in the New Japans are often comfortable with U.S.
business customs and may give you a direct answer in the Western style
some have come to adopt, such acceptance of our preference for frankness
is far from universal even in these places let alone Japan or China, where
it's rarely the norm.

Lars-Erik Lindblad, a travel industry pioneer, has been dealing in
the region for decades. He offers an illustration of East Asian circumlocution in order to save face:

An American was importing wooden toilet seats from Japan. His initial
order was for 3,000 seats at four dollars each. The wooden seats sold
very well, so he sent a telex to the Japanese plant saying that he would
like to increase the order to 8,000 seats per month, and would the
Japanese quote him a new unit price? The return telex said: "Fine. We
will send you 8,000 toilet seats a month. But they will cost you $7.50

each." As this was almost twice the price he had paid for a much smaller order, the American assumed there was some mistake. Again telexes were exchanged. Still the answer was the same: "No mistake. $7.50 per seat." Naturally, that ended their business relationship. Years later, the American told this story to a Japanese businessman, who was not at all surprised. "You failed to realize what was happening," he explained. "The Japanese company could not deliver 8,000 toilet seats a month. It was beyond their production capacity. But if your contact had simply told you the truth, he would have lost face. So instead he quoted an outrageous price, knowing there was no possibility you would accept."

Avoid posing negative questions like "Don't you agree?" or "Isn't it?" East Asian languages are highly complex, and the elaborate grammatical phrasing of the reply will only confuse the answers. In fact, the grammatical structure of languages of the region have evolved to help preserve face. In Japanese, for example, sentences end with a verb. This enables the speaker to gauge the listener's receptivity to what he's saying before actually committing himself to one line of thought or another. If by reading subtle facial expressions or other body language he suspects that what he's communicating is not being well received, he may change the verb at the final instant to soften or completely change the meaning of the preceding words.

If you sense an East Asian is reluctant to answer a question that you've asked, don't press. Let the matter drop if it's not vitally important, or rephrase the question in a more roundabout way if it is.

Never criticize anyone, publicly or privately. Never criticize the competition, American or East Asian; this will cost *you* face.

Even if you know a colleague well, don't mimic, parody or otherwise caricaturize him in a satirical way, as some Americans who are good imitators may do as innocent amusement. In East Asia, someone's feelings may be irreparably hurt.

If you're not traveling as a member of a negotiating team, anticipate that you'll be asked detailed technical questions about all areas of company operations relevant to the business you propose and have the answers. If you're selling consumer or capital goods, specification changes may be necessary to adapt your wares to an East Asian market. If so, you should know what they are and their implications for unit price, delivery time, etc., before you board the plane. The more you have to get back to someone with an important answer that should have been researched in advance, the more you're apt to lose face.

When negotiations begin you should be trying to establish a Confucian-style friend–friend relationship involving mutual reciprocity. By not having key answers, you may cause East Asians to lose face. Just as they will feel embarrassed if you ask questions they can't answer due to lack of knowledge, won't answer for whatever reason, or are unable to answer because they don't understand the question and can't admit it, so they will also feel embarrassed by asking questions *you* can't answer. A frank reply like "I don't know but I can find out" is often unacceptable in East Asia. In fact, it can be a *shocking* admission to make!

### Trust

While East Asian negotiating styles vary from country to company to individual or team, establishing trust is the first order of business. How do you do it?

#### Be Sincere

Don't try to pull the wool over East Asian eyes. Few Americans have the skill to do this in business cultures as different and intrinsically suspicious of foreigners as those of East Asia. East Asians usually leave no stone unturned in investigating your firm and you *personally*. If either has a dubious reputation, count on them discovering it. East Asians also have a highly developed sixth sense for smelling something fishy in a business proposal. Be honest and fair in your business dealings, if not for the sake of morality than for the sake of negotiating success.

#### Put People before Profits

East Asians are just as concerned about making money as Americans are. But in their view, profits are impossible if harmonious human interaction does not precede them. Accordingly, sell yourself before you sell your company, and sell the desirability of dealing with your company before you begin to discuss a specific commercial transaction. After establishing that you and East Asians can get along as human beings, amicably work together, and even help each other out should the need arise, only then does it become possible to speak of making money.

#### Think Long Term

It *is* possible to negotiate short-term transactions in East Asia, particularly in the New Japans, where Chinese capitalists are often in more of a hurry to reach agreements than Chinese Communists or Japanese. Be this as it may, most East Asians, regardless of nationality, are long-term thinkers.

While they may be eager for change in order to progress as individuals and nations, they are less eager for change in the interpersonal relationships that make economic advancement possible. Particularly in highly competitive markets, the person who is patient, moves slowly, avoids pressure tactics, and takes time to prove himself trustworthy—not just in the present but in an unpredictable future—is most likely to achieve his goals.

### Get an Introduction

It's difficult to check into a hotel in an East Asian commercial center and make productive telephone calls sight unseen and without prior warning. A proper introduction from a mutually respected third party is usually the most effective way to open doors; the wise establish their credibility before they arrive. While it's possible to do this after you land, the process can be time-consuming. It may considerably lengthen your trip to the point of impracticality and is still no guarantee that your proposal will interest a local firm.

Because East Asian nations are eager to deal with reputable U.S. companies in certain industries, they have opened commercial offices here, mainly in New York, but often with branches elsewhere. Their U.S.-based officials can evaluate your proposed transaction, find potential contacts in the countries they represent, often arrange your trip (airport transfers, hotels, rental cars, guides, interpreters, business briefings), serve as negotiating middlemen, and may even enable you to conduct business abroad without leaving home. A number of Communist China's Foreign Trade Corporations have representatives in the New York area, among them CHINATEX, MACHIMPEX, MINMETALS, CEROILFOOD, and ARTCHINA. Those of other nations include: the Japan External Trade Organization (JETRO); the Korea Trade Promotion Center (KOTRA), the Hong Kong Trade Development Council, and the Singapore Trade Office. Check the New York Business Yellow Pages and you'll find others. In addition, the U.S. Foreign Trade Administration (see Chapter Three) can be a source of valuable leads.

### Business Customs

While some East Asian business customs are culture-specific and separately discussed, others are not. They prevail in all or most of the region and are important to understand.

### The Red-Carpet Treatment

Out-of-town Americans are usually left to fend for themselves in the U.S. It's expected by both American guests and American hosts that an out-of-towner can find his own transportation from the airport to the hotel and will telephone to announce his arrival and schedule an appointment. It's further assumed here that the workday ends at 5:00 P.M., terminating relations between business host and guest until the new workday begins. Depending on the individuals, a host may invite a guest out for dinner— or vice versa—or a guest may be invited home for cocktails and/or a meal. But if his stay in town lasts a week, his host feels no obligation to entertain him for seven evenings in a row, nor does the guest expect such treatment (or, for that matter, want it).

East Asian hospitality is more comprehensive. Expect to be met at the airport, entertained throughout your stay—often until the small hours of the morning—and driven back to the airport in time to catch your U.S.-bound flight. The Communist Chinese may work a relatively short workday, stopping at 4:00 P.M., but when it comes to showing you the local sights, which they invariably will do, they are tireless guides who think nothing of driving three or more hours *one way* to show you a national pride. Japanese businessmen may be hassled by their wives for coming home *too* early, even on a Friday night. As evening entertaining is an important part of doing business in Japan, a husband who is home by 5:00 or 6:00 P.M. may not be working hard enough in the view of his wife.

### Bowing

Most East Asians—even those who are internationalized—bow to each other and may also bow to you reflexively even though they know it's not an American custom. Bowing is complex. *How* one bows to another depends on whether the relationship is that of superior–subordinate or of equals. Few Americans ever get it right or are expected to, and few East Asians ever get it right with Americans they have not previously met; unless you're elderly or a chief executive, it's hard for them to know your status in a U.S. corporate hierarchy relative to theirs, which determines the form a proper bow must take. (As business cards are normally exchanged concurrently with or after the bow, your company title may not be known.) This makes for an awkward greeting situation all around.

However, most East Asians who have had even the slightest contact with Americans have adopted our practice of shaking hands. The grip is limp and the shaking interval short. Even handshakes can be confusing, as East Asians may try to exchange business cards with their left hands while shaking hands with their right in their eagerness to learn your name and title in order to show you proper respect.

You don't have to return an East Asian bow, but if you reflexively do—even though you may bow incorrectly—it's generally understood that you're attempting to be polite. In most cases, a simple ducking of the head so that your chin touches your throat will suffice. Purists stand with feet together, hands flat against thighs, and double at the waist. Don't be too obsequious. Bowers use peripheral vision. The person who is younger or of lesser corporate rank bows more deeply than his counterpart, and permits a superior to straighten up first. This is true of women as well.

While bowing is usually optional, if you *know* an East Asian is a senior executive or not merely older than you but elderly, a deep bow is in order as a sign of respect that will be noted.

### Coffee or Tea

After bowing, shaking hands, exchanging business cards, and making oral introductions and greetings, you'll probably be taken either to a private office with an informal sitting area (most likely in South Korea, Taiwan, Hong Kong, and Singapore), an informal sitting area with a sofa, chairs, and coffee table that's not part of an office but in a room set aside solely for socializing (Japan and China), or a conference room similar to ours (anywhere in East Asia).

Negotiating team members sit according to rank. At a conference table, the team leader sits in the middle of one long side, not at one short end as in the U.S. The second-in-command sits on his right, the third on the left, and so on. If you're shown to a sofa or a line of chairs, follow the same protocol. East Asians will sit opposite your group in corresponding rank so that their team leader faces yours, their second-in-command faces yours, etc. Only the chief American may be shown where to sit; other team members are simply expected to take appropriate seats.

At this point you'll be offered coffee or tea, more often tea. When you're offered liquid refreshment, accept it whether or not you want it. Particularly in Japan, but in most cases where a woman appears to do the serving, the men will treat her as if she were invisible. No one nods or says thank you, and, the serving done, she will leave the room without a sound.

While tea is being sipped, a ritual "twenty questions," none of which concern business, will be posed to you. Expect to be asked about your flight, the comfort of your hotel, the sights you've seen, the local people you've met, your family, and yourself. This friendly socializing period should last about ten to twenty minutes.

If it's your first meeting and you're not already in a conference room, you may segue into business without adjourning to another place. You'll notice a gradual but easily perceived winding down of polite social talk, often followed by a brief silence. Now you can take the initiative in easing into a business discussion or wait for your host to ask what he can do for you, whichever feels most comfortable.

## Presentation Style

When I worked on Madison Avenue, I used a print broker named Mal. I had a lot of printing to do in those days, and Mal was the person who matched each job to the plant that could produce the quality I required at a price I could afford and still meet my deadlines. Mal knew his business, but he was unaggressive, the antithesis of hard sell, and to be frank I liked having him take me out to lunch; I enjoyed his company. While intelligent, he was naive about much of life beyond printing and was neither ashamed nor proud of it. He was eager to learn things he didn't know and I liked that. It made me feel that I could trust him. He seemed incapable of dishonesty. Mal wouldn't make a promise he didn't sincerely believe he could keep.

Mal worked for the XYZ Company, but I didn't know a thing about it. If I had a problem, I didn't contact XYZ. I called Mal and he took care of it, even though I was one of his smaller accounts. One hot summer Saturday afternoon, when anyone with any sense was at the beach, Mal was at a printing plant making sure my job was done right. What did he gain from such dedication? Not a pat on the back from his employer. Not overtime pay—he worked on straight commission. Not even a "well done" from me, merely a noncommittal grunt. What he gained was a gratifying sense of fulfillment that only comes from doing a job to the best of one's ability, no matter what a client's importance, regardless of praise or political points earned, and despite the size of profits. As Mal saw it, he was free to accept or refuse an assignment. But once he said yes, he made a commitment, not only to me but also to himself. The only thing that mattered was that he gave 100 percent.

Mal would be an ideal negotiator in East Asia. Yes, you do need someone with technical expertise. But equally important, at least one member of your negotiating team should be like Mal, a person who is low-key, sensitive, and so sincere that he seems incapable of dishonesty. East Asians are extremely responsive to such qualities. These traits will win trust more quickly than a dynamic, brilliant, highly aggressive presentation style. Dynamism may get results in the U.S.; in East Asia, it's a turnoff.

Here are other tips for an effective presentation:

It's best to mail ahead a business proposal so that East Asians can study it before you arrive. Even so, in a face-to-face meeting, begin by recapping it rather than assuming the text has been fully understood and launching into your offer in greater detail. The story of your company, its niche in domestic and international markets, your position in the firm, and your responsibilities always seem to make a deeper impression when orally described rather than read.

You'll probably be surprised at how many questions you're asked that you thought were clearly answered in your proposal. This should tell you something: The East Asian concept of what's clear and what's not may be a far cry from your own.

Be prepared to patiently describe the same information from several different perspectives to ensure that it's understood and to specifically spell out all unstated implications, no matter how obvious they would be to other Americans. The more important the point, the more you should take the initiative in doing this whether or not you're asked. East Asians may be reluctant to admit that they don't understand what you're saying for fear of losing face.

Norman Weissman, president of the international public relations firm Ruder Finn & Rotman, New York, explains:

> If you ask a Japanese a yes-no question, you will rarely get a simple "yes" or "no" for a reply. The Japanese are famous for not saying "no." But what is less well known is that they are almost as reluctant to give a direct "yes." What you will get instead is the Japanese *rationale* for a "yes" answer: the logic of it all, without the word *yes* actually being used. For example, a Japanese might say: "You asked me a question. But there are many aspects to the answer. Let us analyze each one of them and discuss which one may ultimately be best."
>
> Often this will not be stated, but it will be *thought*. Americans must learn to take the same approach. By leaving no stone unturned, you are most likely to arrive at the best possible choice. If a Japanese asks you if you like the color *red*—and you reply "yes"—he will be a bit taken

back. He is not quite sure what you mean. How can you possibly say "yes" without explaining the context of your reply? Spelling out the *whys* in negotiations is critical. In Japan, it is not *yes-why* as it is in the U.S.; it is *why-yes*.

East Asians hide their emotions, particularly facial expressions. They are often described as being blank- or poker-faced. You should be, too. Don't contort your face in anger or frustration. Don't look confused, even though you may be. Frankness is seldom a virtue in East Asia; it's impolite and can cost you face.

Don't talk quickly or loudly. Don't be intense. Don't be overly enthusiastic. In most countries, you'll be taken out for evening drinks. *Then* let some emotions show, not in the office.

Talk with your hands as little as possible. Most East Asians are not used to it. Some will find the practice so odd that they will stare at your hands—fascinated, almost hypnotized—as you talk. An East Asian who is staring at your hands is not listening to what you're saying.

Don't tell jokes. They won't be understood. For the same reason, avoid American idioms. "No way," "bottom line," "buck"—as in "passing the buck" or "making big bucks"—"coming up," and "tab" instead of "cost" are often unfamiliar terms even to colleagues who were Western-educated.

East Asians enjoy gossip, but never knock the competition, either in the U.S. or locally. It may cost you serious loss of face.

Prepare your presentation in brief segments rather than talking on and on for an hour and saving the question-and-answer period till later, as Americans commonly do. You may be the only one in the room who knows what you're trying to say. Pause every ten minutes or so to let your information sink in.

After you've completed your fourth or fifth presentation segment and are pausing, don't get frustrated if you're asked a question about Segment One or Two. Don't sigh, a sign to many natives that you refuse to answer. Patiently reexplain the information requested from several angles. If your colleagues give up-and-down nods of the head or answer yes in English, it means "I see"; it does not mean "I agree." An East Asian may understand what you're saying without agreeing with you at all.

Having answered questions about material covered earlier, skip ahead to where you left off. Unless requested, it's not necessary to reiterate everything discussed in between.

Particularly in Japan and China, but potentially anywhere in the region, you may deal with a group rather than an individual. Five, ten or fifteen people may be included. Think of yourself as a public speaker addressing an audience. Look around the room as you talk, randomly singling out individuals on which to momentarily fix your gaze. Don't leave anyone out. Don't address your remarks solely to one individual.

As a sign of respect, the chief negotiator on the East Asian side should be directly addressed more often than his subordinates. Do so when making your most important points. Even East Asians who understand little or no English are quick to catch on. It conditions them to know when something you consider vital is being said, as you consistently direct it to the most important person in the room.

Novices often conduct their presentations as two-way conversations between themselves and the interpreter on the East Asian side, who may be the only one in the room who speaks English, ignoring the non-English speakers. An interpreter may play an integral role in the decision-making process, or he may play no role at all. He may be present at the meeting merely because he speaks better English than anyone else in his firm, or he may be an outside professional called in to do a translating job. If the interpreter poses questions of his own to you, rather than merely translating the questions of others, this is a sign that he is *more* than just an interpreter.

Still, if a non-English speaker asks a question in his native tongue, and the interpreter gives you the English translation, address your reply directly to the original questioner, not the interpreter.

You may make a statement calling for a response or ask a question and be confronted by a silence that may last several minutes. Don't automatically assume this is the negative reaction it might be in the U.S. Often you're seeing what the Japanese call "belly art" at work. In this, each member of the East Asian side analyzes what you've said, decides on the *only* appropriate response, waits for other team members to draw the *same* conclusion, and then lets the team leader—who seemingly "divines" the unanimous conclusion of the group—orally express it, even though nothing has been spoken or traces of facial expression shown. Is the team leader psychic? No. One result of the extreme homogeneity of Japanese culture is that everyone is conditioned to think alike as one; in order to preserve group harmony, individuality must be suppressed as much as possible. To preserve *wa* (harmony) the team leader waits for each group member to undergo an identical thought process resulting in a unanimous conclusion so that everyone feels he has contributed silently but equally to the leader's ultimate response. A prolonged silence may result because some people are naturally faster thinkers than others.

A silence in Communist China may have different cause. In the PRC team leaders are usually autocratic. Subordinates may be present at negotiating sessions merely to take notes and act as sounding boards or serve as witnesses later on. Often they speak only when spoken to and otherwise keep their opinions to themselves. A chief negotiator's silence may result from extended deliberation in formulating a carefully worded response to a key issue, so as not to draw criticism from superiors. Such criticism can get him transferred from Beijing or Canton to a remote, dismal Autonomous Region frontier outpost for life.

In the New Japans there may be fewer silences, less indirection, and less caution among businesspeople in general due to national character or Western education. Still, even in South Korea, Taiwan, Hong Kong, and Singapore, tact and prudence rather than blunt honesty are advised, at least initially. If someone is going to be frank, let your colleague do it. The more direct he is with you, the more direct you can be with him.

### Lawyers and Contracts

While lawyers exist throughout East Asia, their number compared to national population size is but a fraction of what it is in the U.S. Here there are nearly twenty lawyers for every 10,000 people, compared with only one per 10,000 in Japan.

The whole idea of lawyers as litigators who represent plaintiffs and defendants in breach of contract lawsuits is anti-Confucian. In the Confucian context of morality and group harmony, lawyers represent suspicion, the possibility of immorality in commercial dealings, and the potential for discord in business relationships. Few East Asians will deal with you if this is sensed. It's a reason why bargaining sessions tend to be extensive and often require several trips. The longer they last, the better each party gets to know the other, and the more secure each can feel that the other is worthy of trust.

Similarly, East Asian contracts are not usually the elaborately detailed legal instruments common in the U.S. While this is slowly changing, most remain short, vaguely worded documents that state the general principles governing a business relationship rather than spelling out every if, and, or but. They are a symbol of good faith. They are *not* weapons to be used later on to force one party or the other into submission against its will. If an East Asian is going to screw you, he'll screw you, contract or no contract. Nurturing a trust relationship is your best assurance that this won't happen.

When a conflict in a negotiated agreement arises, everyone is expected to reconvene and settle the matter within the context of the good-faith spirit implied by the general principles set down on paper. If the dispute cannot be amicably settled among yourselves, an impartial third-party arbitrator is likely to mediate an agreement. Going to court is a seldom-used last resort. For this reason, you should have an expert on local law examine and interpret the unstated implications of a Chinese letter of intent or a Japanese heads of agreement—terms for native con-tracts—before you sign one. But do it privately, not in the conference room for the East Asian side to see.

Even if you do manage to bring an East Asian to court for breach of contract, and even if you're armed with an inch-thick document full of clauses, riders, and warranties, the dispute is apt to be adjudicated *philosophically* according to ethical Confucian precepts. A panel of local judges may render a verdict based on how *human beings* not firms should harmoniously interact with each other.

Few Americans can boast that they have taken an East Asian to court on his native soil. Fewer still can say they have won the suit. And even fewer can claim to have received their money's worth in damages. More often the result is a complete and permanent severing of the relationship between plaintiff and defendant, and it may become impossible to deal *anywhere* in the country ever again.

Most old hands feel it's wise *not* to bring a lawyer with you on your first business trip to the region. They also counsel to seek *impartial* advice—that is, advice from an expert on East Asian business other than a lawyer—as to whether or not one should be present at future meetings. The larger the financial risk of the transaction, the more likely lawyers are to get involved. But even multimillion-dollar deals have been con-cluded in East Asia without lawyers ever being physically present at negotiating sessions for either side.

# CHAPTER SEVEN

---

# Making It
# in Japan

"My introduction to the Japanese was one of the more
painful and awkward experiences in my professional
career."

MITCHELL F. DEUTSCH,
former national advertising manager for au-
dio products at Sony Corporation and author of *Doing Business with the Japanese*

More Americans have more problems trying to negotiate in Japan than in
any other place beyond our national borders. The U.S. Department of
Commerce estimates that for every successful trade agreement between
an American and a Japanese firm, twenty-five commercial transactions
fall through. In some cases this may be due to technical matters: market-
entry barriers to foreign exporters, inability to find local distribution channels, etc. Nevertheless, a major culprit in the high failure rate is culture.
Most Americans board their Japan-bound flights with little or no comprehension of what makes the Japanese "Japanese."

## Portraits of a Businesspeople

It's sobering to realize that 110 million people crowded onto a mere
one quarter of one percent of the world's land are producing one tenth of
the world's GNP. The Japanese achieve this remarkable feat by bringing
the basic human activity of productive work to a precise level of organization, discipline, and efficiency without parallel in the U.S. How do
they manage it?

## Corporate Structure

When Americans talk of Japanese business culture, they are usually referring to the top 40 percent of Japanese firms, not the lower 60 percent. While even inexperienced U.S. negotiators are now generally aware that major firms in Japan function in ways quite different from ours, many are surprised to find corporate hierarchies are similar to those here. At the top is a chief executive, and beneath him are vice-presidents, senior managing directors, managing directors, directors, department heads, and section heads within departments. Beneath them are rank-and-file personnel.

One difference is that boards of directors, which are above presidents in U.S. firms, may not be senior in authority to presidents of major Japanese firms. Board chairmen are usually retired presidents and board members directors who work full time within the company; corporate outsiders are rarely appointed to a Japanese board as is common in the U.S.

Other significant differences cannot be gleaned by studying the organizational chart of a Japanese concern. They include personnel practices in hiring and administration, homogeneous conditioning of employees in unity of purpose to achieve corporate goals, variety and effectiveness of communication channels, and the key role of middle management.

## Personnel Practices

Competition for positions in Japan's top organizations begins in kindergarten. By the high school and university levels, there is a recognized hierarchy of educational institutions from which the best companies and government ministries recruit new personnel each year.

At each tier of Japan's educational system, the emphasis is on rote learning, not conceptual thinking which American schools try to stress. For example, while it's now common for Japanese students to study English, instruction is usually limited to reading and writing, which can be memorized, not conversation, which calls for more creativity. Even university professors who teach English may not speak the language well. Hence, proficient English speakers in Japan are few, although they far outnumber Americans who are fluent in Japanese.

At each stage of their school careers, the cream of Japanese students is weeded out by a series of ruthlessly competitive examinations—students call this "examination hell"—which requires enormous sums of information to be memorized and reproduced on paper. Excellence on these tests gets a handful of students into influential high schools and then prestigious colleges. By rising together as a select group, Japan's young elite is conditioned to share a high morale and unity of purpose, as the coterie is closed to all but the brightest and toughest young minds in the nation.

Selection by Japanese companies and civil-service organizations is based solely on academic performance and recommendations of teachers, not on perceived but latent individual ability, personality traits like leadership, or extracurricular activities such as excellence in sports. Starting salaries are usually equivalent, regardless of the company or the industry; in 1981, Japan's industry average of starting salaries for college graduates was less than $6,000 per year. Perks, including expense accounts and housing subsidies, make the figure not nearly as low as it may seem.

In the U.S., who gets hired is predicated on company needs. American firms tend to be less interested in the person than in the job that needs doing and the individual's ability to do it. Performance is evaluated mainly within a short-term financial context; for example, in publicly owned firms by quarterly earnings per share of company stock. As such, U.S. companies are primarily concerned with hiring *specialists* rather than generalists. Particularly in highly competitive industries where there is a glut of job applicants, there may be no formal training program for new employees, and the first question often asked in personnel interviews is: "What's your previous experience?"

Japanese companies seldom hire specialists. They seek generalists who are viewed as human resources to be molded to meet corporate needs. Once a student has been chosen solely on the basis of high marks in college or high school, *then* individual ability and potential are closely observed within a corporate context.

In the top 40 percent of Japanese firms, personnel are usually hired for life. In return for a student's commitment to work for his employer until retirement age—usually between 55 and 60—the company provides broad but in-depth training based on job rotation. Personnel are transferred from one department to another every three or four years, giving them a much greater perspective of overall company operations than is typical in the U.S.

Promotion within a Japanese corporate hierarchy is not based only on technical ability and performance as it is here. Other factors considered are the ability to develop good rapport with as many members of the company as possible, and the skill with which an individual uses these personal relationships to form a system of intelligence for extracting information from and contributing information to immediate superiors, peers and lower-ranking personnel. All relevant data is then passed on to upper management. While American company personnel from secretaries on up are encouraged to make value judgments and screen data so as not to burden superiors with trivial matters, a Japanese manager who is unsure of the importance of a piece of information is encouraged to send it upstairs for evaluation rather than make a value judgment himself. Failure to share even potentially insignificant data may lead to suspicion from superiors that he can't be trusted to convey all important information. Such mistrust can prevent career advancement. Because so much data—the importance of which is uncertain—is passed on in this way, the process by which decisions are reached is inevitably slowed.

### Unity of Purpose

New employees in Japan are already homogeneous in a cultural sense— being raised by their parents to think and act alike, have the same motivations, and share the same values—as well as educationally. Japanese firms build upon this sense of oneness. New entrants into the public and private sectors begin work on the same day, April 1st. They enter an organization as a group, are paid identical salaries, often wear matching uniforms, and may even sing a company song and recite a company creed daily. For instance, every day at 8:00 A.M., 87,000 employees throughout Japan sing Matsushita Electric's song and recite the following text*:

*Basic Business Principles*
To recognize our responsibilities as industrialists, to foster progress to promote the general welfare of society, and to devote ourselves to the further development of world culture.

*Employees' Creed*
Progress and development can be realized only through the combined efforts and cooperation of each member of our Company. Each of us, therefore, shall keep this idea constantly in mind as we devote ourselves to the continuous improvement of our Company.

---

* *The Art of Japanese Management*, Richard Tanner Pascale and Anthony G. Athos, Simon & Schuster, New York, 1981.

*The Seven "Spiritual" Values*
1) National Service Through Industry
2) Fairness
3) Harmony and Cooperation
4) Struggle for Betterment
5) Courtesy and Humility
6) Adjustment and Assimilation
7) Gratitude

Unity of purpose is also fostered by the office layout. In the U.S., offices are walled or closed, as each manager is an individualist who thinks independently of his peers and subordinates. Analogous offices in Japan are unwalled and open. The working unit is a group of about ten people who sit at a double row of abutting desks facing each other, with the manager's desk at one end of the row. This is intended to foster face-to-face communication within and *between* departments. This arrangement has historical as well as Confucian roots. Over the centuries, Japan has been heavily devastated by natural disasters and wars. In addition, it's a heavily populated country with few natural resources. From time immemorial, at the heart of the Japanese psyche has been a passion for human endurance over harsh adversity. The essence of Japanese survival has been and remains the ability of individuals to work together as groups, and of groups to work in harmony for a common good.

Advancement within a Japanese corporate hierarchy is slow. For much of their careers, employees who entered the firm on the same day in the same year are promoted as a group and receive equal upgradings of salaries and perks. As a result, initial rewards tend to be psychological, not financial. They take the form of greater responsibility and the subtle recognition that goes with it.

This threads a tricky needle in preserving group solidarity. While being given more responsibility can hardly be kept secret, it's an intangible reward and does not separate an individual from his peers as would a dramatic change of title, salary or perks. Moreover, with increased responsibility comes an increased obligation to maintain good rapport within and between groups if an individual is to continue to rise.

Thus, actual changes in corporate titles come slowly, and correlate more closely with age than with performance. A Japanese section head (*kacho*) is usually between thirty-two and forty-two, rarely younger or older. Department heads (*bucho*) range from thirty-nine to forty-eight. Directors (*torishimari yaku*) are generally forty-five or older. However, an individual's ability to assume a given title may antedate the low age in the range. In fact, salary increases don't usually begin to separate a Japanese manager from his peers until he's been with the firm for fifteen years or more. Such wage differentials distinguish those being groomed for further advancement from those who are apt to be forcibly retired at the mandatory age of fifty-five without being appointed to a directorship.

## The Role of Middle Management

Even Americans who regularly deal with corporate officers in the U.S. should be wary of ignoring middle managers in a Japanese firm by trying to go over their heads to the top. Unless your proposal involves a very large investment on the Japanese side or a significant change in Japanese corporate policy, it's usually the middle managers who will sell your idea to their superiors or recommend a rejection that's apt to be heeded, rather than top executives making the decision and autocratically imposing it on subordinates as is customary in the U.S. With few exceptions, decisions in Japanese business are made by consensus. Each departmental staff that will be affected by a given decision is expected to provide input from its own special perspective, as each is closest to a given problem, enabling senior management to render a final verdict based on the collective contributions of all departments involved.

As such, the role of middle managers in making decisions can be vital. They ease the flow of information up and down the corporate hierarchy. One way this is done is by forming a *quality-control circle*, the structure of which parallels the hierarchy of the corporation as a whole. Consisting of workers organized into groups of about ten, each circle is headed by a leader—a middle manager—who aids the group in choosing projects or topics for evaluation or discussion, coordinates the activities of different circles working on a common problem from different points of view (production, marketing, operations, licensing, etc.), and seeks additional technical expertise when required. Each circle is encouraged from above to set its own goals, do its own planning, manage its own link in the chain, and control its own quality of ideas and work. If your business presentation is initially interesting to a Japanese firm, one or more quality-control circles, presided over by middle managers who may also be present at face-to-face negotiating sessions, are apt to be formed to analyze and evaluate it in detail.

If your proposal is approved by middle management, it will be passed on to a quality-control committee, which in turn will route it up to the director level. At any point en route upward, the proposal can be vetoed or tabled. Or company directors may want additional input from other department heads, section heads, assistant section heads, and workers, requiring the formation of still more quality-control circles. This can drag out decision making interminably. It may be necessary for an American negotiator to personally meet with each middle manager who is a circle leader to win his trust or resolve problems that his circle-group members have uncovered. While taking the time to do this is still no assurance of success, *not* taking the time to do it may ensure failure.

## Pre-Trip Research

Failed U.S. negotiators often complain that the Japanese erect impenetrable barriers to market entry. Sometimes they are right—but not always. The proof is the many Western firms that have successfully entered the Japanese market and now control a sizable slice of total market share in the country. For example, the estimated share of Schick safety razors in Japan is about 70 percent, Nestlé instant coffee 60 percent, Olivetti typewriters 35 percent, IBM computers 40 percent, and Coca-Cola soft drinks about 60 percent. Why do companies like these, which consistently face strong domestic competition, succeed in Japan while others don't?

### Marketing Studies

Many Americans try to sell in Japan without taking time to do what they do as a matter of course in the U.S.: *know their customers*. Instead they assume that Japanese and American needs are the same. Not so.

Contrary to popular belief, a survey of Japanese consumers showed that 67 percent made no distinctions between local and foreign-made products when making a purchase, and over 80 percent of young, single Japanese women voiced no such preference. Those who *did* consistently choose domestic over foreign goods cited criticism of Western products that even cursory market research should have revealed: uncompetitive pricing, improper specifications, and poor after-sale service.

Consider improper specifications. It's no secret that the Japanese are smaller in physical stature than the average American. In addition, tiny Japan is the seventh most populous nation in the world. About 75 percent of the Japanese people are packed into cities. Of these, 58 percent are crowded into only three metropolitan areas: Tokyo—with 11 million people, the world's most populous city—Osaka, and Nagoya. Moreover, the design of urban apartments in Japan is still based on the traditional three-by-six-foot *tatami* mat, with six- and 4.5-mat rooms. As a result, most

Japanese consumers live in homes that are considerably smaller than those typical of urban America.

Yet many would-be sellers don't take time to learn these far from esoteric facts of Japanese life. Major opportunities exist in Japan for U.S. manufacturers of household furnishings and appliances. Yet potentially lucrative contracts are lost to American, European, and East Asian competitors who looked before they leaped, conducted marketing studies, and knew in advance that their products required downsizing—with all that size reduction implies in the way of manufacturing, unit pricing, delivery time, servicing, and such—to meet Japanese consumer needs.

### The "Right" Product

Novices often use Japan to test market new products. While this is not necessarily doomed to failure, it usually incurs higher risk for newcomers than for companies already established in the country that know local markets well.

In fact, the Japanese regularly conduct surveys to determine which types of foreign goods are most likely to succeed domestically. Currently on the optimistic list for consumer products are low-priced, medium-class goods for everyday use like underwear and certain packaged foods; high-priced, high-quality prestige items like designer fashions and accessories; and Scandinavian furniture, porcelain, wine, cashmere apparel, and fur coats. In each case, imported products that have sold best in Japan were already successful in their native countries due to proven quality, performance or unique features. They either had established brand images or ones that could be established via mass-media advertising. Or they offered distinct alternatives to domestic wares in design or finish.

Similarly, on the most-wanted list for production materials and capital goods are items for which production technology is not already available in Japan like trimellitic anhydride; imported items that undercut domestic prices for the same items; items with too small a market to be economically produced in Japan like helicopters; and products clearly different from domestic goods due to their unique technology like high-speed automatic presses and minicomputers with high-quality software. Concerning the latter, U.K.-based Sinclair Research is a case in point. Sinclair began exporting its moderately priced, multifunction personal computers to Japan through Mitsui & Company in 1982, and easily reached sales objectives of 20,000 units within the first year.

Complaints about domestic distribution barriers to foreign products frequently stem from the fact that many U.S. goods are innately uninteresting to Japanese distributors, who, in their indirect ways of communicating, may not spell this out so that Americans get the message. As a result, unsuccessful sellers probably lay the blame for their failures on the Japanese distribution system more often than it deserves.

### Product Quality

The Japanese are among the most quality-conscious people in the world. Visit the furniture department of a major Tokyo store and you'll see shoppers on their hands and knees looking *underneath* tables to check out how the corners were mitered or chairs to see how the stuffing has been reinforced. When the Japanese examine a product with a fine-tooth comb and find fault, they often want to know why the defect exists, why it wasn't caught during the production stage, what you intend to do about it, and how you can guarantee that it won't happen again. As Americans tend not to be this fussy, even goods that sell well in the U.S. may fail to meet the exacting standards of the super-fastidious Japanese. Even a meticulous West German electronics concern like Semikron International conducts much more stringent tests on its modules or elements bound for Japan than it would for equivalent items to be distributed in the U.S.— or, for that matter, in West Germany, and Germans are among the most quality-conscious of all Europeans.

### Delivery

If inability to find local distribution channels is a major complaint Americans have about Japan, inability to keep delivery deadlines is a big gripe the Japanese have about foreign exporters. A survey of 1,000 Japanese businesses showed that nearly half listed shorter delivery times and delivery on agreed-upon dates as the main improvements they wanted most from foreign exporters, after more competitive pricing and higher quality. Japanese consumers will buy a lesser product available right now rather than wait months for a potentially better version that they want today. For Japanese manufacturers prompt delivery is equally vital, as overly long or late arrival of production materials keeps costs and inventories high.

### Service

Pre-, point-of- and after-sale service demanded by Japanese consumers and producers may exceed what is needed to make sales in the U.S. To further fluster American sellers, the nature, degree, and cost of these services usually require creative marketing strategies. Such strategies begin with awareness of their need. Their basis is research on what competitors are doing. Too often, neither awareness, research, nor creative strategies exists.

It's important to understand how Japanese think when making a purchase. Americans negotiate contracts. Japanese negotiate *relationships*. Similarly, Japanese consumers view the act of buying as establishing a relationship with the manufacturer or supplier. When a product is faulty or breaks down, the Japanese don't merely shrug their shoulders and let it go at that. To them, a violation of trust has been committed—a serious matter if not remedied.

The expectation of service before, during, and after the sale underlies the assumption that honesty, integrity, and sincerity are mutual between buyer and seller. Pre- and point-of-sale service may mean giving customers adequate product information or permitting them to test-use products at no charge. After-sale service, particularly of capital goods, often requires regular maintenance checks that must be anticipated, budgeted for, and offered at the outset to make the sale.

This should come as no earth-shattering news, yet many Americans are surprised to hear it. I use an IBM typewriter partly because I like the machine but mainly because the company offers the best after-sale service. When the machine malfunctions, an IBM repairman usually shows up to fix it the same day. With other typewriters, I'd have to cart the machine back to the store at which I bought it and wait for several days until it was repaired. Meanwhile, my production operations stand still.

However, I pay an annual fee for my IBM service contract. In Japan, more often than not regular maintenance checks are free. It's expected that you stand behind what you sell—with no strings. When malfunctions or breakdowns occur, repairs, parts replacements—sometimes even providing extra parts with the initial purchase—or replacement of entire units may be mandatory to sustain the relationship. Whether you bear the whole cost, or the customer bears it, or you share it, varies from one situation to another. Whatever, the scope of after-sale service is generally much greater in Japan than in the U.S. If you're a seller, count on the Japanese raising it as a negotiating point.

### Distribution

Everybody complains about the difficulty of tapping into Japan's distribution channels: Americans, other foreign businesspeople, and expatriates working in the country. Exporters say that long, complex distribution hassles force up retail prices, weakening price competitiveness. They create the need for major marketing efforts at major costs. And they block even the most effective marketing strategies, because products are not in stores when customers appear to buy them.

Although the Japanese government claims that distribution problems are highly overrated, such complaints are too numerous to be universally dismissed as illegitimate. While there are no foolproof keys to breaking distribution barriers in Japan, here are ways U.S. firms have successfully used to get their foot in the front door.

Form a partnership with a sole import agent, a Japanese firm that knows the country's laws, is strong in marketing, has a Japanese staff— which is vital in a land that remains highly xenophobic—and is granted *exclusive* rights to market your company's products in Japan.

Getting a sole import agent saves you the time and frustration of having to negotiate with middle managers, government officials, and a parade of other intermediaries, and it frees you to focus on marketing your wares. You also can piggyback onto a sole import agent's strengths: in advertising, inventory supply, after-sale servicing, and established sales network. In return, the agent expects good profit margins, a stable product supply, and in the case of high-quality imports, often social prestige—of no small importance in a country where face comes first.

Japan's top nine trading companies (*sogoshosha*), which are huge and responsible for 26 percent of GNP, are popular choices for sole import agents by American and European firms. They provide financing for Western partners, furnish information to both partners and suppliers, guarantee stable supplies, and absorb risk in other ways; they also make purchasing easier for partners.

In addition, many smaller trading companies coexist beside the nine giants. They can also serve as sole import agents. Specialized trading houses (*senmonshosha*) may have the know-how not only to boost sales but also to generate new market demand, as well as participate in joint new-product development with a U.S. firm.

However, sole import agents may create more problems than they solve. Investigate any potential Japanese partner before you sign a contract, and then be sensitive to any changes in the relationship from then on. Don't sit back, as Americans do, and assume that operations in Japan will run smoothly thereafter. A sole agent may lose interest in marketing your wares, or its selling strategy may fail, and you may learn of this not by direct communication but by suddenly seeing your profits plummet. Or, at times, contractual restrictions may prevent a sole agent from quickly

shifting sales tactics or switching to a different mode of market participation without bringing the matter to your attention (often for reasons of
face).

Common criticisms of affiliating with *sogoshosha* are that they raise
product prices arbitrarily; they are so large and general that their knowledge
of specific foreign products is limited or nil; their real role is merely to
process paperwork; and they significantly reduce profit ratios in Japan
below those obtainable in other countries. Bigger is not necessarily better.
In many cases *senmonshosha*, precisely because they are smaller and more
specialized, can be more effective partners than the general trading giants.

Another way to break the distribution barrier is to work with a Japanese firm that's *not* a specialist distributor or deals in the same product
lines. Such companies may have parallel or analogous marketing expertise
in a seemingly unlikely area that can open new channels of distribution
for your products. For example, General Foods' early success as a producer
and seller of instant coffee in Japan, beginning in 1954, suffered a plunge
in market share to 8 percent by 1970 due to intensified competition from
other instant coffee makers. By teaming up with Ajinomoto, a Japanese
manufacturer of chemical seasonings, with Ajinomoto handling distribution through its extensive network and General Foods focusing on technology, its Maxwell House brand of coffee regained its 20 percent market
share, with sales climbing sixfold in less than a decade.

But you don't have to form joint ventures to make it in Japan, as
Tupperware has proved. Tupperware established a fully owned Japanese
subsidiary, solving distribution problems in the same unique way that has
been effective in the thirty-seven countries in which the company deals:
the Tupperware Party. In this, a housewife who represents the firm and
acts as the party hostess invites a group of her friends from the neigh-
borhood to her home. While serving refreshments amid coffee-klatch
gossip, she demonstrates and explains the benefits of Tupperware food
containers and other products. Orders are delivered via the party hostess.
This concept of personalization, sincerity, and trust in selling is ideal for
the Japanese. It should serve as a lesson for negotiators of any firm in
any industry. Tupperware, Japan, boasts the highest sales volume of any
Tupperware operation outside the U.S.

Licensing can also make distribution inroads. Production of Western
products under license in Japan has risen sharply in recent years. Licensing
has many virtues. It strengthens cost competitiveness with local products
by eliminating currency-exchange fluctuations and price hikes due to home-
country inflation. It lowers transportation costs. It may improve product

quality, as Japanese quality-control techniques are often superior to those in the U.S. Because the licensee has a more intimate understanding of his native market, he can better meet Japanese requirements. And licensing ensures the swift, stable supply system that Japanese consumers and producers demand.

But licensing is not the answer for everyone. Exporters new to Japan should first test the waters by selling directly, and consider production under license only after they have gained some understanding of how Japanese marketing and distribution works. One needs to hold a tight rein on a licensing agreement. More than a few Japanese licensees have tried to sell their own products under a Western-licensed brand name—particularly when the brand was prestigious and had a well-established market image—hoping to make a quick profit, often by selling goods of lesser quality. This has been done without the licenser's approval. If the unauthorized Japanese products are inferior, the licenser's reputation suffers.

## Two Myths about Japanese Business

Many books and articles praise Japanese business culture, and there is much about it worthy of admiration. But American readers are often left with the impression that everything about Japanese business is superior, and that by simply adopting the country's management methods, U.S. economic woes would be solved. Authors frequently point to the "Japanese miracle"—a war-torn economy in 1945, that now accounts for 10 percent of the world's GNP—as proof that the Japanese are doing something right that Corporate America is not. It's true that U.S. management is far from perfect. But what many publications about Japan neglect to consider is *how* the Japanese miracle took place, and the *cost* of Japanese management methods to Japanese society. Here two experts address these issues.

Sol Sanders, International Outlook editor, *Business Week*, on the Japanese miracle:

All this nonsense about Japan Incorporated and the superiority of Japanese management techniques is just that: bunk! In the postward period, the U.S. made the largest transfers of capital and technology in history to Japan. Japanese steel mills were built with subsidized public funds from the World Bank. Every Japanese steel mill has been built since 1950. Of course they are going to be more efficient than mills built in the U.S. before World War II.

Yes, there is enormous collaboration between Japanese business

and government. The Japanese are islanders. They have intense nationalistic feelings and xenophobia. They do stick together. But the Japanese
planning system has made colossal mistakes time and again. It's not
something ten feet tall.

American companies sold the Japanese research and development
throughout the late 1940s and 1950s at idiotically bargain rates, as it
turned out. U.S. manufacturers were short-sighted. Their company accounts and R&D budget projections had never figured the Japanese
component into their costs. Profits from selling R&D were initially
considered found money. It was unexpected. When it started to roll in,
U.S. businesspeople thought it was marvelous.

Most of our problems in competing with the Japanese today—what
we call the "Japanese advantages"—were created by the circumstances
of this postwar rehabilitation, not by anything endemic or intrinsically
superior in the Japanese system.

**T. O. Beidleman, professor, Department of Anthropology, New York
University, on the societal cost of Japanese management methods:**

Americans read into Japanese companies what they want to see. Most
of the really negative studies done on Japanese firms have been conducted
by the Japanese themselves, not by Americans. Many of the awful books
published on Japanese business culture in this country are based on
projective techniques. Their authors look at a couple of Japanese firms
through the wrong end of the telescope, and then present the Japanese
system as being ideal for American needs.

Almost all the research done on Japanese companies has dealt with
large firms, which represent about 40 percent of Japanese business. The
upper 40 percent subcontract to the lower 60 percent, feeding off them
like parasites.

Consider a large Japanese automotive manufacturer with lifetime
employment, strong worker loyalty, and all the rest. The manufacture
of its little red tail lights is likely to be subcontracted to some small,
broken-down Japanese company out in the sticks, with maybe 200 employees or less. *Its* personnel don't get lifetime employment. They have
no job security at all. Women get a raw deal. Pensions are rotten. Japan
has one of the worst social-security systems in the world. Hospitalization
plans are terrible. Old-age retirement benefits are poor. And lots of small
parts are farmed out in this way.

But, to date, the research has focused on a particular aspect of
Japanese business—one with many attractive qualities. It has yet to look
at the broader reality: this great base of workers who support the structure, and who live in conditions no American would tolerate.

When one talks about Japanese business, it's not merely the big, terrific companies with lifetime employment and great worker loyalty. It's also the many little firms supporting each of the giants, and they are barely able to survive. But that doesn't interest us, so there has been very little study on it yet. As a result, we've developed an incredibly idealistic view of how wonderful and effective the Japanese management system is. However, if you look behind the success stories to the reasons for their success, you begin to realize that the price is steep, a lot steeper than any American would be willing to pay.

## Business Customs

A survey by Japan's Manufactured Import Promotion Committee found that 80 percent of foreign businesspeople thought business practices in Japan unique compared to those of their home countries and other fully industrialized nations; 70 percent felt they should be modified to conform with international standards; 60 percent maintained that they should be fully changed; and only 30 percent asserted that it was the obligation of cultural outsiders to understand and accept them as is. Why do twenty-five out of twenty-six American transactions fail in Japan? This is a major reason. Japan's business customs today are the result of centuries of evolution. The Japanese are unlikely to change or even modify them in the foreseeable future to suit American or anyone else's convenience. (Are we prepared to change our business methods to suit Japanese convenience?) U.S. negotiators who subscribe to the minority view—that Japanese methods and manners should be respected *as is*—will have a significant edge on competitors who stubbornly insist on fighting city hall. The bottom line is: You have no choice.

### *Language*

Japanese is among the world's most complex writing systems. A modern Japanese typewriter must be able to reproduce some 3,000 characters! Ancient Japanese scholars devised the system by adapting Chinese writing to their own language needs—a remarkable feat as Japanese is multisyllabic with many verb inflections, while Chinese has only one syllable per character and no verb inflections. Today, the Japanese continue to use Chinese ideographs (*kanji*) plus two phonetic alphabets. One, *katakana*, is mainly used for the many English and other foreign words now incorporated into the language. The other, *hiragana*, expresses the grammar and pronunciation of Japanese words and sentences.

Increasingly in Japan's major cities, placards, billboards, and street signs are bilingual, including Roman characters, evidence of the growing importance of trade and tourism from the West. To Americans visiting Japan for the first time, this may suggest that most Japanese are fluent in English. In fact, few Japanese can read and write any language other than their own, and those who can speak fluent English are fewer still. Even Japanese–English interpreters who represent Japanese negotiating teams are often far from masters of our language—particularly when it comes to understandable pronunciation, even though grammar and wording may be correct.

The Japanese may prefer to speak in roundabout ways that Americans find confusing. Adding to confusion, the Japanese language is ideographic with each symbol often representing several objects or ideas, depending on the context of the conversation in which it's used, rather than having specific words to convey specific meanings as English does. This encourages U.S. negotiators to think that both the Japanese people and language are incapable of precise communication. Yet the Japanese can communicate with knife-sharp clarity in writing or speech if they choose. Says a former American resident of Tokyo: "Japanese can be almost brutal in its quick, sharply defined modes of description."

However, despite the Japanese ability to clearly communicate, often they choose not to be precise. Sometimes this is due to native mores on politeness; it's discourteous to be blunt, especially when the news is less than best. But it may also be a reluctance by the Japanese to make definite commitments that may later prove embarrassing if they can't be kept, causing loss of face. The Japanese may strategically keep their options open by indirect communication. As a result, rather than specific questions and answers being exchanged, a kind of thought stream of discussion develops and propels negotiations forward.

For example, it's common in Japanese conversation for Mr. A to introduce a topic like the crisis in Central America. To which Mr. B replies: "Mmm, yes," adding, *"Tai-hen densai." Tai-hen* is an adverb that loosely translates simply as "very." It does not imply very *what*. Mr. B may mean "very difficult," "very good," "very bad," "very ominous," "very perplexing," "very problematic," or "very" *anything* else. It often takes a lot of patient probing to find out what the Japanese really mean. Many Americans go awry by assuming that "very" *something* is implied.

Another reason for the Japanese tendency for circumlocution is to preserve group harmony. In Japan, minority opinions are not usually abruptly overruled by superiors in the American individualistic fashion. Rather, they are respected and either incorporated into the majority view or gently, sensitively, and politely altered through discussion to reach a group consensus. For such gentle persuasion to occur in front of you—the Japanese often refer to Americans as "Roundeyes" or "Red Ones" (due to their perception of our skin color), nicknames that suggest how alien we seem to them—would be akin to airing one's dirty laundry in public, extremely embarrassing as the Japanese see it. Instead, feelings that are closer to the truth are privately expressed when negotiators can confer more freely among themselves and with their quality-control-circle members. For any one individual—unless he's a high-ranking director—to take charge and publicly speak for the group before private conferences have been held with everyone involved would erode the group's team spirit and unity of purpose. Sometimes this does happen, but it's not an everyday event.

Furthermore, middle managers must speak in carefully worded vagaries so as not to alienate their superiors. Japanese middle managers usually compose the majority of negotiating-team members. They may spend much time conferring with subordinates in their quality-control circles to formulate suggestions that will please superiors. Few would dare to speak for top management unless specifically delegated to do so.

The Japanese know that few Americans speak their language. If you're dealing with a major firm in Japan, it will usually supply an English-speaking interpreter. Be this as it may, it's wise for most Americans to bring their own interpreters. Japanese interpreters may speak English imperfectly. An interpreter of your own can help clarify thoughts for both sides which the Japanese-furnished interpreter may unintentionally translate in vague, incomprehensible, or incorrect English.

To complicate communication, the Japanese language is full of honorifics that can turn what in English would be a simple statement into a seeming speech. Or, conversely, a single Japanese "word"—that is, the verbal expression of an ideograph—may say a good deal; a mere handful of words may describe volumes. Add to this the fact that many Japanese expressions have no easy analogs in English and the potential for confusion even among interpreters is great; two interpreters are safer than one.

However, bringing your own interpreter may be viewed by the Japanese as suspicion of them by you. To dispel doubts, your interpreter should play a subordinate role in discussions, allowing the interpreter representing the Japanese side to do the most translating. If you've hired a top professional, he should be taking detailed notes throughout a meeting. Afterwards, debrief him privately to learn what was really meant within the context of a given conversation. What you may be told by a Japanese company's interpreter is merely what was said. Often what was said and what was *meant* are two entirely different things in Japan.

Given the complexities of mastering Japanese, does it pay to take language lessons? Yes. While you may never learn enough Japanese to actually negotiate, it makes a good impression in social situations where trust can be established or destroyed. A favorite question the Japanese ask of Americans is: "Are you studying our language?" But those with some conversational instruction should not show off; it's very bad form.

James R. Ladd, managing partner of the Tokyo branch of Deloitte Haskins + Sells, an international accounting firm, explains:

> Self-effacing talk is very well-received by the Japanese, especially when it comes from foreigners who are making an attempt to speak their language. You don't have to go into details about your Japanese lessons. A simple—"I've studied a little bit, but it's very difficult"—is a standard, acceptable reply. I've been studying the language for several years now, and when anyone asks if I speak Japanese, I usually answer, in Japanese: "Only a little, I'm afraid." One should express it almost in the form of an apology. The Japanese will not normally test you beyond that. But they do appreciate knowing that you've at least made an effort.

Even if you don't make an effort, there's one word in Japanese probably used more frequently than any other and it's handy to know: *dohmo* (pronounced "doe-moe"). Like many Japanese words, *dohmo* has a variety of meanings. Depending on the context in which it's used, *dohmo* may mean "well"—as an exclamation of surprise or agreement, or a noncommittally neutral response—or "thank you," "good morning," "excuse me," or even "good-bye." In fact, *dohmo* is so versatile that it can signify either acceptance or rejection, based on the tone of voice in which it's spoken and on the situation. And yet, even when *dohmo* is used to mean "no," it's a courteous no, not an offensive refusal.

## Collateral Materials

Decision making in Japan may involve dozens of people, many of whom understand little or no English. You'll only further slow a process that most Americans already consider interminably slow by not supplying first-rate translations.

Because the Japanese language is ideographic, and ideographs are pictorial representations of words or concepts, the people of Japan are highly visually oriented. As such, visual aids can help to effectively make your case. Product samples, working models, diagrams, charts, tables, photographs, and drawings can be liberally used to clarify, enhance or even replace printed text.

Similarly, Japanese of all ages and I.Q.s enjoy comic books and comic strips. This may seem childish to Americans, but in Japan comic illustrations are often used to convey serious concepts of ethics and to entertainingly dramatize moral dilemmas that have no easy solutions. Comics designed for commercial purposes—like those occasionally used by mail-order record clubs in the U.S.—can also be employed to illustrate key presentation points.

The logic of using comics becomes clear when you recall that face-to-face meetings primarily include Japanese middle managers who are quality-control-circle leaders. After a session, they will circulate your collateral materials to their circle members for collective consideration. Your materials should be designed to clearly convey your selling story to the lowest common denominator in the Japanese decision-making process, not the highest. If your firm has an advertising department or agency, an art director's story board (which is usually used as the basis for something more elaborate like a television commercial) can simply be photocopied in color; it may drive a point home more effectively than the costlier film.

However, slides, films, and film strips are effective, too. In fact, they probably make more of an impact in Japan and elsewhere in East Asia than they do in other parts of the world. But voiceover narrations and superimposed words should be translated into Japanese. For the equipment needed to stage a successful audiovisual presentation, see Chapter Three.

You can't bring too many copies of translated collateral materials. Not only will you need a complete set for each member of the Japanese team, but you may accelerate the decision-making process at the quality-control-circle level if each member of each circle has his own set to study, rather than the circle leader having to pass around the one set he received during your presentation. In addition, if you show slides or films, be prepared to leave them *and* the equipment required to view them behind so that all circle members can see them later on.

Americans often assume that because their film or slide equipment bears the name of Sony, Panasonic, or some other Japanese firm that they don't have to lug it along. Many find too late that their U.S.-purchased Sonys or Panasonics were made for *export only*, and that their slide trays or film reels are not compatible with Japanese equipment made by the same manufacturers for domestic use.

## Forms of Address

Don't address your Japanese colleagues by their first names. Kunihiko Kobayashi is Mr. Kobayashi. When you get to know him better after the first meeting or during evening entertainment, and want to be respectful, call him Kobayashi-*san*. This will make your relationship a bit more personal but *san* should not be added to a person's last name without knowing him at all. To use the appellation *san* with everyone is a sign of insincerity.

However, a Japanese executive whose status is equivalent to yours, or who outranks you, or an individual who is clearly your senior in age, (especially if he is elderly), or any male member of a negotiating team if you're a woman, needs no further acquaintanceship to deserve the respect that *san* after his name conveys.

## Negotiating Notes

Despite their reputation for being excessively polite, the Japanese are not as polite as Americans in some respects. An American, for instance, will meet with a businessperson before knowing in detail what he has on his mind, and will often hear him out even if there's no interest in the offer. The Japanese won't. If an audience has been arranged through a third party with a Japanese negotiating team, it's safe to assume there's sincere initial interest in your business proposal. Expect to face a group of the world's most attentive listeners and thorough questioners.

A ritualized format has evolved for opening a business presentation in Japan. You don't begin by bluntly stating your offer, followed by an itemized listing of the terms and conditions attached. Instead, your introduction should be philosophical. Cultural anthropologist T.O. Beidleman elaborates:

> You begin with an expression of great pleasure: the joy you feel in having been invited to discuss business with such a well-reputed Japanese firm, and how honored and delighted you are that this is happening. It develops into a kind of fugue. Your key themes—in this case, the benefits of doing business together—are repeated and successively developed by continuous interweaving into the conversation so that they merge into a single well-defined message. The Japanese will usually respond in kind. You praise each other. You rhapsodize about the virtues of your company, the virtues of the Japanese company, and how well-suited both are for

what you propose, which is why you think they would make an ideal business marriage.

Then you switch philosophical gears. Business isn't really about making money. It's about people being *decent* to each other. Now, implicitly, if people are decent to each other, they will make money, a line of thinking with Confucian roots. Good people are rewarded; the bad are punished. The Japanese believe that morality and profit should go hand in hand. It's important to position yourself and your firm within human, societal, and ethical terms. You must introduce yourself within the contexts of human decency and personal loyalty. The Japanese may seem superficially reserved, but beneath their unemotional facades they are a highly emotional people. Approach the Japanese as human beings first, then as managers. Even in business, there's a well-defined moral component you must establish at the outset for negotiations to proceed.

Hence, it's less the wording of a contract in Japan than it is the *process* leading up to it—the way in which both sides exchange ideas, compromise, and reach final agreement—that forms the basis for the business relationship to follow. Americans often use rhetoric to persuade, to convince, to *push* a point across to the Japanese. Japanese communication is based on *pulling* out another person's views through intuition. The Japanese assume that a group of people should be able to *perceive* each other's views without direct expression. An American who remains closed to such sensitivity may earn himself the nickname *henna gaijin* ("vexing foreigner") due to his unpredictable or offputting behavior.

Americans favor arguments based on rationalism, logic, and facts, not emotions. But Japanese rely more on interpreting feeling and sentiment. They place a higher premium on people than on corporate image. They expect more from you as an individual than just a recitation of cold facts. The whole idea of argument smacks of one person trying to *force* his feelings onto another and this is alien in Japan. The American practice of attempting to influence people through emphatic words is un-Japanese.

In their propensity for speaking in vagaries and abstractions, the Japanese may use metaphorical aphorisms to make a point indirectly. A common aphorism is: "The able hawk hides his talons." This is similar to Theodore Roosevelt's famous advice: "Walk softly and carry a big stick." If you're told something like this during a meeting, it means you're coming on too strong, being overly aggressive, and perhaps trying to exact concessions from the Japanese side via a power play. This is not how to get what you want in Japan.

The best way to get cooperation from the Japanese is to develop *amaeru* (pronounced "ah-my-roo")—that is, a trust relationship based on *amae* ("ah-my"), the basic way a Japanese individual relates to the people around him. *Amae* has been defined as passive-object love or indulgent love. It's a fundamental longing to be looked after, to be protected in a paternalistic way, which to the Japanese is necessary for psychic survival. This is partly why titles within a Japanese corporate hierarchy from *kacho* (section head) on up are closely correlated with age. Seniority of rank based on age rather than merely performance breeds a feeling of paternalism that lower-echelon employees want and need. A company president is said to be the *oyabun* or "parent role" of the relationship. The employee plays the *kobun* or "child role." Traditionally, the *oyabun* does all he can to ensure his employees are housed, content, and not lacking in basic life needs. He may even help an unmarried employee find a spouse, or help the child of a member of the "company family" get into a prestigious school.

Similarly, Japanese middle managers foster a familylike atmosphere within their departments. To increase goodwill among subordinates, they regularly attend drinking parties with their staff members, listen to the problems of subordinates—work-related or otherwise—much like priests in a confessional, accompany their staffs to company-sponsored events at hot-spring resorts, country clubs, or picnics, and even make social calls to employees' homes. In return, the *kobun* feels great loyalty and dedication toward his immediate superior, as well as those above him right up to the chief executive.

Of course, for an American—a "Roundeye," a cultural outsider—to develop *amaeru* with a Japanese takes time, often years. But once a trust relationship of such depth has been established, it requires something cataclysmic to break the bond. *Amaeru* involves mutual obligations. Each party in the relationship looks out for the other. Thus, even if you have financial difficulties at a future date, a Japanese firm may come to your aid, as long as help is not clearly futile.

Michael A. Seamark, vice-president of operations for Canada Dry International, tells this story:

> About ten years ago, we were going to launch a new product line in Japan. One of our suppliers incurred a cost of about $150,000 to develop molds for the packaging that was required. Then market circumstances changed, and, ultimately, the new product line was never introduced.
>
> Quite rightly, the supplier came to us and asked to be reimbursed for his expense. We sat down to negotiate, and made a commitment to continue to use him as our Japanese supplier. We could not guarantee

what volume of business there would be in the future, of course, but we could guarantee *our* loyalty, as well as to suggest to other members of our Japanese production network that they use this particular supplier.

In the decade since then, that supplier has never come back to us and asked for his $150,000 back. I would guess the amount of business we've actually done with him in that time is considerably less than that sum. But he has yet to even try to bill us for it.

That would never happen in the U.S. If I contract for your services, and you provide them, but then they don't meet my current needs, you still have every right to charge for the costs you've incurred to deliver the services at my request and on my behalf.

But the Japanese see things differently. In the same situation, they'll say: "Okay, it's true that you owe us money. But if we can continue to do business with you in the future, even though our present business volume may be small, it may become larger later on. With this in mind, we'll amortize the cost we've incurred in doing business with you initially against the potential for future profits."

As a result of this business philosophy—predicated not on relationships between abstract corporate entities but between flesh-and-blood human beings—it's common in Japan to find commercial ties stretching back over generations.

In judging the Japanese, don't underestimate the capability or authority of the managers with whom you deal. Unlike U.S. business norms, the Japanese place more emphasis on gaining experience in a variety of company operations rather than spending an entire career refining expertise in only one area, understated leadership qualities that don't disrupt group harmony, and ability to develop and maintain good rapport among personnel at all organizational levels, below as well as above. There's less stress on minute specialization, individual achievement, and personal dynamism. Don't be fooled by Japanese politeness or the inability of individuals to speak fluent English. Often it's no indication of intellectual inferiority, fear, lack of power, or incapacity for cunning.

### The Decision-making Process

Undoubtedly, most Americans consider this the most confusing and frustrating aspect of doing business in Japan: getting—and waiting endlessly for—the Japanese to say yes.

By now most everyone is familiar with the term *bottom-up decision making* as it applies in Japan. But many novices think it means that once a suggestion made by lower-echelon personnel has successfully climbed to the upper rungs of the corporate ladder, top management passively and routinely accepts it, and that Japanese company decisions are *never* issued as top-down directives, as they are in the U.S.

It's true that probably most suggestions that become decisions in Japanese companies originate somewhere in the middle company ranks, often at the initial instigation of even lower-ranking employees. It's *not* true that company directors automatically buy them. They are accepted, rejected, tabled, or routed back down for further consideration as top management sees fit.

It's also false that Japanese top executives *never* issue directives, or *always* include the company family in their decisions. Setting major investment goals and managing significant crisis situations are usually the sole purview of the president and board of directors.

When a directive from above *is* imposed arbitrarily or a suggestion originating from below is arbitrarily overruled by corporate higher-ups, the pride of underlings may be wounded. This puts middle managers on the spot. Their task is to convince their staffs of the rightness of executive decisions, reestablish willingness to carry them out, show sympathy for employee feelings, and if push comes to shove to request them to abide by a directive in which they did not participate whether they like it or not. Unlike their opposite numbers in the U.S., Japanese middle managers have no power to hire and fire; therefore, developing strong social bonds with their staffs is a practical necessity. They don't give orders; they must *mediate* to preserve harmony within their groups. A middle manager's effectiveness at his job is directly related to his mediation skills.

Be this as it may, most decisions in Japan *are* made by consensus. While individualistic Americans analyze hard facts and make quick decisions—often ones that are wrong precisely because they were too hastily made—Japanese managers place their confidence in the broader knowledge and wisdom of the group. Usually they favor carefully thought out and unanimously reached conclusions, no matter how long they take. The pressure to shoot from the hip and make quick decisions is rare in Japan, where the meaning of *long-term* may encompass five or ten years, not twelve months or less as is common in the U.S.

Reaching a consensus involves a long process of individual discussions, group meetings, inter-group coordination, compromises, evaluations, and reevaluations. In the way everyone plays a part in the decisions affecting his area of company operations, a Japanese firm more closely resembles a political party than it does an army with a rigidly stratified chain of command, the American corporate model.

Once a general consensus has emerged at the mid-levels of the company with input from lower-echelon personnel, a formal document is drawn up requesting a decision (called *ringi-sho*) which is routed up the corporate hierarchy, collecting everyone's stamp of approval along the way. The stamp is in the form of a "chop" or seal. Any manager against the decision being requested or who feels some aspect of it should be reconsidered may stamp his chop on the *ringi* document sideways or simply leave his space blank. *Ringi-shos* arise from quality-control-circle discussions and may contain dozens of pieces of information, which is why decision making in Japan may take so long. A typical *ringi-sho* includes the following personal stamps:

- The section originating the request
- Other divisions consulted
- The person who drew up the document, usually a young man in the office
- Section chiefs responsible
- Most closely related division
- Division originating the request
- Section chief
- Director in charge
- Senior managing director
- Vice-president
- President
- Opinions concerning the decision, each with the seal of the writer
- The Directors' Committee decision

The *ringi* system enables the section closest to a problem or opportunity to suggest a course of action, while still permitting top management to maintain control of the company overall. Because the list of signatories is so extensive, considerable time must be spent on research, analysis, and intra- and inter-group discussion (called *nemawashi* or groundwork) if a *ringi-sho* is to successfully run the gauntlet from the bottom to the top of the corporate hierarchy. *Nemawashi* has been compared to the slow, patient removal of a precious tree for transplanting, by meticulously digging around the roots so that none are harmed in the process. The "harmed root" is a metaphor for a flaw in the suggestion, causing loss of face for all who initiate and approve a *ringi* document that's ultimately rejected. Thus, while top management in a Japanese firm *always* has the last word, the right of veto is not used everyday. This is not merely to spare the feelings of subordinates but primarily because the request for a decision has been exhaustively thought out by many people, rather than capriciously initiated by one or two; a suggestion so carefully made is usually sound. The *ringi* system—a specific, formal process for generating solutions to problems at lower- and middle-management levels—is a major difference between decision-making styles in Japan and the U.S.

An important implication of the *ringi* system is that decision *making* and decision *execution* are not the two separate and distinct steps that they are here; in Japan, both are part of the same process and happen concurrently. While an American executive may be able to make a quick, autonomous decision, the implementation of the decision often takes a long time. While Japanese collective decision making may take longer, implementation of the decision happens faster; as the decision is in the process of being reached, in effect it's simultaneously being executed—department by department throughout the company—as if the green light had already been given to go ahead. As a result, it may take a while to get your initial order in Japan, but the second order often comes quickly; sometimes your goods are already sold before they even arrive.

A Japanese who begins a new business in Japan is often given this advice by his friends: *"Shobai wa akinai."* *Shobai* refers to the art of doing business. *Akinai* is a play on words. Its old-fashioned meaning is similar to that of *shobai*. But *akinai* is also a homonym for the same word with a different, modern definition: roughly, "not to give up." The message is equally relevant to Americans hoping to deal in the country for the first time: In Japan, perseverance and patience pays off.

### Body and Unfamiliar Oral Language

Just as Americans may be put off by Arabs and Latins who converse practically nose to nose, feeling their sense of personal space has been invaded, so Japanese attitudes of reserve (*enryo*) are expressed in mannerisms that guarantee inward privacy. Americans are generally most comfortable talking to each other at about arms-length distance. In Japan, this is perceived to be uncomfortably close. Don't feel rejected if your colleague stands several feet outside your normal range of conversational sphere. For him, double or triple the distance at which Americans comfortably talk is his cultural norm.

Other than initially shaking hands, which remains a foreign custom the Japanese have adopted, the Japanese shun physical contact. Don't tap a colleague on the chest to emphasize a point, pat him on the back, touch him on the shoulder, or squeeze his arm. Public displays of affection even between husband and wife are considered indecorous in Japan; for a married couple to kiss in front of their children is shameful conduct.

Americans laugh to express mirth, humor, happiness, irony, etc. In Japan, a laugh usually signifies embarrassment, confusion, dismay, even shock. If a Japanese laughs during a negotiating session, it's probably not because you've said something funny and you would do well to get to the root of it at once, with suitable apologies.

Apologies are liberally interlarded in Japanese conversation. When asking for a favor, show restraint by begging forgiveness before you pose the question. When you're paid a compliment, which will probably happen often, deny your worthiness or bow your head humbly and offer sincere thanks. Similarly, the Japanese may belittle everything that's theirs. What belongs to you is marvelous; what belongs to them is so humble as to barely suffice. This requires no supportive response for you. It's merely *enryo* at work.

Modern Japanese beckon by fluttering the fingers palm down, the way we say good-bye. When referring to themselves they point to their noses. Pinching the nose indicates a person who is disliked. A fist to the nose means a braggart. A crooked index finger conveys dishonesty. A little finger extended signifies a girlfriend. Grinding a fist into the palm is a sign of flattery. Two fingers tapping the palm refers to sushi, a traditional dish of bite-size slices of raw fish atop small shaped beds of glutinous rice; it's a popular lunch or a dinner appetizer. Twiddling thumbs with clasped fingers indicates sumo wrestling. Some Japanese count with their fingers, using only one hand. Fingers are bent into the palm one by one, starting with the thumb; at six, the pinky is re-extended first, and so on.

If you encounter silence in a meeting, it may be because the Japanese are practicing "belly art"; to interrupt the silence is rude. But often a silence results because the Japanese expect you to guess what is on their minds. It may also occur if they feel uncertain or indecisive. Use your own discretion in interpreting the meaning of and breaking a silence, but if you don't know why the conversation has stopped, it's usually best to be patient, avoid feeling uncomfortable simply because no one is talking, and let the Japanese speak first. Silence is not anathema in Japan; it's golden.

If you speak some Japanese, and a colleague addresses you in English, to answer in Japanese is an insult. If a Japanese *thinks* he speaks some English but you can't understand what he's trying to say, *never* reply: "I don't understand your English." This may cause loss of face. Ask him to repeat what he has said, or rephrase what you think he might be trying to communicate in the indirect form of summary statement, like: "I see. In other words..." Don't say: "In other words, *you* mean..." At this point, your interpreter, if you have one, or the interpreter for the Japanese side, will probably intervene.

## Social Customs

After-hours entertainment is an important part of Japanese negotiations. If things go well, expect to be invited out for a night on the town soon after meetings begin. The Japanese have a saying: "You get through to a man's soul at night." The primary purpose of evening entertainment is for both sides to get to know each other as human beings so that they are better able to trust each other. Japanese managers from the *kacho* or section-head level on up may have expense accounts that approach, equal, or exceed their annual salaries. Today, Japanese companies spend some $37 million a day on wining and dining after dark. If this seems surprising, one *torishimari yaku* (director) of a large corporation explains it like this: "You Americans spend more than that each day on legal fees. We prefer to take the money that would otherwise be spent on lawyers and invest it in more pleasurable enterprise that enables us to find out if a person has personality traits worthy of trust. If there is trust, the need for lawyers is greatly reduced or eliminated entirely."

Evening entertainment usually involves restaurant meals and nightclub hopping. Contrary to a widely held belief in the U.S., geisha parties are mainly arranged for old friends, not new acquaintances (unless they are making offers the Japanese are exceptionally keen on accepting, which is not usually the case).

Rarer still for newcomers is a dinner invitation to a Japanese home. Japanese often feel embarrassed that their homes are so small by typical American standards. Or an invitation home may be impractical, as many managers live a three-hour train ride away from the overcrowded, expensive commercial centers where company headquarters are located.

In addition, the critical bond in Japan is between mother and child, not husband and wife. To this day, male chauvinism in the country rivals that of the Arab world. Japanese women remain second-class citizens, receiving lower salaries for equal work, fewer perks, and little or no opportunity to climb the corporate ladder like men. In business, most are employed as technicians, receptionists, typists, clerks, and tea servers rather than as fledgling managers. The expectation is that they will soon marry, begin families, and permanently retire from corporate life—even though this is not what statistics show. A male manager in Japan won't usually consider inviting you home for dinner and an evening with his wife and children.

Most Americans who are invited to geisha parties or Japanese homes are either expatriates stationed in Japan whom the Japanese deal with on a regular basis or U.S.-based negotiators who have traveled to Japan many times. Such invitations usually indicate that a trust relationship has already been established; rarely does this happen overnight. Most Japanese entertainment in which you're likely to participate is intended to lay the groundwork for a trust relationship. It does not indicate that your colleagues particularly like you, trust you, or are even willing to do business with you. However, whether or not such feelings develop may well be predicated on how you behave at restaurants and nightclubs.

Unless you're dealing with top executives, lunch is not the business opportunity in Japan that it is in the U.S. Generally, even managers at the *kacho* and *bucho* levels in major firms eat with their staffs in company cafeterias for convenience and to foster group solidarity. Or they order out for sushi and dine at their desks while they work. It's best to invite most Japanese to dinner rather than lunch.

Since World War II, the Japanese have proven their remarkable ability to adapt. Only yesterday, evening entertainment, particularly nightclub hopping, was strictly a male-only affair, which put American businesswomen in Japan at a distinct disadvantage in negotiations; it's hard to form trust bonds if denied the main opportunities for doing so. This has largely changed, primarily because so many Japanese are being educated in the U.S., and most of the rest—at least in major companies—learn about American culture by reading newspapers and magazines like *Time* and *Reader's Digest*, and by watching American movies and television shows broadcast via satellite. Increasingly, American women are regarded as being sexually neuter. They are simply *American* and are now often included in evening entertainment to which Japanese wives would rarely, if ever, be invited. If you're a top executive wondering whether to send a well-qualified female negotiator to Japan, the answer is *yes*.

However, if you're a male negotiator who has brought along his wife, it's best not to include her in initial evening entertainment if you're the host, or to ask if she can accompany you if you're the guest. Her presence may interfere with business. Similarly, if it's you who is doing the inviting, don't ask a male Japanese colleague to bring *his* wife. He won't want her to be present.

Many Japanese will automatically take you to a Western-style restaurant, thinking you won't like Japanese food. If you're among the Americans who do enjoy Japanese cuisine, tell your host that you would prefer to sample native dishes. He won't feel insulted if you don't make this request, but he'll probably feel complimented if you do.

Similarly, if you're playing host it's fine to take a colleague to a Western-style rather than a traditional Japanese restaurant. Those at international hotels are best bets.

Let the Japanese play host first, which they will probably do soon, and then reciprocate. If you do the initial inviting, you'll obligate them to reciprocate. The Japanese may be extremely reluctant to feel obligated to strangers in any way, and as you're a guest in their homeland, it may cause them to lose face.

You'll usually go out with a group of people from a Japanese firm. Conversely, when *you* are the host, don't invite *only* the chief negotiator for an evening meal. Invite the most important members of the *team*. It may also be necessary to extend dinner invitations to section or division heads who may not be present at negotiating sessions yet who still require extra convincing that your proposal is sound and that you can be trusted. A third party representative who makes your initial introduction or possibly your interpreter can often learn who in the firm you have yet to meet may be roadblocking the *ringi* system by which your proposal is being evaluated.

When your turn comes to play host, the cost of a dinner party even at a Western-style restaurant in a major city may approach or exceed $100 per person, depending on the wine. As you may take five, ten or more Japanese to dinner within a single trip, the price of playing host can be steep. If you run your own shop, grin and bear it; at least it's tax-deductible. If you answer to superiors at home, be sure they know in advance that evening entertainment in Japan is neither optional nor cheap. You'll find this easier to explain and have resignedly accepted up front than leaving everyone unaware and having to defend your expense report when you return.

### Chopstick Etiquette

You don't have to eat Japanese food with chopsticks, but it makes a good impression. Sometimes Japanese themselves mix utensils, using knives and forks to eat steak and chopsticks to eat rice and vegetables. The wooden, half-split chopsticks found in restaurants (*waribashi*) may be separated by your colleagues by gripping one side with the teeth and breaking off the other by hand. You don't have to do this. Splinters are removed by rubbing one stick against the other.

It's bad form to leave chopsticks crossed on your plate or standing upright in food like a bowl of rice. Don't lick or scrape them to remove sticking food. When eating rice, Japanese lift the bowl toward their mouths, but hunching one's shoulders or putting one's face directly over the bowl is indecorous. When using chopsticks pay attention to your food. Don't glance around the room. Sushi, which may be served as an appetizer, is eaten by hand, not with chopsticks as is common in the U.S. However, use chopsticks for the salad portions of a sushi platter.

Hold chopsticks so they extend one-third above and two-thirds below your hand, with ends even. The lower stick is held stationary with either the third or second and third fingers. The upper stick does the clamping by manipulating it between your thumb and first two fingers. *Waribashi* come in a paper envelope. Don't crumble it into a ball when you remove them. At the end of the meal, replace them in the envelope.

If you're eating Japanese food, let your hosts order first. If you're invited to order before everyone else, politely decline. The senior-ranking Japanese at the table is usually the first to tell the server what he wants. Then subordinates will probably order the same thing—whether they want it or not. Such is the extent to which group harmony may be carried; to do otherwise would make a person stand out as an individual. As an American you can order what you want, but this pressures you to follow suit. Most Americans succumb not only because they would feel uncomfortable being the only ones in the party eating something different, but also because they too are seeking group acceptance.

## Nightclubs

After dinner, you'll probably be taken to at least one Japanese nightclub. The ones Americans visit most are called *karoke* (pronounced "car-okay") bars. A *karoke* bar is a hostess club. When you're seated at a booth or table, some hostesses will join you; the number depends on the size of your group. Most are Japanese, but they may be of any nationality, including Americans. While some *karoke* hostesses are also prostitutes, they work at low-class establishments, not at the better places you're likely to frequent. At top *karoke* bars, their function is simply to help everyone relax, keep the conversation going, tell adorable jokes that you probably won't understand, initiate silly games that everyone plays, and most importantly, ensure that liquor flows steadily among members of your party (which is how *karoke* bars make their biggest profits).

*Karoke* bars enable Japanese not just to drink but to get *drunk*. Per capita consumption of alcohol in Japan is among the world's highest. One must get drunk in so repressed a society to erode the otherwise impermeable psychic walls behind which feelings are kept bottled up. By letting out some emotions, a degree of intimacy can take place between people impossible to establish in formal office situations. Such shared intimacy becomes the basis for feeling trust.

At *karoke* bars, the standard drink is Scotch and water, or *mizuari*, meaning "diluted with water" (the Scotch is implied). If you prefer a liquor other than Scotch you must request it; otherwise you'll automatically be served *mizuari*.

Even if you're not fond of hard liquor at home, it's important to seem to drink with your Japanese colleagues should the opportunity arise. At least accept *mizuari* and after a while pretend to act somewhat inebriated. Many Japanese start to relax and open up only after their faces turn red with a tipsy flush, a sign of sincerity. Some Japanese worriedly consult their physicians to find out why their faces don't turn red after extensive imbibing, implying they are incapable of being sincere.

When Japanese get drunk, they fool around. A popular diversion is to place a paper napkin over a glass and put a coin in the center. Everyone takes turns burning cigarette holes in the napkin around the coin. The one who burns the hole that makes the coin fall into the glass must drink the drink. It may seem silly now, but everyone laughs heartily, has a few more drinks, and after a while, just about anything seems funny.

*Karoke* bars take their name from *karoke* sound systems with outlets at each table. A hostess will bring a small tape recorder to the table with a few cassettes and plug in the machine. The cassettes contain only background music. The party also gets a song book and a microphone, which are passed from person to person. Everyone must sing a song—including you. Intermingled with Japanese song soundtracks are usually some American songs. They may range from oldies but goodies like "My Darling Clementine" to fifties rock 'n' roll like "Love Me Tender" to hits by contemporary artists like Michael Jackson or Elton John.

If you're a college glee club veteran or sing in a church choir, show your stuff. If you sing "You Ain't Nuthin' but a Hound Dog" like you aren't kidding, no matter. As in other areas of Japanese negotiations, the process matters more than the result. Don't be afraid to seem foolish.

This is a way to express your humanity to the Japanese. Many will sing their own songs no better than you do yours. Some Japanese executives take professional singing lessons in order to master one or two songs to preserve some semblance of self-respect.

In between singing and playing silly games, it's usually permissible to talk shop. After a day of prolonged bargaining, the session may continue in the informal atmosphere of a *karoke* bar. While drinking, business can often be discussed more frankly than at the office. If you say something that would have been rude earlier, it will probably be forgiven. In Japan, drunkenness excuses almost anything. Normally shunning physical contact, Japanese may throw their arms around you in boozy camaraderie. They may also get unabashedly sick in public. As a people, they don't hold their liquor well.

However, drinking may also be used as a ploy to get the upper hand in negotiations. Americans sometimes visit *karoke* bars with a half-dozen Japanese colleagues, five of whom proceed to get quite drunk and one of whom only acts the part. He's the one to start talking shop. While you can feel freer to say what's on your mind, be wary of making commitments until you're once again sober. A promise is a promise in Japan, drunk or not. Counsels one veteran of *karoke* bars:

> I'd recommend that anybody who wants to do business in Japan be prepared to get drunk *a lot*—if you're a good drinker. But you must be able to drink without ever losing that little interior part of yourself that's still in control. If you can't do that, you'll get into trouble. You must *look* drunk. You must *act* drunk. If you don't, you're obviously not getting on well with the boys. But the Japanese don't ever get so drunk that they totally lose control. You get drunk to say things that are on your mind and can say under no other circumstances. But you're still dropping depth charges. You can say things when drunk that you could never get away with sober. But you never really tell the absolute truth. Even when one is drunk in Japan, complete frankness is nearly always a mistake.

Don't be disconcerted when you return to a Japanese company the morning after an evening of drinking to find that your buddies of only a few hours before are back to their normal, formal reserve. They may not even acknowledge your presence as you pass them in the hall or face them again at a conference table. Don't remind them of what was said or done at a *karoke* bar, or ask if their hangovers are as bad as yours. Once again, their personal feelings are shored up behind thick mental walls. They have ceased to be the jovial individuals you partied with last night. Their personalities are again submerged into a harmonious group in which individuality is suppressed.

What about your efforts to be friendly, sincere, and worthy of trust? Don't worry. They haven't been forgotten. Next-day aloofness is how the Japanese behave with each other as well as foreign guests. This is their situational ethics. On subsequent trips, as your relationship with your colleagues deepens, you'll still find the Japanese running hot and cold. When you revisit a *karoke* bar, your previously experienced camaraderie will probably resume where it left off.

Repay a visit to a *karoke* bar with a restaurant meal, rather than hosting a drinking party yourself at a similar establishment. *Karoke* bars are expensive. You usually pay a cover charge to enter, buy Scotch by the bottle (often at $100 a liter), pay another fee for setups, yet another for the companionship of hostesses, and then you're supposed to generously tip them as you leave. The tab for entertaining a few Japanese at a *karoke* bar for a couple of hours can top $1,000! *Karoke* bars are Japanese turf and are best left to them. They don't expect you to take them there, and most Americans are grateful for that.

## Gift Giving

Japan is the most gift-giving business culture in the world. Says one American who works in Tokyo: "If there's even the slightest occasion for giving a gift, the Japanese will do it; if not, they will invent it."

Do come to Japan bearing gifts. The preferred gifts at the outset of negotiations are collective, presented to a Japanese firm as a whole rather than to an individual. You won't usually deal with individuals in Japan; you'll deal with groups, which can be large. While logo gifts are fine to give, you may have to bring a dozen or more to present to the Japanese who compose a negotiating team, as well as to others whom you don't initially meet but later learn are bottlenecking progress.

A group gift should symbolically reflect your firm as much as possible. One U.S. automobile manufacturer gives gold-plated models of his latest cars. A banker gives old U.S. twenty-dollar gold coins, embedded in lucite. Executives of a department-store chain headquartered in its own U.S. skyscraper give metal replicas of the building. But a suitable gift can also be a bottle of Johnny Walker Black or Chivas Regal Scotch, two brands universally known to Japanese and which everyone can enjoy. Bring the Scotch from home or buy it at an airport duty-free shop; Chivas costs $45 a fifth in Japan.

Group gifts need not cost a fortune, but if you shop at a prestigious store, so much the better. Says an American manager working in Osaka:

Gifts for the Japanese should be made in America, and are best wrapped in paper patterned with the logo of a well-known store. When we first opened negotiations in Japan, we presented the Japanese team with a sterling silver bowl. We bought it at Tiffany's. It came in a Tiffany's box and was wrapped in distinctive Tiffany's paper. When the chief Japanese negotiator unwrapped the gift, he saved the paper. He carefully reassembled the entire package so that he could show it to his superiors as it was presented to him. That's half the significance of the event: seeing where the gift was purchased.

However, let the Japanese initiate the gift-giving exchange. Don't surprise them with a gift. If they don't have something to give you in return, they lose face. Leave your gift at your hotel until you receive something—and you customarily will. Then, at a future meeting, present your gift. This is why it's important to bring a gift that was clearly made in the U.S. It shows you had the foresight to be sincere. If you purchase even a lavish gift at a store in Japan on the spur of the moment, you lose points.

As for lavishness, don't overdo it. If you give the Japanese a better gift than they give you, they lose face.

If you decide to give corporate mementoes, check Chapter Three for suitable suggestions. Be sure logo gifts are not made *anywhere* in East Asia: South Korea, Taiwan, Hong Kong, and China as well as Japan. This may be a slap in the face.

While the wrapping paper of a high-class store is important, it's best to leave off bows and ribbons. The Japanese consider American bows unaesthetic. Crossed ribbons imply bad wishes.

Present a gift with *two* hands. If it's a collective gift for a firm, present it to the chief negotiator. He will hesitate to accept it. Don't be offended. To accept something as soon as it's offered shows overeagerness, which is bad manners in Japan. Continue to offer your gift while apologizing for its unworthiness. A Japanese who presents a gift to you will do likewise, and you should not accept it at once. One can never be too humble in Japan or too reserved.

Eventually your gift will be accepted. To refuse it would mean a loss of face for you, which no Japanese will intentionally cause. When the situation is reversed, you must also accept a Japanese gift after it has been offered to you two or three times, for the same reason.

When presenting your gift, don't make a big deal out of it. Don't give a speech. Underplay the act. Don't expect to be thanked for the gift. This isn't rudeness, just not custom.

Depending on the situation, some Japanese may unwrap your gift at once; others won't. They will open it when you're not present. This saves face. If a Japanese doesn't like your gift, he may feel compelled to compliment it insincerely to save face for you. But if he *knows* he's being insincere, *he* loses face. Nor are you obliged to open a Japanese gift in the presence of the giver.

Even if you shop at a quality store, buy something relatively inexpensive. Once you have a prestige name, it's the thought that counts more than the content. The less you spend, the better. Ideally your gift should be equal in value to whatever the Japanese give you. Unless you're psychic, you won't be able to second-guess what the value of a Japanese gift will be. It's always better to give the Japanese a lesser gift than they give you, rather than a better one. You may lose a little face, but if someone has to lose face in Japan, it had better be you.

Gift giving in Japan may seem like a delightful custom to the inexperienced, but it makes many old hands groan. It can easily turn into an endless, increasingly expensive cycle. Here, I give you a gift, you give one to me, and we're square. One is never square in Japan. The Japanese gift you, you gift them, now they must re-gift you, you must re-gift them, and it goes on interminably. If you give the Japanese a better gift than they initially give to you, count on getting a still more expensive gift on a future trip. Now your next gift must be more expensive, to save face. If you give too lavish a gift at the outset, the cost of gift giving can soon get out of hand.

# CHAPTER EIGHT

---

# Chinese Checkers

"An open door is not always an invitation to enter."

*Chinese fortune cookie fortune*

Japan is probably the world's most puzzling place for U.S. negotiators because of the sheer number who try to deal there. But the People's Republic of China (PRC) is catching up fast as more Americans set their sights on a market of over one billion Chinese. This is because China is among the most mystifying blends of old and new to be found in global commerce.

In some ways, the Chinese can claim technological advancement that modern industrial societies cannot. For example, in Sichuan Province lies an engineering marvel: the Dujiangyan Irrigation System. This vast network of canals, ditches, reservoirs, dams, and dikes waters over 1,300,000 acres of arable land that once thwarted cultivation due to alternating cycles of floods and droughts. The system is now being studied by agronomists the world over. With all the aids of modern technology at their disposal, they have yet to devise a network as efficient in their own countries.

Even more remarkable about this engineering feat is its origin. The Dujiangyan Irrigation System was begun in 250 B.C., when the emperor Qin Shi Huangdi—who, as an adult, would order a major part of the Great Wall to be built—was still a child. The main canal cuts more than 6,000 meters through Long Quan Mountain. The mountain was cleaved by heating its rocky slope with burning logs, then dousing the smoldering surface with cold water to crack the otherwise unbreakable stone. Over 2,000 years would pass before dynamite was invented.

However, as a modern nation China lags behind industrialized Japan and its newly industrializing neighbors in living standards and economic development. Even so, there are dramatic improvements. Xishuangbanna, near the borders of Burma and Laos in Yunnan Province, had a primitive culture only thirty years ago. The natives were slash-and-burn farmers who lived in bamboo huts set on stilts for protection against marauding boars and tigers. In the 1950s, when infantrymen of Mao's army first entered the region, they received the hospitality traditionally accorded to cultural outsiders: death. When a subsequent mechanized military unit was dispatched, the inhabitants acquiesced, not due to Mao's superior force but because they had never seen motorized vehicles before. Thinking they were being visited by horse gods, they rushed out with offerings of food and fell to their knees in reverence.

Today the region boasts a thriving city in which residents study ballet, play basketball, watch television, seek foreign tourism, and are developing the infrastructure to maintain it. In addition, advanced agricultural techniques like crop rotation, fertilizer technology, and hydroponics are now used to grow a greater variety of crops and increase crop yields.

Still, China has a long way to go to catch up with other East Asian countries and with the West. Despite the nation's current plan for rapid industrialization and improvement of living standards, in many respects the PRC remains the "sleeping giant."

In 1978, when China reopened its doors to Western tourism and commerce, Li Qiang, Minister of Foreign Trade, proclaimed: "By and large, we now accept all the common practices known to world trade." But years later, as Americans are increasingly discovering today, this announcement was premature. More often than not, what the Chinese consider common international practice is common only from a Chinese point of view.

## Portraits of a Businesspeople

In *Birds*, Aristophanes wrote: "The wise learn many things from their enemies." Despite ardent assertions of friendship and a real desire for Western trade, Chinese government officials do consider us enemies; we are decadent capitalists, and China has a long history of exploitation by the West. The Chinese are also wise. They have devoted much time to studying the U.S. and sometimes have an edge on us in understanding as a result. Yet this edge is often counterbalanced by the inefficiency of China's bureaucracy and the rigidity, obtuseness, and paranoia instilled by its brand of Communism, which retard negotiations in a nation seeking foreign commerce in order to progress. Political ideology also makes the Chinese a baffling businesspeople. Many Americans who struggle to understand them are left knowing little more than when they began, for acceptance of all the common practices known to world trade notwithstanding, negotiations in the PRC abound in contradictions that defy U.S. business logic.

### Bureaucracy

Superficially, the public sectors of China and Japan may seem similar because both are collectivistic; one deals with groups, not individuals. In major transactions, a negotiating team in Beijing may be larger than in Tokyo.

But one of the most distinct traits of Japanese companies and government agencies is that communication channels run horizontally as well as vertically throughout a hierarchy, and down-up as well as up-down. This efficiently supplies decision makers with maximum intelligence in order to make the most informed decisions.

However, information sharing is not the norm in Chinese bureaucracies. Government agencies tend to be secretive, closed societies, suspicious of each other. Their members may confine fraternization to each other not only in professional but also in social situations. Because horizontal communication is poor, after having met with representatives of Agency A you may find the officials of Agency B intensely curious about what you learned. Often the easiest way to find out what parallel agencies are doing is by questioning foreign businesspeople in China!

Vertical communication is also poor in Chinese government. Subordinates are often kept in the dark as to what the economic and ideological mandates are of those above them. In this sense, decision making in China is autocratic. As a result, subordinates are often unaware of how the decisions they must implement fit into the grand scheme of China's economic future.

Ostensibly, the Chinese negotiate agreements based on what is best for the country as a whole. But how this can be done with poor lines of communication horizontally and vertically is anyone's guess. Better cooperation and unity of purpose based on knowledge rather than ignorance would seemingly be required.

Under Mao Zedong, this cumbersome decision-making situation was made more time consuming by being centralized in Beijing. With the opening of China to international trade, it has since aroused complaints from within the country itself. Deng Xiaoping, China's current vice-premier, experimented with bureaucratic decentralization to speed up decision making, respond more quickly to market opportunities, improve production, and accelerate modernization. But without a codified plan for the diffusion of power, the result was chaos.

For example, foreign tour operators—who generate a sizable part of China's much needed foreign exchange—found that a block of hotel rooms in Shanghai or Guilin, booked through the China Travel and Tourism Administrative Bureau in Beijing, had often been independently sold to someone else by the tourism agency of a local municipality or even by the hotel itself, with no cross-communication. As a result, the tour operators were left with fifty stranded, angry customers who had no place to stay.

On a larger scale, lack of cross-communication in China's newly decentralized bureaucracy caused the cancellation of a $250 million foreign trade center in Beijing, negotiated by Americans with China's Ministry of Foreign Trade. First, the National People's Congress had not been consulted; it frowned upon the venture because of its high cost. Then the municipal government of Beijing itself, which was not represented in negotiations, opposed the plan mainly because it failed to incorporate direct financial benefits to the city. Meanwhile, the Ministry of Foreign Trade had already invested $7 million in the project before it was stopped.

The upshot of such fiascos was reported in the *New York Times* (March 15, 1984):

> China announced today that it was returning to tight state control over foreign trade. The reason, it said, was "confusion" brought on by China's opening to the outside world in the past five years.

What effects the shift back to centralization will have on intercity and interfactory trade competition in China remains to be seen. But it's less likely to have detrimental effects on U.S. firms with already well-established relations with the Chinese than on newcomers. For first-time negotiators, quick decisions in China remain rare.

## *Fear*

In a bureaucratic environment with poor communication and mistrust from within, the main priority of Chinese team members may not be to consider their country's best interests but to look out for their own. Fear of criticism from superiors verges on paranoia in China, and with good reason: The consequences of incurring disfavor from above can be severe. It may stymie career advancement, cause demotion and loss of face, or result in a job transfer from an important commercial center to an inconsequential wilderness outpost for life.

## *Passivity*

American negotiators are typically aggressive, goal-oriented, and prepared to make commitments. The Chinese are usually passive, reactive, and noncommittal. Bargaining sessions are often one way, with you talking and the Chinese listening. Dynamic individualists who thrive on having the center stage, many Americans are not good listeners. However, the Chinese are adept at keeping their ears open and their mouths closed. This is often for fear of saying something open to criticism by superiors later on. But it's also an effective tactic for eliciting one-sided commitments from Americans, or learning and copying technologies protected by U.S. patent without remuneration; this is not considered unfair practice in China. The Chinese are hungry for knowledge, a trait we admire. But they may continually ask probing questions that entice Americans to reveal too much. Many U.S. negotiators, who are fond of elaborating on the virtues of American technology and what it can do for China, take the bait.

## *Aggressiveness*

On the other hand, Chinese negotiators can be quite aggressive in exploiting a weakness revealed by the American side. And, unlike the Japanese, they don't always try to appear emotionally reserved in bargaining sessions. If they feel the "spirit" of a relationship has been violated by you, and so vague a concept can be interpreted many ways—to Chinese advantage—your counterparts may be quick to respond with stern rebuke. Outbursts of anger and criticism are also tactics used by the Chinese to throw Americans, who are eager to be liked, off balance. Many U.S. businesspeople have been made to feel that they have unwittingly done something wrong, despite their good intentions. Such intimidation tactics can be highly effective in winning concessions that the Chinese seek.

### Responsibility

The Chinese may state at the outset of negotiations that they merely represent higher decision-making bodies and thus have no authority to make commitments themselves. At other times, however, they may give the *illusion* that they wield true decision-making power. This may be due to personal egotism. Or a seeming commitment may be made at one level of discussion to proceed to another in order to extract more information—knowledge that can be used to gain advantage in subsequent bargaining sessions. Or, occasionally, the Chinese may feel secure that they are committing themselves in a way that will meet with approval from superiors—based on prior consultations with them—and then it's still poorly received.

In addition, fostering the illusion of decision-making power may be used as a tactic to lead Americans into overestimating expectations concerning decision-making speed, scheduling, production capacity, future profit potential, and general cooperation from the Chinese. Once this information is reported to the home office, which in turn is usually quick to share it with stockholders, the U.S. negotiators are in a bind. The Chinese can then exploit the situation to exact further concessions if premature American claims are to be validated.

For whatever reason, in subsequent meetings the Chinese may suddenly switch gears and disclaim or evade the responsibility they implied they possessed earlier. In the U.S., the link between power and responsibility is assumed. In China, it's increasingly, intentionally blurred as the accountability for making a decision is passed from one committee behind the scenes to another at ever-higher levels of the bureaucracy. Experienced Americans take what they are initially told in China with a grain of salt.

### Bigger Is Better

To avoid criticism from superiors, the Chinese may insist on dealing with the Number One firm in a given field. In the Chinese mind, one should only deal with the best, and often *best* is equated with *biggest*. Thus, multinational giants in the West and Japan may have an automatic edge on smaller competitors based solely on their size, not on whether their goods, services or terms are best for China. Bad deals are often made by the Chinese because of this myopia.

## *Ethnocentricity*

While Americans are ethnocentric, our cultural chauvinism is often inadvertent. Many of us don't realize that our attitudes and actions *imply* feelings of superiority. Not being introspective enough, we don't carry the logic of our thinking to its inevitable conclusion.

The Chinese resemble the French in being quite conscious of feeling themselves to be a people culturally superior to all others. Such feelings stem in part from a justifiable pride in China's heritage. Today's Chinese are heirs to one of the oldest and richest civilizations on the globe, a civilization that has made many important contributions to the world, among them the invention of gunpowder, the compass, and the printing press.

However, ethnocentric feelings are intensified by Marxist dogma, which holds itself to be moral and pure and capitalism to be immoral and decadent.

Convinced they are culturally and morally superior to decadent capitalists, the Chinese may try to cast U.S. businesspeople in the role of beggars, not choosers. As they often see it, *you* have come to China. The Chinese did not come to you. This *proves* that you need them. Whether or not they need you remains to be seen. Hence, for the Chinese to condescend to negotiate, you must be prepared to make concessions that justify their cooperation without expecting to get something in return for each item you give up.

By extension, the Chinese deem it their natural right as a superior people not merely to reap a fair share but the *lion's share* of gain. Often it's not sufficient for the Chinese merely to get enough of what they want. While they accept that you, too, must make a profit, you must not profit perceptibly *more* than the Chinese. To reinforce feelings of superiority, the Chinese must "win" negotiations in order to save face. Even when a business proposal is clearly mutually advantageous, if it's *perceived* that what you gain is more than what you give, the Chinese lose face. Losing face is a serious concern in China, and may draw criticism from superiors.

## Xenophobia

Paradoxically, the Chinese may feel superior to decadent capitalists yet at the same time fear them. Such fear is based in part on a culturally inculcated paranoia toward the West and Japan arising from their exploitation of China in centuries past. The Chinese are convinced that capitalists will take advantage of them if they drop their guard.

But their fear goes beyond the lessons of history. Most Chinese you'll face across a conference table have agrarian peasant roots. People with a poor-farmer mentality have an intrinsic mistrust of prosperous merchants, and by extension of wealthy capitalists. This is because businesspeople don't earn a living by sweat and physical toil for the good of the family— the basic unit of Confucian society—or any larger social entity. Instead, by a mysteriously relaxed process, they reap an overabundance of material reward with no discernible effort. Moreover, they selfishly hoard their wealth rather than altruistically sharing it with the group. Chinese logic follows that the rich but idle and miserly few *must* be taking advantage of the needy many by the very fact of this inequity in the distribution of wealth, unconscionably prospering at their expense. This generations-old feeling of outrage and mistrust is manipulated by Marxist dogma into a sense of moral indignation and self-righteousness.

As such, the whole concept of earning a profit makes the Chinese suspicious. Often they draw no distinction between profiting and profiteering, seeing both as being fundamentally greedy, conniving, treacherous, and immoral. Believing they are motivated by a higher moral purpose fuels the Chinese conviction that they are ethically superior, and feeds their need to feel they get more than they give in dealings with the West.

They justify their unbalanced expectations in negotiations as self-protection against calculating Westerners who seek to manipulate the morally pure Chinese for *their* unfair gain. The Chinese are convinced that no capitalist would continue to negotiate if there wasn't plenty still at stake. Accordingly, they may try to push you to the limit with their demands for concessions, believing that as long as you're still willing to bargain, they are not acting unfairly—by definition.

## Friendship

When a U.S. negotiator new to China first steps off the plane, the Chinese will strive to develop good interpersonal rapport, putting friendship before business. Indeed, the Chinese excel at being delightful hosts. Novices are often beguiled by initial shows of courtesy and generosity into believing the Chinese have taken a special shine to them as individuals. This is just what the Chinese want you to think.

Because the Chinese are innately xenophobic and their political ideology holds that capitalism is basically immoral, expect to be mistrusted at the outset, despite the friendliness you're shown. Americans are frequently quick to forget that China is a Communist state. Many take for granted that early shows of generosity—like personal gifts and lavish banquets—are paid for by individual hosts. But in a country that officially shuns materialism and the vanities of private ownership, the government pays the bills.

It's precisely by being charming, giving, and polite that the Chinese may intentionally try to put you at ease as a negotiating tactic, not out of genuine friendship. Once you're relaxed and off guard, they can better size you up as an adversary, appraise your intelligence, gauge your reliability and sincerity, probe for weaknesses, and decide how to exploit them effectively when bargaining begins.

To the Chinese, friendship with Westerners does not imply intimate personal relationships between *individuals* as it does in the U.S. Instead, it involves harmonious cooperation between abstract *entities*, an American corporation on one side and a Chinese bureaucracy on the other. The Chinese are one exception to the otherwise nearly universal rule that you're not regarded as a symbol outside our borders. In China, you're initially that—a symbol—rather than being viewed as a unique human being. Years can pass before a bona fide friendship develops between individuals, if it ever does.

In fact, the Chinese system is set up to discourage the possibility of a true friendship forming between you and a native. Countrymen are urged to inform on each other when they witness an unauthorized breach of thought or conduct. For this reason, each time a Chinese visits you at your hotel, he must register at the front desk. If the desk attendant suspects that his visit is personal rather than official, he will telephone his work unit or other organization to check.

Be this as it may, the Chinese *are* susceptible to human emotions. It's possible to meet individuals who honestly do like you and seek to socialize with you without authorization, often out of curiosity to learn more about the U.S. However, if this should happen, be aware that such unsanctioned fraternization may get a Chinese into trouble, and it won't help you to achieve your business goals.

Not only are the Chinese conditioned to avoid empathy with Americans, but if you respond too enthusiastically to early overtures of friendship—as U.S. negotiators may innocently do—you may exacerbate the instinctive suspicion Westerners often arouse in China. The Chinese know their initial courtesies are merely routine cultural formalities—largely empty gestures—and perhaps attempts to gain tactical negotiating advantages. But they are often unaware that Americans don't see through them and realize what is going on. When you make much ado about what they consider nothing, the Chinese may interpret your overexuberance as a cunning counter-tactic, masking your true intent to take advantage of them by a duplicitous display of camaraderie.

Don't be misled by this state of affairs. The Chinese *do* sincerely seek trust relationships with Americans. But their fear of foreigners is not easily or quickly overcome, and friendships usually form much more slowly than U.S. businesspeople are encouraged to believe. Furthermore, the conditions for friendship in China may lead to an exaggerated dependency of the Chinese on you that few Americans anticipate or desire.

Dependency implies obligation. But unlike the situation in Japan, the Chinese concept of obligation may *not* be mutual. As the Chinese define friendship, the haves in a relationship give selflessly to the have-nots with no expectation of repayment. As a result, many Americans find themselves caught between a rock and a hard place. On one hand, they are cast in the role of supplicants seeking Chinese benevolence; on the other, as members of a wealthy capitalistic society, they are *rich* supplicants. Hence, it becomes their moral duty—if they are sincere friends—to give to the poorer, purer, more deserving Chinese, be it in the form of gifts, better terms, price reductions, free training of Chinese personnel, or even free or bargain-priced transfers of technology.

In this way the Chinese may manipulate their American "friendships" to gain negotiating leverage. If their demands on the relationship are denied, they may quickly retaliate with outraged accusations of "false friend!"

Yet the Chinese themselves are not above being expedient friends. Americans sometimes establish officially sanctioned friendships with the Chinese at much time and cost only to lose business they had taken pains to cultivate to a larger (and therefore *better*) competitor that entered the negotiating arena late. This is something smaller exporters in particular should keep in mind. It's not sufficient merely to try to sell the Chinese goods or services you know they lack and are convinced they desire. Quality, rightness for Chinese circumstances, even preferential price are no guarantees of a sale if a much bigger company with comparable wares exists.

### Patience

Stephen Soule, an importer of products from the PRC for over six years, offers a perception widely held by U.S. businesspeople who regularly deal in the country:

> China has really changed in the past few years. Part of me says: "You've got to be kidding. Nothing in China changes that fast." But clearly it's a different place in which to do business now than it was on my first trip in 1978.

Soule's is the voice of experience, and beginners should be cautious for just this reason. Americans with years of negotiating practice in China have typically endured so many frustrations in the past that the genuine improvements today tend to overshadow fundamental difficulties that still exist, which savants have come to take for granted. Once a business relationship has been well-established, it may now be possible to reach agreements in China with previously unheard-of speed. Says Soule:

> My last trip to China was terrific! I was in Peking for two days, Shanghai for two days, Hangchow for two days, and then I returned to Shanghai for another meeting and left. I accomplished more in a few days than I was able to do in *weeks* at any other time.

Unfortunately, such efficiency does not usually await newcomers. Another U.S importer with over a decade of China experience describes his early years of dealing with the Chinese, and his account is probably closer to what first-timers can expect in China today*:

> We buy fifty-pound cartons of Product X, packed forty-eight to a wooden pallet. The Chinese wanted to sell us 100-pound gunny sacks that were not palletized, and the goods were of a type that had never been used in the U.S. So we had to get the Chinese to make X to American specifications, which they resisted for a year. When they finally agreed to the specification changes, they still wanted to ship the goods in gunny sacks. Nobody here will buy X in gunny sacks. At last we got the Chinese to pack them in cartons. But then they didn't want to put the

---

* The actual product is not identified to protect the informant's anonymity. He was extremely sensitive about jeopardizing a relationship that took years to establish.

cartons on pallets. Finally we got them to agree to the pallets, but the pallets were made of concrete, not wood—which makes no sense. But the Chinese didn't know about wooden pallets. After all the patience in the world, we got the Chinese to do exactly what we wanted them to do, and now China is our single largest supplier of X.

This anecdote is instructive for two reasons. First, it's a *success* story, but it's not a story of *easy* success. After years of outwardly calm, endlessly tolerant negotiating, and coping with an array of unforeseeable frustrations, this chief executive—whose company has gross annual sales of over $100 million, mostly from selling China imports—found that persistence and patience pays off in the long run. Other Americans who succeed in China agree. Very few make money there fast.

What's also significant about this story is that it's told by a *buyer*, not a seller. Compared to what exporters often endure to develop profitable relationships with the Chinese, he had it easy!

## Business Customs

Not long ago, Americans ran into their first roadblock in dealing with the Chinese when trying to secure a commercial visa. Issued by invitation only, this alone could take up to a year—if it was granted at all. Today the Chinese have considerably eased visa issuance. In fact, it's now possible for U.S. businesspeople to visit China as members of tour groups or as independent tourists and simply drop in at an appropriate government ministry or other agency in a commercial center without a prior appointment. For example, five of China's Foreign Trade Corporations (FTCs)—independent state entities empowered to handle foreign trade for the products they represent—are headquartered in a single building at 82 Dong'anmen Street. Use the lobby telephone to announce your presence. A representative will appear to hear you out.

In addition, a few FTCs have opened branches in the U.S. The China Investment and Trade Office and the Consulate General of China may also help. Such organizations are mainly in New York. Trade missions to China are increasingly being sponsored by both the U.S. public and private sectors; participation is among the best ways for newcomers to gain business experience in the PRC.

American corporations are fostering trade between China and the U.S. business community at large. Chemical Bank, for instance, has proposed sponsoring seminars to introduce firms in the New York area to business and investment opportunities in China. From the Chinese side, a growing number of organizations like the Chinese Overseas Shipping Company are opening branches here.

China is showing new flexibility and scope in business dealings with the West in other ways, too. A recently concluded agreement between the PRC and the Columbia Broadcasting Network will permit the airing of sixty hours of CBS programming on Chinese television, including documentaries, football games, and even TV commercials.

Developments like these lead sinologists to be guardedly optimistic about the future of U.S.–China trade. Their reservations are partly political. For example, U.S. treaties with Taiwan concerning the sale of American military aircraft and other weapons to the Taiwanese remain a festering sore spot in our diplomatic relations with China, which considers Taiwan to still belong to it. Politics and trade are integrally linked in China, not separate issues as they often are here. Also, despite encouraging signs, decision making in China continues to be a long drawn-out process. The Chinese are swamped with business proposals from all over the world. There's a chronic shortage of personnel qualified to evaluate them. And despite the ambitious goals of the Four Modernizations—China's plan for economic development—the Chinese are not workaholics; quitting time is 4:00 P.M.

## Pre-Trip Research

If you've never dealt with the Chinese before, it's wise to seek expert *American* advice before making initial overtures. It usually saves time, expense, and frustration. Foreign Trade Corporation officials in the U.S. may serve little more than public relations functions and have no authority to negotiate. Will you be told? Probably not. While it's possible to meet with an FTC representative in China without an appointment, there may be no interest in your proposition. Will you be told? Probably not. Or your offer may draw no reaction not because it's uninteresting but because you're addressing it to the wrong organization. Will you be told? Probably not. If you specifically ask, you may find that the representative of one agency has no idea where to send you next, as horizontal communication channels in China are poor; this too may not be readily admitted.

In so uncommunicative an environment, U.S. experts can be a godsend. Places to turn include the U.S. Department of Commerce's Industry and Trade Administration, Office of East-West Country Affairs, PRC Division, or the Office of East-West Trade Development, Trade Development Assistance Division (both in Washington, D.C.). Private organizations like the National Council for U.S.-China Trade (Washington) or the U.S.-China Industrial Exchange (New York) can also help. Finding China expertise is easy. The challenge is choosing from the many options available.

## Business Proposals

Business proposals written for Chinese readers frequently come on too strong. Instead, they should explain in an objective, factual, soft-sell way what the size and reputation of your firm are and what makes it Number One in its field. *Number One* refers to size as well as quality. If you're not plainly first in quality, if you're the best but only within a certain market context, or if you manufacture goods of comparable quality to those of larger companies, without the counsel of an expert you may find yourself leaping off a diving board into an empty pool.

Don't try to dupe the Chinese by omitting this information from your proposal, or using tricky wording to make your company seem bigger and/or better than it really is. You won't fool the Chinese for long if at all. Large cadres of Chinese technocrats are employed solely to gather and evaluate data on companies the world over. It won't take them long to cross-check your facts and figures against theirs. An effective proposal should not dwell on basic information it's safe to assume the Chinese already know but rather expand on it.

In addition to citing the specification requirements in *metric* measurements of desired purchases, importers should tell the Chinese what their sales volumes are, the extensiveness of distribution channels, and their financial reliability. Annual reports, bank references, and Dun & Bradstreet ratings will satisfy the latter requirement.

U.S. firms commonly suggest how their product lines or services will fit into China's general modernization goals. A more effective tack is to research known Chinese development plans, assume the Chinese will know what they want to buy when they see it, and match your offering to a *specific* economic objective. This helps mid-level bureaucrats convince superiors that your proposal is worthwhile. The more conclusions you must draw because they are not apparent, the more your chances of success are reduced in China.

However, some conclusions that Americans take for granted as being obvious are not obvious to the Chinese, particularly when it comes to commercial considerations less tangible than technology transfers, quality or price. Often overlooked is the creation of badly needed jobs in the PRC. Arne J. De Keijzer, a China business consultant, recalls:

> I had a client who was in the tourism business. We were proposing something to the Chinese that had never been done before in the country, and the idea initially met with a stone wall. Finally, we talked with the head of the Peking municipality and his staff, who would be responsible for project implementation if it ever got off the ground. What eventually began to win the Chinese over was when we discussed the plan from the point of view that it would employ X number of people. These people would be trained as part of the transaction not only as bureaucrats but also as technical personnel. The Chinese replied: "Oh, we hadn't thought of that." So it may not have been the service itself that was of primary interest. Perhaps more importantly, we were trying to help the Chinese justify the project within their own bureaucracy, culture, and economic needs.

The Chinese usually need twenty or more photocopies of a business proposal. They will be distributed by your initial contact to other members of his organization, and possibly to municipal agencies and factories as well, as a variety of entities may participate in decision making. Despite China's proliferation of new hotels stocked with modern office equipment, photocopying machines remain in short supply.

## Collateral Materials

As many colors have symbolic meanings for the Chinese, limit color in collateral materials to that of photographs. Yellow, for example, the color of emperors, won't be well-received in the now Communist People's Republic. Purple, a preferred color in Japan, denotes a barbarian in China. In general, the Chinese are unimpressed by splashy literature. It's not necessary to invest in color printing.

The Chinese don't respond well to purely imagistic messages. Product shots showing pretty girls will either seem puzzling to them or be turnoffs. Purple prose should also be avoided. Stick to facts.

Pragmatism, not showiness, marks the most effective literature. No-nonsense graphs, charts, tables, diagrams, and case histories are what Chinese want to see.

Be cautious when using geopolitical maps, particularly if color or gray shading separates national entities. Maps indicating that Hong Kong is a British colony and Taiwan an independent country won't win negotiating points in China.

Use approved terms of national reference in text and conversation. They include the People's Republic of China, the People's Republic, the PRC, or simply China. They do *not* include Mainland China, Red China or Communist China. Never refer to Taiwan as the Republic of China, the ROC or Free China.

## Dress

Chinese negotiators usually wear drab, monochromatic shirt jackets, buttoned to the top and not tucked in at the bottom, and matching pants— the all-purpose utilitarian costume favored by Mao Zedong and popularly known as the "Mao suit." It may seem like informal attire, but it's no less casual than a dress suit is in the U.S. It does not imply that you can adopt unbusinesslike attire in China. Men should wear conservative suits and ties, women their equivalent.

As Chinese women either wear Mao suits or blouses and slacks, slacks and pantsuits are okay for American women. Although there's no taboo against it, few women in China show their legs, and most of them are foreign tourists, not natives.

It's best not to look fashionable. Don't bring expensive designer clothes. Chinese women wear flat-soled shoes. American women can do likewise or wear low or half-heels; high heels are out of place. Both men and women should pack a pair of comfortable walking shoes. Business travelers do a lot more sightseeing than they often expect, at the insistence of Chinese hosts. Visiting the Great Wall from Beijing takes a full day, and a guided tour of the Forbidden City can last hours. Conservative, casual wear is acceptable for sightseeing.

Regardless of your sex, tone down jewelry or eliminate it altogether. A wristwatch made by Timex is preferable to one by Piaget. Handbags and attaché cases should not look like they cost more than what your Chinese colleagues earn in a year. Something well-worn is better than something new.

Women who want to make the best impression should not wear cosmetics, including lipstick. Beautiful clothes, opulent jewelry, makeup, and luxury items like gold or silver pens are signs of decadence in China. They may be secretly admired but officially they will earn disapproval. The Chinese with whom you'll negotiate will adhere to the authorized party line. Evidence of materialistic vanity won't be overlooked and may hamper an already difficult trust-building process.

## Small Business Gifts

Wherever you go in China you'll probably receive small gifts: carvings, textiles, ceramics, fans, chops (seals), etc. The larger your company, the higher your rank, the more important your business proposal, and the more eager the Chinese are to accept it, the more lavish the gifts you may receive. For instance, double-sided silk embroidery from Suzhou is world-renowned and a prestigious gift. In China, the most prized of semiprecious stones is jade, which comes in many colors. White jade, ranks first in value. Receiving an object made of it can be a good sign; the Chinese don't give white jade to just anyone.

Despite antimaterial party policy, the Chinese appreciate gifts from Americans. Gifts should have practical or intellectual value that recipients can cite to justify their acceptance. Lavish, expensive or ostentatious gifts, or items with no obvious use for education or work, may be criticized— not necessarily from the recipients, but from countrymen who watch and inform on them. *Everyone* is under scrutiny in China.

Logo gifts are acceptable. Items made of plastic, wood, vinyl, leather, or nonprecious metals are preferred over gold or silver objects. Most gifts suggested in Chapter Three are appropriate. While clocks—particularly digital clocks with LED displays—are popular logo gifts in the U.S., the English word *clock* is a homonym for the Chinese word *funeral*; gifts of clocks may be misinterpreted for this reason and should be avoided. It's also best not to give commemorative medals or coins, even ones made of brass, bronze or other nonprecious metals. The Chinese are forbidden to accept foreign currency; medals may be mistaken for money.

Best bets for non-logo gifts are classical records, picture books about the U.S., illustrated volumes on just about any interesting nonpolitical subject like nature or geography, and English or Chinese-English dictionaries, as many Chinese are trying to learn our language. With any gifts presented to individuals rather than symbolically to an organization or the nation, you should have something for each member of the Chinese team or nonrecipients lose face. Experienced Americans may bring one or two dozen gifts to distribute on a single trip, which is why—if you're giving books—paperbacks may be more practical than hardcovers; it's the content that counts. Don't bring gifts of food. Chinese tastes are not American. Natives may find gift foods like cheese as offputting as you'd probably find stir-fried bees or anteater which are local delicacies.

Often overlooked yet perhaps a gift more desirable than any other is a year's subscription to *Reader's Digest*. Probably the two most popular magazines in China of U.S. origin are *Time* and *Reader's Digest*. *Time* is ill-advised because it covers political and social issues that may conflict with Communist ideology. *Reader's Digest*, however, is safe. In fact, according to Joan Mills, associate editor of *Reader's Digest International Editions* (of which there are forty-one, printed in seventeen languages, including Chinese), 2,000 issues of the Asia Edition are sent to China from Hong Kong each month, the result of an official agreement between the Chinese government and *Reader's Digest*. In addition, over 200 monthly subscriptions are mailed to China from the magazine's headquarters in Pleasantville, New York.

*Reader's Digest* subscriptions are ideal gifts because they meet all criteria for effective gift giving in China. They are inexpensive. They are politically sanctioned. After you've left China, recipients are reminded of you on a monthly basis. And they are highly coveted by the Chinese. It's estimated that the few copies of the magazine now sent to China have a passalong rate of 100 people; each issue is passed from one Chinese to another until it literally disintegrates.

It's probably most practical to have subscriptions sent to an *organization* at its China address rather than to individuals, whose names you may not know even after you've met them (subordinates may not be introduced), or who may not play a role in decision making. Organization personnel will circulate the issues. Six to twelve subscriptions should be a sufficient show of generosity.

Subscriptions take time to process, but *Reader's Digest* will send you samples to distribute on your initial visit to China, along with gift cards. For details, contact John Condon, Special Services Accounts, *Reader's Digest*, Pleasantville, NY 10750; (914) 769-7000, extension 2752. That's for English-language editions mailed from the U.S. For faster delivery of *Reader's Digest*'s English-language Asia Edition, which is mailed from Hong Kong, contact Victor Laniauskas, editor-in-chief, at this telex number: LANIAUSKAS (780) 63222 DIGEST HX HONG KONG. For Chinese-language editions mailed from Hong Kong, contact Lin Tai-yi, editor-in-chief, at this telex number: LINTAIYI (780) 63222 DIGEST HX HONG KONG.

All gifts for the Chinese (including sample copies of *Reader's Digest*) should be *wrapped*. Gift wrapping shows you planned ahead, and that the enclosed items are intentional gifts, not bribes, forms of charity (about which the Chinese are highly sensitive), or makeshift gifts thoughtlessly given at the last minute. The best color for wrapping paper is red, a lucky color in China; white is funereal.

As the Chinese are not permitted to accept tips, you'll also need a supply of small wrapped gifts to replace the cash you would normally give people who perform personal services for you elsewhere in the world: hotel chambermaids, drivers, guides, etc. Inexpensive calendars, pens, key rings, memo pads, and such will do.

## Negotiating Teams

The Chinese expect an American board chairman, president, or at least a senior corporate officer to open negotiations, even though a top Chinese official may not be present at initial meetings. At the outset, the Chinese want to deal with key U.S. people as well as the largest U.S. firms. A top executive in your company must appear before their equivalent appears, giving the Chinese a symbolic victory that wins face for them from the start. Sending your chief executive is also a sign of your sincere wish to do business. In addition, it protects Chinese negotiators from superiors' criticism, as dealing with top people in top firms is approved conduct.

American CEOs, particularly those who have yet to visit China, are usually eager to go, as the trip is alluring and prestigious. Many travel on their own or with only one other corporate companion. As they often lack specialized knowledge of company operations, they may fall prey to easy manipulation. The Chinese encourage them to make broad commitments in the spirit of good faith. Such sweeping statements of intentions would be innocuous and unbinding in the U.S., but in China they are frequently interpreted at future meetings with American subordinates to limit their bargaining ability.

CEOs are usually expected to take only two mandatory trips to China: one to launch negotiations and another—which may be months or years off—to sign the eventual agreement as a symbolic gesture, when a high-ranking Chinese official will also be present. In between, teams of American middle managers usually shuttle back and forth between the U.S. and China working out transaction details. When sales of just about any technology—high, medium or low—are involved, American technical personnel are "invited" (that is, expected and required) to conduct educative seminars, often in several Chinese cities.

Chinese negotiating teams can be huge, containing dozens of people, depending on the nature of the business. In addition to representatives of a national government agency, there may be members of municipal government agencies and officials of specific factories who may have a say in decision making. However, when the group is very large most people are probably not actual team members. Often university professors and other non-negotiators are invited to sit in for their own enlightenment. This is particularly true during technical seminars.

Regardless of the number of people on the Chinese side, it's common for only one person to do the talking: the chief negotiator. Subordinates may be present merely to take notes and speak only when spoken to.

## Protocol

The Chinese team will enter a room in order of rank, with the highest-ranking member entering first. Your team should do the same; the Chinese will assume that the first member of your group to enter a conference room is the chief negotiator, which can lead to confusion and embarrassment if a subordinate enters first. Business cards may not be exchanged all around but only between negotiating heads. In fact, subordinates may never be introduced, just as American executives don't normally introduce their secretaries to office visitors; subordinate team members may serve little more than secretarial functions in China.

Chinese business cards are usually translated into English on the reverse side. Business cards will probably contain three names, as in Wang Yen-shou. *Wang* is the family name, *Yen-shou* the given name. Wang Yen-shou is addressed as Mr. Wang, not Mr. Yen or Mr. Shou. When addressing a Chinese woman named Wang Li-ping, call her *Miss* Wang; Mrs. is not used to distinguish married women in China. Unlike Americans, who move quickly to a first-name basis, the Chinese *rarely* call anyone other than children and relatives by first names. Don't call them by theirs or invite them to call you by yours.

After entering a meeting room, the Chinese side will show your team where to sit. Early sessions may be informal, taking place in large, sparsely furnished rooms with coffee tables and overstuffed chairs lining the walls. The chief American negotiator usually sits to the right of his Chinese counterpart, with higher-ranking members of each team sitting closer to team leaders than subordinates. At more formal sessions, chief negotiators may face each other across a conference table, with second-in-commands sitting to their right, third-in-commands to their left, and so on. Interpreters generally sit near team leaders to help them communicate.

Tea will be served and small talk exchanged. Then, if you've requested the meeting, the Chinese team leader will make a short welcoming speech and give you the floor. State what's on your mind concisely but without being blunt. The Chinese prefer to hear you out and react to what you say rather than vice versa. Few Chinese have mastered English, and Chinese interpreters are often little better. If you're going to make related points, summarize the issues in your opening remarks, then address them one by one. If you skip from one unrelated point to the next, pause every few minutes to give the Chinese a chance to digest the information and respond.

Regardless of the number of people present, the conversation will mainly be two-way between team leaders, probably with the chief American doing most of the talking. The Chinese may be shocked by the rudeness of an American subordinate who enters the conversation without permission, especially if he interrupts a superior in mid-sentence. Hand signals should be used by American subordinates to indicate they have something to contribute, and the American team leader should respond by asking a subordinate a specific question like "What do you think about that?" as if he's requesting input. The leader should not ask "Yes?" as if he has no idea what a subordinate wants to say, even though it may be the truth. These are matters of face.

Either side can conclude a meeting, but as the guest you should be sensitive to how much of the host's time you're taking up. If you're overdoing it you may be given indirect clues. The host may suggest that *you* must be tired, or in a hurry, or very busy, or he may muse that lunchtime is near. If the session occurs in the afternoon, remember that the Chinese workday ends at 4:00.

If you get a hint, take it. Both teams rise and shake hands, and hosts escort guests to the door or to their cars.

## Technical Seminars

Once a top American executive has visited China and convinced the Chinese that a business relationship is worth considering, the Chinese may invite you to conduct a technical seminar. Many U.S. firms include this offer in their business proposals as it can be an effective way to whet Chinese appetites. It's tacitly understood by all that technical seminars also serve as sales presentations. Americans are often expected to "perform" in China to prove their value as business partners.

The Chinese usually are less interested in what's newest in a given

field than in what's best for China. For example, most of the country's
billion-plus population is composed of farmers, yet only 11 percent of the
nation's land is arable. Thus, modern, efficient, labor-saving farm machinery is of little interest to China, where there is already a chronic
shortage of jobs. Similarly, a technology like robotics that reduces factory
workforces does not meet China's economic needs. The Chinese want
more employment opportunities, not less.

As in business proposals, the most effective seminars assume the
Chinese will know what they want when they see it, and stress how a
U.S. firm is best qualified to help them attain their goals. This often
requires a greater up-front research investment into China's economic and
political objectives, but the expense can be amortized in the long run.
Short-term thinkers rarely succeed in the PRC.

The Chinese may show no reaction to a technical seminar. Despite
greater freedom of speech permitted by Deng Xiaoping's administration
than by Mao's, years of anti-intellectual conditioning under Mao are not
easily forgotten. Even today speaking out uninhibitedly can be unwise,
drawing criticism from superiors and incurring political disfavor. However, sometimes Chinese do assert themselves. Recalls one China business
consultant:

> I once had an experience with an advertising delegation in China. We
> were the first advertising group in the country. We gave three days of
> seminars in Peking, and each day there was an opportunity for the
> audience to ask questions. The Chinese had no questions. For the Amer-
> icans, it was very frustrating. Then we went to Shanghai, put on the
> same show, and opened the floor to questions, expecting nothing again.
> For a while there was only silence. Then one man stood up and asked:
> "In the case of billboards, how do you account for the psychological
> effect of factor X?" Everyone's ears perked up, for here was a person
> who not only knew what he was talking about but was not afraid to
> speak. If your Chinese audience is totally dead, it doesn't necessarily
> mean that your presentation bombed. The most effective seminars are
> simple and well-organized, with a logical progression. Introduce your
> company. Explain its product lines. Then move to the specific proposal
> you've come to discuss in relation to China: how it fits into your com-
> pany's needs, and how you think it meets Chinese goals. Finally, give
> the details of the product itself.

Sometimes the Chinese react with uncharacteristic speed. Technical
seminars may be so effective that the Chinese are ready to begin negotiating
at once. In anticipation of this possibility, at least one top executive with

the authority to make on-the-spot decisions, particularly regarding price, should accompany the technical team. Inability to negotiate costs immediately (often without consultation with the home office, which may not be easy to reach from China), may be interpreted by the Chinese as insincerity, result in your loss of face, and lose business you're in China to land.

However, it's more common for technical seminars to represent the second phase of a four-part bargaining process. First, your chief executive makes a symbolic visit to get negotiations started. Then, technical seminars are held. Third, middle managers travel to China to work out the details. Finally, the CEO returns to sign the agreement.

Chinese agreements are termed protocols or letters of intent. They are not lengthy legal documents. They can't be used in a Chinese court to force your colleagues to comply with commitments they make and then fail to honor. There are only 6,000 lawyers in China. (There are over 600,000 in the U.S., over 40,000 in New York alone.) Lawsuits are rare. Hence, protocol or no protocol, negotiations with the Chinese never really end. As long as your business relationship lasts, they continue. As problems arise, they are expected to be amicably settled by the parties in disagreement without outside intervention. If push comes to shove, a third party, who will be Chinese, mediates a settlement. But even this happens rarely, and when it does, Americans often find themselves short-shrifted.

### Interpreters

While the Chinese will supply an English-speaking interpreter, the savvy bring their own as well. Even Americans who grumble about the expense of hiring a top interpreter are glad they did when they discover how poorly many Chinese-furnished interpreters speak English; some are merely English majors still in college. In fact, one yardstick for measuring your importance in Chinese eyes is the quality of interpreter they supply. If your business is less than major, their interpreter will probably be less than best.

The best interpreters for Americans are Overseas Chinese (OC). Many experienced negotiators hire an OC interpreter in Taiwan, Hong Kong or Singapore before visiting China. Being bicultural as well as bilingual, an OC can be a priceless asset not just in translating what your colleagues in China actually say but also in reading between unspoken cultural lines. In addition, an OC often helps natives of China overcome some of their xenophobia for Westerners. Even Chinese interpreters born in Taiwan,

Hong Kong, Singapore, or the U.S.—all capitalistic societies—are considered by Chinese Communists to be brothers under the skin, inextricably bound by blood and heritage. OCs are felt to have a natural affinity to mainland Chinese not shared by *kweilos* (foreign devils—a common nickname for Westerners) who compose a negotiating team.

Overseas Chinese may even be regarded by Chinese Communists as double agents in negotiations, outwardly representing Americans but secretly favoring the Chinese side. Of course, this is anything but the case. Yet proof of the partiality shown to OCs in China is the discounts of 10 to 40 percent they receive on hotel and restaurant rates over those charged to business and leisure travelers of other cultures.

This bond of fellowship that Chinese negotiators perceive between themselves and OCs can be useful to U.S. negotiators. While the Chinese may be unwilling to reveal information during formal bargaining sessions, an OC interpreter can meet with the Chinese team *after* a session to elicit facts, learn true feelings, or uncover problems not communicated earlier in response to direct questions from you. These informal, between-meeting sounding-outs can yield more intelligence than anything said or implied at a formal session just held, and may help explain surprise moves the Chinese make as tactical ploys to gain negotiating advantage.

## Negotiating Notes

Americans usually think short-term and want to get down to business details right away. Then later, generalities regarding the future of a commercial relationship can be discussed. We see this as a logical progression. Why waste time discussing the future when one is not yet certain that there's even a present?

The Chinese think just the opposite. Their first priority is to clarify general principles that will govern the relationship in spirit, assuming that if it gets off the ground at all it will intrinsically be long-term. This logic is akin to that of American marriage vows, in which spouses-to-be promise to love, honor, and cherish each other for life. Just as the meaning of love, honor, and cherish is not defined during the wedding ceremony, and in reality remains to be seen, in like manner the Chinese will postpone discussion of specific business terms until future trips to China are made by U.S. subordinate specialists, after an American chief executive has laid the groundwork for further negotiations and returned home. At the outset, the Chinese view detailed discussions as being potentially provocative, bothersome, nitpicking, and discordant. Once general principles of good faith have been established, so their thinking goes, the details will work themselves out as a matter of course. Or, to continue with the wedding analogy, once you've sincerely declared your love for each other, then you move into the same house and proceed to evolve an amicable modus operandi for daily interaction.

However, the flexibility of this philosophy enables the Chinese to use a variety of ploys to throw unwary Americans off guard in bargaining sessions. These ploys are the basis for demanding concessions that the Chinese want without giving anything in return.

### The Presidential Ploy

American chief executives, overeager to open negotiations in China, are often too quick to agree to the general principles the Chinese propose without understanding their implications and without the expert advice they would routinely seek at home. After all, the principles are so vaguely worded that they seem harmless enough. Certainly they would never stand up in a U.S. court. And because the Chinese refuse to discuss details at this early stage, the safety of agreement lies in lack of clarity, or so many CEOs think as they board their flights for home.

But on a subsequent trip when American subordinates arrive in China to negotiate a commercial strategy, they find the Chinese ready to discuss details, as if a strategy had already been worked out and agreed to earlier by their corporate president. When they try to negotiate specific terms equitable to both sides, they are informed that their chief executive has already committed the company to specific obligations; these were implied by his agreement to the general principles governing the relationship.

In reality, the Chinese may interpret the agreed-upon principles to mean specific commitments that are anything but apparent from actual conversations or signed documents, but which tilt the negotiating seesaw unabashedly in their favor. Moreover, the interpretations presented to American subordinates may not even have been apparent to *Chinese* negotiators when they met with the American CEO. Instead, they were formulated by committees behind the scenes later on; frequently they show the U.S. chief executive to be generous to a fault.

For example, an American CEO might agree in principle to train Chinese workers as part of a transaction. At a future meeting with American subordinates, the Chinese may insist that in keeping with the spirit of the training principle, transfers of classified technology were tacit in the agreement. Otherwise, how can native personnel be properly trained? Because the details of training were neither discussed nor probably even considered by the American chief executive, the Chinese press their advantage by forcing onto American subordinates their own itemized definition of what a sincere training program must necessarily include, a definition they strategically avoided clarifying when the CEO was present. Furthermore, the Chinese may contend that the CEO was well aware of what a commitment to training implied—even though the Chinese themselves did not know the implications at the time, but rather decided what they were later on to suit their convenience.

This ploy puts mid-level U.S. negotiators on the spot. Either they must cause their chief executive to lose face by insisting that he didn't know what he was doing, implying that he's not only incompetent but also insincere (and in fact a liar), or they must give in to Chinese demands for concessions that would blow the roof off the home office. Attempts to reinterpret the general principles on a more equitable basis are often met with angry Chinese accusations that the Americans are flagrantly violating the spirit of the agreement.

Top executives who begin China negotiations should know that it's necessary to convince the Chinese only that the principles of a harmonious business relationship *can be reached*. It's not mandatory to reach the principles *themselves*. Once you've proved that good faith in commercial dealings is possible, your job is done—unless you have the knowledge and corporate mandate to carry negotiations further. Executives new to China business should make no commitments or sign any documents, no matter how vaguely worded, without conferring with an expert first.

### The Patience Ploy

Knowing that Americans are usually in a rush to conclude business, the Chinese may try to tax your patience to the limit. Many Americans are impatient before they even get to China, as it can take a year or more from the time a business proposal is submitted to the Chinese for consideration to the time an invitation to visit the PRC is actually extended.

The Chinese, in contrast, are among the world's most patient people. Americans often find their hosts initially more eager to take them sightseeing than to talk shop. Well, a day of sightseeing is pleasant enough. But after two, three or more days of playing tourist, trip costs begin to mount and pressure from the home office to start getting results becomes intense.

When business meetings finally begin, Americans, their impatience overwhelming, tend to be overly aggressive, talkative, and committal.

Meanwhile, the Chinese remain calm and passive, listening, asking probing questions, making no promises, and volunteering little information in exchange for what they learn. Such unresponsiveness throws any U.S. negotiators off balance. Rather than a bargaining process of give and take, they find themselves in a situation of give and give.

To make matters worse, Americans have a compulsive need to feel that something concrete is getting done, while the Chinese consider abstract, symbolic gains to be concrete. U.S. negotiators want direct feedback. Instead they are told the Chinese side is not empowered to make decisions, draw conclusions or even speculate about outcomes. These are the sole purview of committees behind the scenes.

Hence, by Chinese calculation, Americans find themselves lurching from one emotional extreme to another. Initially they are treated with courtesy, friendliness, and generosity. This makes them relaxed. Then, when negotiations begin, they are frustrated by the Chinese refusal to reveal hard facts, giving them little or nothing substantial to report to superiors in the U.S. Continued lack of results makes them look incompetent.

Naturally, this causes anxiety, which the Chinese tactically instill and nurture. Overstressed Americans often begin to make exaggerated claims and promises to fill communication voids, hoping to get a rise out of the Chinese. Meanwhile, Chinese subordinates are scribbling away on their legal pads, noting everything that was said in order to hold loquacious Americans to commitments—whether explicitly stated or implied—that many regret once their composure is regained.

The only way to fight impatience is with patience. Anticipate that you may encounter the situation described and stay calm. Be sure your superiors know in advance what you're apt to face in China so that *their* expectations are realistic and they don't pressure you unfairly. You'll probably have to travel to China several times before the outline of an agreement is reached. Accept it, and limit your agenda for each trip to resolving a few key issues rather than trying to sign, seal, and deliver the whole deal at once. Also keep your return date open; it's hard for newcomers to accurately gauge how long a China trip will take. But if the Chinese continually use stalling tactics during your stay, put your foot down; give them a firm date on which you're going home. This may draw a response. If it doesn't, their true desire to deal is suspect.

Ironically, once you reach agreement, the Chinese are often as impatient as Americans to get things going right away.

### The Technology Ploy

Many Americans assume that a Chinese invitation to conduct technical seminars is a sure sign that a sale can be made. It isn't. The Chinese may try to get something for nothing rather than pay for it. Chinese technocrats will attend your technical seminars, try to learn ever more confidential information, and react to your replies of "Sorry, that's classified" with hard looks, because they view you as a profiteer hoarding knowledge that should rightfully be shared with all. However, information that *you* request from the Chinese may be denied because it's a matter of state secrecy and in the public interest. The Chinese see nothing contradictory about that.

They may also invite two or more competing foreign firms to conduct technical seminars at the same time in the same city, shuttling back and forth between them and trying to play one off against the other by intimating that Firm A is revealing knowledge that Firm B is not. How much you succumb to these pressures by way of leaking classified information depends on how badly you want to do business in China. Some U.S. companies use fallback tactics, assigning technical intelligence different grades of confidentiality like governments do, revealing knowledge one level at a time in strategic increments, up to the point at which they draw the line.

Where you draw the line depends on the policy of your firm. But be careful not to reveal too much. The Chinese make no secret about their desire to copy foreign technology without recompense. In their ethnocentric view, it's their right. Such U.S. business concerns as the need to get a return on investment in research and development, the moral duty of all nations to honor the protection of U.S. patents, or entitlement to licensing fees elicit little sympathy in China. Cognoscenti don't assume that such stipulations are naturally acceptable to the Chinese. Instead they tactfully try to justify these requirements at the outset of negotiations.

For example, one American softened his demand for payment by assigning what he was prepared to give the Chinese in return—including intangibles like new jobs—a dollar value that was calculated by an economist. The total amount was greater than the cost of his licensing fee, satisfying the Chinese need to out-bargain him in negotiations. He explains that success in China often depends on profit margins being flexible enough to satisfy the Chinese desire to get more than they give, and yet still produce acceptable income for your firm.

U.S. companies that deal in China learn to live with the situation by making long-term profit projections rather than futilely insisting on large quick gains. Measured over years, doing business with the Chinese can pay off handsomely. But initial profits may not justify what you must do to earn them.

### The Shaming Ploy

U.S. businesspeople tend to ascribe their own negotiating logic to non-Americans, the Chinese not excepted. For their part, the Chinese often make the same mistake in reverse. Because face is so serious a matter in China, the Chinese find it hard to believe that face is not equally serious in our country, resulting in wrecked careers or social ostracism if it's lost.

When Americans are rebuked for violating the spirit of an agreement (as it's arbitrarily interpreted by the Chinese), this results in serious loss of face in Chinese eyes. Accordingly, the Chinese expect rebuked Americans to feel as deeply ashamed as they would feel were the shoe on the other foot. They assume Americans and Chinese think as one, that Americans will automatically accept Chinese condemnation as being genuinely deserved, and desperately eager to regain face, they will gratefully agree to Chinese demands.

Ironically, Americans often *are* embarrassed by Chinese accusations even when they have bent over backwards to act in good faith. Abruptly faced with severe criticism, they suppose there must be *some* basis for it, that they must have committed *some* inadvertent but serious faux pas. Otherwise, the intensity of Chinese ire would be irrational. But Chinese ire is not irrational. It's another tactic to get what they want, and it frequently works. Out of unjustified guilt, novices often feel they must make some concession by way of atonement for unknown sins.

The basis of this tactic is hyperbole, a trait of the Chinese language. Use of hyperbole may encourage the Chinese to make demands so unrealistic that not even *they* expect them to be met. Usually what they want is a smaller concession, but to ensure they get it, they begin by insisting on something larger, then allow themselves to be bargained down to what they really seek. In the end, Americans often give them what they want, considering it minor when compared with their initial demands, and breathe sighs of relief. In this way, the Chinese protect themselves from losing face by avoiding the risk of being told no if they simply asked for what they really sought, and they gain face by ultimately getting it.

To clarify what's actually going on, an Overseas Chinese interpreter can intercede privately on your behalf. While the Chinese won't tell *you* what they are up to, they often will tell an OC, out of kinship feelings

previously discussed. It's common for minor concessions that Americans
would be willing to make if directly approached to be exacted in this
circumlocutious way.

### The Good-Cop, Bad-Cop Ploy

The Chinese may try to create the *illusion* of friendship as a negotiating
tactic. Often the person who meets you at the airport or a Chinese-furnished
guide/interpreter will play the good-cop role. This individual tirelessly
takes you on day-long sightseeing tours and is offended by nothing you
say. He's curious, interested, and interesting himself. He's a warm, gra-
cious, sympathetic escort.

But later, when you meet the *other* members of the Chinese team,
the air in the conference room takes on a sudden chill. Earlier, if you
behaved like a typical American, discoursing freely about any subject you
were asked, the Chinese will probably have compiled a substantial dossier
on you based on the daily reports of your "friend." And when you're
suddenly accused of violating the spirit of an agreement, who will you
turn to for sympathy and understanding? Your friend, who, in his gentle,
benevolent way, will "advise" you as to the "right" thing to do. The Chinese
are skilled at getting what they want this way, so be aware. Don't assume
an extra-national friendship is forming between you and a member of the
Chinese team. Despite what you may be encouraged to think, the chances
of a true friendship forming in a few days—while possible in the U.S.—
is remote in China.

### The Publicity Ploy

As doing business with the Chinese can be prestigious as well as lucrative,
overeager Americans may jump the gun, assume that negotiations in China
are going well—which in fact they may be—and be too quick to order
press releases written and stockholder meetings called to announce im-
minent agreement. Often they find that the initial prestige gained by
making public announcements of the impending success of their China
dealings is soon lost.

Sometimes this is because the time anticipated to conclude a transaction with the Chinese was underestimated. By raising everyone's expectations prematurely, they put U.S. negotiators in China under pressures
to perform that are beyond their ability to meet, often due to deliberate
stalling tactics used by the Chinese once they get wind of what is going
on. As a result, home-office decision makers become vulnerable to Chinese

demands for new concessions if their public promises are to be realized.

The Chinese prefer their foreign business dealings to be kept confidential unless consulted first. It's wise to ask for their approval before making public announcements, and invite them to read the text of press releases and speeches. Even if the Chinese grant such requests, the prudent refrain from going public until a formal agreement is reached and symbolically signed by an American chief executive and a high-ranking Chinese official. As long as negotiations preceding such an agreement are going on, the Chinese may use any public declaration you make about your relationship with them—whether or not they grant approval—to drive a harder bargain, forcing you to acquiesce to additional demands if they are to help you live up to your words.

## Social Customs

As in the Arab world, there is little to do at night in China. While it's now possible for foreign tourists to spend a night in a private home, business travelers are unlikely to be invited to a Chinese home for dinner. This might make the host's neighbors suspect that he's conducting unauthorized, personal activities with you, a breach of rules that may get him reported and punished. You'll probably feel bushed most evenings anyway; China negotiations and sightseeing are exhausting for most people. Plan on several evenings with time on your hands before going to bed, and pack an entertaining book or something diverting to do to take your mind off business. You'll do a more effective job the next day if you give your batteries a chance to recharge.

### Lunch

China's commercial centers—Beijing, Shanghai, and Guangzhou (Canton)—now have modern Westernlike hotels, each with a choice of international restaurants. As a result, formerly rare business lunches have become common, often replacing elaborate evening banquets, for which Americans with years of China experience are usually grateful.

Either you or the Chinese may host a lunch. If two teams are negotiating, it's acceptable for the chief negotiators of each side to lunch together (with their interpreters if communication is a problem), saving larger group affairs for evening banquets; China newcomers will probably be guests of honor at at least one banquet.

If there is a second occasion for chief negotiators to lunch together, whoever was guest first should be host next, picking up the check, so that hospitality is balanced and no one loses face.

### Banquets

Novices commonly give Chinese banquets too much importance. Because banquets are elaborate, gala, ceremonial meals, Americans often mistake them for signs that things are going well and an agreement is close to being reached, even after only a few days of negotiating. This is rarely the case.

It's traditional custom for the Chinese to host a banquet at the end of American business visits, even if the stay is short. As a newcomer visiting several cities, you may attend a banquet before leaving each. The lavish feast is usually nothing more than a good time for all, at posh French restaurant prices that are billed to the state. This way, the Chinese can enjoy exotic local delicacies well beyond their normal means to afford; a banquet is as much for their own pleasure as it is for yours.

The rules of banquet etiquette dictate that hosts arrive before guests, and that the business protocols described earlier are observed. Everyone usually sits in a large anteroom, is served tea, and engages in polite conversation before entering the dining room.

Banquet tables are large and round, seating about twelve people, with a lazy susan in the center. Initially the lazy susan will contain a variety of cold dishes. If the party is large, there will be more than one banquet table with place cards showing everyone where to sit. The Chinese will direct you to your seat in any case. As the guest of honor, you'll sit to the right of the chief host, traditionally facing the door, which historically gave the main guest the first chance to escape if an enemy assailant invaded the room. Your second-in-command sits to the right of the Number-two person on the Chinese side, and so on.

Your place setting will include a plate, a pair of chopsticks leaning on a small stand, a water glass for beer or *qishui* (an orange-flavored soft drink), a wine glass (the wine is usually syruplike), and a small cordial glass for mao-tai (a 120-proof liquor made from sorghum). Chinese chopsticks are round-edged rather than square-edged like those of Japan. Unlike Japanese *waribashi*, they are not disposable, don't come in envelopes, are already separate rather than having to be broken apart, and are slipperier to handle, but otherwise the good manners for their use are similar. (See *Chopstick Etiquette* in the chapter on Japan.) You may be offered a fork in place of chopsticks, but if you're adept at handling them the Chinese will be pleased and probably make a fuss about it.

The chief host will serve the guest of honor from the lazy susan first, then other subordinate guests within reach. Subordinate Chinese hosts will do likewise. After this initial ritual of hospitality, help yourself. Sometimes, when a new course is served or at intervals during a course, your host will replenish your plate, whether you want more or not. It's impolite to refuse.

After cold appetizers, the procession of courses usually covers the five basic tastes of Chinese gastronomy in this order: sweet, spicy, sour, bitter, and salty. A banquet can include ten or fifteen courses, so pace yourself. It's polite to eat less as the meal progresses.

Chinese food in China bears little resemblance to Chinese food in the U.S. Sichuan cuisine alone is said to include over 2,000 dishes; most are made with ingredients unavailable at home. Each province or region has its own multitudinous specialties. Some you'll probably find delicious. Others may make you ashen-faced—like sea slugs, bear paws or pangolin (anteater). If you're not an adventurous eater, don't ask about the contents of a suspicious dish; you may not like the answer.

If you find duck brains or fish gizzards on your plate, and they aren't two of your favorite things, *pretend* to eat them by pushing the food around with your chopsticks rather than turning green and not going through the motions. Don't pick through a dish on the lazy susan to find an ingredient that you especially like. Choose your target first. Don't take the last morsel of any communal dish, a sign that there wasn't enough food, causing your hosts to lose face. Unless you want seconds, leave some food on your plate or your host may automatically help you to more. Once you have a second helping, you're expected to eat some of it.

You can drink *qishui*, beer or wine whenever you want, but mao-tai is usually saved for toasting, which the chief host will initiate. He will rise and raise his little mao-tai glass. Everyone else does the same. Then he will make a short speech, announce *ganbei* (pronounced "gon-bay," meaning "dry glass," the Chinese "bottoms up"), and empty the glass. Everyone follows suit. The ritual ends with each person either turning his glass upside down or open end out so that everyone can see the contents have been drained. This shows you're macho in China, and you need a cast-iron stomach to drink mao-tai. Some people, particularly vodka drinkers, like it. For most, though, the experience is akin to eating fire; mao-tai is potent enough to make your scalp sweat. To make a good impression, try to drink at least one glassful. Even though it will be promptly refilled, you can use another beverage for subsequent mao-tai toasts. American women are absolved from drinking mao-tai if they wish, and Chinese women who attend banquets may avoid it altogether.

After the chief host has made the first toast, the guest of honor should also make a toast, followed by *ganbei*, repeated two or three times. For example:

> I'd like to thank you for this wonderful banquet. Here's to the growing friendship between our two countries. *Ganbei, ganbei.*

It's appropriate to make a couple of short speeches and toasts along such lines during the meal. But if you're one of the few Americans who like mao-tai, don't try to outdrink the Chinese. If you continue to make mao-tai toasts, your hosts will be forced to join you in order to keep face; even the Chinese can only stand so much mao-tai at a sitting.

A fish dish is usually the last main course served, often followed by soup and finally fresh fruit. About ten or fifteen minutes after dessert is served, it's polite for guests to take the initiative in making their thanks and saying good-bye.

In China, one banquet deserves another and is considered a gift. If time permits host your own; otherwise, do it on your next trip. Banquets come in several classes, based on per-person price. About $25, $50 to $60, and $100 per person are the usual price categories. Host a banquet of the *same* price category as the one you were given. To host a less or more expensive meal makes the former hosts lose face. Inform your interpreter or the interpreter for the Chinese side that you would like to host a return banquet; he'll see to the details. Remember, as the host, you must show up first. If the banquet time is 7:00 P.M., be at the restaurant by 6:30.

As banquets can include a dozen or more guests and hosts at $100 per person, entertainment expenses in China can be high. Alert your superiors. As you move from city to city, each new Chinese delegation may throw you a banquet. If you host a return meal at each place, costs can get out of hand. Inviting a Chinese chief negotiator to lunch is a suitable substitute, if time and money make it impractical for you to host banquets throughout China.

### Symbolic Banquets and Big Business Gifts

When agreement has finally been reached, a lavish banquet will be thrown by the Chinese to symbolically seal the deal. Your chief executive is expected to be there, and a top Chinese official will be present if your firm is large and the transaction major. Each gives a formal speech, after which a contract is often publicly signed.

Symbolic gifts are normally exchanged. Your company may be given an exquisite tapestry, statue or intricately carved screen as a gift from China. In the past, U.S. firms presented something equivalent. But the appetites of today's Chinese have grown considerably. Particularly for joint-venture partners, sellers of capital goods, and buyers whose needs require the Chinese to build a new factory or transport workers from their homes to a distant manufacturing site, a gift the Chinese increasingly desire and expect is an *automobile*. This is a practical group gift as cars are in short supply in China. They are government owned—private own-ership is forbidden—and the Chinese normally walk, ride bicycles or take buses to work. The gift of a car can cut one-way transportation time in half.

Of course, a car is justified only by a multimillion-dollar deal, but if negotiations involve big money, particularly if the transaction requires worker transportation, such a gift can get your new relationship off to a good start. The sturdier it is, the easier parts can be replaced or repairs made, and the more passengers it can hold, the better. Don't give an automobile that's not American-made. Don't give a status-symbol car like a Cadillac. You'll only embarrass the recipients and earn their contempt. In China, think minibus or Jeep.

Otherwise, banquets thrown to celebrate a meeting of the minds follow the same procedures as ordinary banquets that are merely excuses for everyone to have a good time at the state's expense.

### Conversation

Safe conversational topics at premeeting socializing, lunches, and banquets include the weather, the sights you've seen, the cities you've visited or will visit, any of China's historical or cultural prides (knowledge of Sun Yat-sen, the father of modern China, is always impressive), and life in the U.S. that's not described in a boastful way. Avoid discussion of politics—the U.S.'s or China's—although the Chinese may bring it up. If they should, even if you're knowledgeable about the issues involved, keep your opinions to yourself. Instead, hem and haw. If you say something wishy-washy, the Chinese will usually back off rather than press. If you make a pronouncement, you'll lose points no matter what you say. For example, if you defend U.S. foreign policy concerning Taiwan, you'll alienate the Chinese. If you disagree with it, you'll only make them suspicious, as the Chinese tend to regard all Americans as secret agents of a capitalistic government rather than as independent, apolitical entrepreneurs. No amount of persuasion to the contrary is apt to change their minds.

At lunches and banquets—not during preliminary tea but during the actual meal—you can talk shop. However, be wary of making commitments, especially after drinking several glasses of mao-tai. The Chinese will keep track of them. Sometimes one member of the Chinese party only pretends to drink mao-tai. When everyone else is starting to feel pretty good, he'll be the one to introduce negotiating issues and try to persuade you to at least tacitly agree to something you might not say yes to sober. Then, at a subsequent meeting, it will be presented to you as a fait accompli. In China, prudent Americans stay alert and measure their words carefully at banquets and all other times.

# CHAPTER NINE

---

# Selling
# in South Korea

South Korea's Government worries—perhaps more than many others—about its reputation abroad, especially in the United States. One official lamented in private what he called his "M. and M. problem." It was his conviction that when the subject of Korea arose, many Americans thought first of *M\*A\*S\*H* and the followers of the Rev. Sun Myung Moon and his Unification Church.

CLYDE HABERMAN,
*The New York Times*
(March 21, 1984)

The Republic of Korea—or ROK—South Korea's official name, is in a curious position regarding its international image, particularly among Americans. While movies about Americans fighting in Europe during World War II are automatically considered period films, reruns of a popular television series like *M\*A\*S\*H* are often not.

This is partly because Americans, whether leisure or business travelers, are more familiar with post-World War II Europe than they are with post-Korean War Korea. But it's also because Korea has lived up to its nickname, the "Hermit Kingdom," through most of its 5,000 years of history, shunning cultural outsiders with new and subversive ideas that threatened to undermine the traditional, Confucian way of life. While Japan, the U.S., and several European powers forced Korea's opening to international trade in the nineteenth century, the nation failed to enter widespread American consciousness until the Korean War; for many, it remains frozen in 1953, when the war ended.

Similarly, as Sun Myung Moon is a native Korean, the general American lack of awareness of life in modern Korea may lead some to believe that a nation of 39 million people is largely composed of brainwashed "Moonies." In fact, there are over 11 million Buddhists in the ROK, over 9 million Christians, over 22,000 Muslims, and most other Koreans are

*245*

worshippers of *Tonghak*, *Wonbulgyo* or *Taejonggyo*, all native religions. The number of Moonies in South Korea is proportionate to their number in the U.S., a mere handful of adherents.

As for still being the war-torn country depicted in *M\*A\*S\*H*, even in the wake of Japan's "economic miracle," Korea's recovery by industrializing and modernizing is remarkable. Only twenty years ago, the ROK was among the world's poorest countries with a per capital GNP of $82, near the international bottom. Most Koreans were struggling to farm a land that's 80 percent hills and mountains and scant in natural resources. Unemployment was widespread. Domestic savings and exports were insignificant. And the nation remained in shambles after the Korean War.

In the two decades since, South Korea has skyrocketed to become the world's tenth largest producer of electronic goods, from silicon wafers to color televisions. The ROK is second in international ship building, fifteenth in iron and steel production, and among the five world leaders in overseas production. Seoul, the capital—with 9 million residents, about the population of New York—has become as modern and glitzy an international center of commerce and tourism as Tokyo, Hong Kong or Singapore. As newcomers discover at once, South Korea today is vastly different from the country once known as the "Land of the Morning Calm."

## Portraits of a Businesspeople

Probably most Korean businesspeople are among the easiest of East Asians with whom to deal, but some can be perplexing. Increasingly, Koreans are adopting Western business manners, being Western educated, learning English, and following international commercial practice. But a minority are Japaneselike in their behavior, which is why Americans bound for Seoul or Pusan should also read the chapter on Japan. Of this minority, many have evolved individual compromises between Western and Japanese ways of doing business. Yet all Koreans continue to belong to a culture unique to East Asia.

### Koreans and Japanese

In the nineteenth century, after years of upheaval and uncertainty in Korea due to the country's forcible opening to trade with Japan and the West, Japan made Korea a military as well as a commercial target and launched a successful invasion, annexing the nation in 1910. The Japanese subjugation of Korea lasted until Japan's defeat in World War II.

Japan's domination of Korea was cruel. Not content to exploit the country for its mineral resources, steal land from its people, and drain profits from its markets, the Japanese imposed their own rigid system of conformity on the inhabitants, instituting a campaign to systematically eradicate Korean heritage. Traditional Korean customs were outlawed. Korean children were denied education. Even speaking the native tongue was decreed a crime. It became mandatory for all Koreans to learn Japanese, and, at least in public, to speak the language of the conquerers.

As a result, an entire generation of Koreans grew up speaking, acting, and thinking like Japanese. Their own language and culture were clandestinely kept alive. But for over thirty years the modus vivendi of Koreans was the Japanese way.

After World War II, Korea was divided along the 38th parallel, initially to make the disarmament of the defeated Japanese forces in the country easier for the U.S. and U.S.S.R. to implement. But the Soviets had plans for expansion east as well as west, and, three years later, a joint U.S./U.S.S.R. commission and the United Nations were unable to reunify the country. With a Communist regime now well-established in the north, general elections were held in South Korea on August 15, 1948, and the Republic of Korea was born. The U.S. declared the new republic to be the "sole legitimate Korean government on the peninsula," and the Western forces in the country were sent home.

Two years later, the Korean War erupted. Over one million American troops poured back into South Korea, led by Douglas MacArthur, who sought to "Americanize" Korean culture as he had tried and failed to do previously in U.S.-occupied Japan. But for the South Koreans, the attempt caused cultural chaos. Still not permitted to be themselves, they reverted back to the Japanese system. It may have been hated, but at least it was familiar. For many Koreans, it was all they knew.

What of South Koreans now, over thirty years later? Robert H. Kwon, senior partner, Coopers & Lybrand, an international accounting firm, is a Korean American who has worked in both the ROK and Japan. He offers this perspective:

> Japan modernized before Korea. But in the past ten or twenty years, Korea has been moving faster than Japan in adopting Western business practices.
>
> I consider Japan much more conservative than Korea. In Japan, if you deal with top executives, most will be old: in their sixties, seventies, even eighties. In Korea, you will not find many top people in their sixties or seventies. Most will be in their forties or fifties. Being younger and

more flexible, their thinking is more modern than that of executives in Japan.

Lawrence V. Fairhall, senior consultant, Korea Trade Promotion Center (New York), feels the implications of Korean decision makers' youth today are crucial to understand.

> For the older generation of Koreans who grew up under Japanese occupation, it was too difficult to change. They continued to speak Japanese as well as Korean. They thought like Japanese. That's the way they had been brought up. And they were the founders of many large Korean corporations.
>
> But the younger generation, now in its thirties, forties and fifties, is composed of Western-educated, English-speaking people who are very alert to modern ways of doing business and basically run things today. The older founders are taking a back seat and letting the younger men assume control.

Taking a paternalistic back seat and letting younger protégés manage their companies, then resuming corporate power when necessary, as in crisis-management situations, are distinctive traits of Japanese chief executives. Explains Scott Kalb, a business and political analyst at Harvard's School of East Asian Studies, who has lived in Seoul:

> Many Koreans have used a Japanese model for their corporate structures, methods of doing business, and general plans for economic growth. But even in companies with Japanese frameworks, the Koreans have placed their own strong stamp.

What's the nature of this strong Korean stamp?

## The Irish of Asia

So the Koreans have been nicknamed, and the epithet fits. By East Asian—particularly Japanese—standards, Koreans are independent, individualistic, and autocratic in decision making, less oriented toward group harmony, often to the dismay of older parents. They may speak their minds directly, pay less attention to facework, are more openly competitive, and are quite capable of losing their tempers, most un-Japaneselike behavior.

Koreans are also less xenophobic than their neighbors across the Sea of Japan. (In South Korea, this body of water is called the "East Sea.") They are friendlier to Westerners, and are good-humored, hard-drinking romantics who love music, sentimental singing, and telling tales, especially sad, nostalgic stories. But far from a glum people, they are great kidders who love to tease and have no hangups about laughing at themselves as well. Contrasting them to the Japanese, many Americans describe Koreans as being a bit rougher around the edges, but much easier to get to know and like.

Historical and geographical associations make comparisons with the Japanese inevitable, yet U.S. negotiators experienced in both countries cite the same observations. Says one:

> Compared to the Japanese, Korean business style is more aggressive. The Koreans are trying harder to succeed. It's a cultural trait. In South Korea, it doesn't take as long for business decisions to be reached. It's not as essential to get an enormous consensus that you usually seek in Japan. One may encounter similar problems in that Korean managers need approval from superiors, which can take time. But in Japan, no one will stick his neck out for anything. In Korea, there may be a bit of reluctance to make an individual commitment. But it's not as tightly controlled. The Koreans are more willing to take risks, to go ahead and implement a project. Korean lines of communication are not as elaborate as they are in Japan, which facilitates decision making. Japan is the most protocol-conscious nation in the world. There's no place that pays as much attention to face and form. In Korea, you may see many of the same forms, but their source does not seem to run as deep. You don't find the same kinds of conscious attitudes toward face. Koreans are generally earthier than Japanese.

While circumlocution to save face may not be as strongly inculcated in modern Koreans as it continues to be in Japanese today, Tae-wan Yu, former director of the Korean Cultural Service in New York, adds:

> It is preferable for businesspeople to learn cross-cultural currents. If time is of the essence, it may help those trying to do business in Korea to realize that Koreans are the most straightforward of all East Asians. They will answer direct questions with direct answers. Consider how direct I am being with you now. However, one cannot speak for all members of a race. I suspect you will find many Koreans still expressing negatives indirectly in order to save face. A sensitive American should be able to understand what is being communicated. An American firm that wants to do business in Korea would do well to select its representatives with cultural sensitivity in mind.

Earthiness probably accounts for the greater affinity Americans say they feel for Koreans than for Japanese; Americans are an earthy people, too. Thomas Kutzen, vice-president, Chase Manhattan, who was stationed in Seoul, recalls his impressions of both countries:

> I found Korea very comfortable, but it was more difficult in Japan. When I visited Japan, the separation between foreigners and Japanese was very strict. Japanese hospitality toward foreigners comes out of a sense of awkwardness. With Koreans, it's more genuine in the sense of friendship and trust. The glib sense of humor that Koreans show in *M\*A\*S\*H* is relevant. Koreans have a marvelous sense of humor. They are very sociable people, whether you're dealing with an individual or a small group. In Japan, you rarely deal with individuals. The Japanese usually do everything in large groups, and you must relate to the group as a whole, which makes getting to know individuals more difficult.

While less xenophobic than the Japanese or the Chinese Communists, Koreans may have mixed feelings about cultural outsiders. And despite the Korean stress on individual accomplishment, Confucianlike feelings of group spirit and national unity do persist. One American observes:

> The Koreans are in a rush. There's an anxiety driving them. First, there's the struggle to survive as a people. Then, there's the struggle to prove oneself as an individual. A great deal of face is gained in Korea by being a person who succeeds. This source of pride in self-achievement is something Americans can relate to; it can be used to form a common bond with Koreans. It would be futile to relate to the Japanese in this way, as their system stresses *group* achievement. The Chinese Communists wouldn't even tolerate it. Even among the Chinese capitalists, who have their own stock exchange in Hong Kong, when an American enters the building he's a *kweilo*, a foreign devil. But the Koreans like to mix. They feel that by rubbing elbows with cultural outsiders they are going to learn something new and be better able to progress.
>
> At the same time, however, Koreans can be very defensive. This defensiveness has historical roots. The country has been invaded and exploited time and again. Koreans don't want to be taken advantage of. On one hand, they like Americans, because of what we've done and can do for them; there's a sense of gratitude that you won't find in Japan, even though the U.S. has done a lot more for the Japanese. On the other hand, Koreans don't want you in their country longer than they feel is necessary. Once a project gets underway, they often want to take over completely and implement the rest themselves. If you consider recent history, this is understandable. Unlike post-World War II Japan, which received the largest transfers of U.S. capital and technology in history, Korea got where it is today mainly on its own.

This strong sense of self-reliance is a Korean trait repeatedly noted by Americans who have lived and worked in the country. Explains one U.S. expatriate now working in Pusan:

> The Koreans are survivors. They are very humble about it but intensely proud of it as well. They love sad, mournful stories because theirs has always been a world demanding incredible perseverance and endurance against all odds. Even modern Koreans are relatively new to Western influence; most of it has taken place since 1953. The Koreans take enormous pride in their ancient inventions, from block printing to the first armored naval vessels. But this has been their first chance in recent history to present themselves to the world in a positive light, rather than having to defend themselves against military invaders. It brings a great deal of energy to their mission. Koreans are mission-oriented, which is why they can be highly sensitive about their international image today.

## Business Customs

The larger the Korean firm, the more likely its executives are to have Western educations and speak English. You may negotiate with an individual or only a couple of people rather than a large group, as in Japan. However, elderly founders of small concerns or companies located outside the ROK's commercial centers (Seoul, Pusan, and Inchon) may resemble the Japanese in their business methods, including group negotiating. In addition, many customs common to other East Asian countries also exist in South Korea.

### Introductions

Make initial contact with a Korean firm through an introduction by a mutually respected third party rather than arriving in the country totally unknown. In the U.S., there are many Korean professionals who can open doors in their native land: bankers, lawyers, noncompetitive businesspeople, even former politicians. Robert H. Kwon advises:

> Contact a Korean of rank who will give you a reference. Korean society is tightly knit. Everyone knows everyone else. All influential people are acquainted. When an introduction comes from one of them, it gives you needed credibility.

While it's hard to deal in Japan without being properly introduced, it's possible in South Korea, although using an intermediary is still preferred. Tae-wan Yu explains:

As in America, it is always better, if possible, to be introduced by a mutual friend. Relationships are highly valued in my country. But I see nothing wrong with sending a letter outlining the benefits of a proposal to a potential Korean business partner, followed by a telephone call asking for an appointment for a personal discussion.

Probably the easiest way to make business contact is through the Korea Trade Promotion Corporation (KOTRA). "We can provide all kinds of services for American businesspeople," says senior consultant Lawrence V. Fairhall. "Those going on their first trips to Korea can come to any of our offices in this country—in New York, Atlanta, Chicago, Dallas, Detroit, Los Angeles, Miami, New Orleans, Seattle, San Francisco, and Washington, D.C.—and we will advise them what to do." Among KOTRA's functions are:

• Supplying foreign businesspeople with information about Korean products, exports, and imports
• Helping executives visiting Korea to pursue their business activities
• Organizing and participating in international trade fairs and exhibitions
• Supporting international cooperation in such fields as Korean investment in joint ventures abroad and foreign investment in Korean domestic industries, the employment of skilled manpower, and technology transfers
• Managing the Korea Exhibition Center—KOEX, in Seoul—which organizes and hosts domestic and international trade fairs and exhibitions

Continues Fairhall: "If you talk to a KOTRA specialist, he will advise our head office in Seoul of your business interests and your arrival date. Introductions and office visits will be *prearranged*. If necessary, we will provide an interpreter. We will supply a car for the foreign visitor to be driven to the various plants. Our operation is totally organized. We will even book your hotel reservations. We will pick you up at the airport, take you to your hotel, and give you a briefing before your appointments with X, Y, and Z potential clients, which have already been scheduled. I can't tell you how many monthly inquiries we get from future business travelers to Korea—a *lot*—and they are all handled similarly."

## Business Cards

Koreans often feel that American business cards need not be translated, as English is widely spoken and understood in the country's public and private sectors. Says one ROK government official: "Unless you speak our language, it makes no sense to me to have business cards translated. Would that not indicate that you understand Hangul?"

Hangul is the official language of South Korea. Invented in the fifteenth century by King Sejong, it incorporates elements of Chinese and Japanese, yet it's a unique tongue. With only ten vowels, fourteen consonants, and twenty-four characters, it's among the simplest, most comprehensive, most efficient alphabets ever devised, and the easiest of East Asian languages for Americans to learn.

But despite what English-speaking Koreans insist, have business cards translated into Hangul on the reverse side. You may deal with local decision makers who don't understand English or read it well.

Americans may combine visits to Japan and South Korea in the same trip, often traveling to Tokyo first, then Seoul. Don't hand a Korean a business card printed in Japanese on the reverse side, or vice versa. Even though Japan is the ROK's major trading partner (the U.S. is second), ill feelings between Koreans and Japanese still run deep.

Like the Chinese, most Koreans use three names. Westernized Koreans may put family names last, as Americans do, but it's traditional for the family or surname to come first. As there are about 300 family names in South Korea, the sequence of names on business cards can be confusing. But only a few are used by most natives: Kim, Lee, Pak, Ahn, Chang, Cho, Choe, Chung, Han, Kang, Ku, Ko, Im, Oh, Noh, Shin, Yu or Yun. If you see one of these names on a Korean business card (usually translated into English on the reverse side), it's probably the last name, regardless of where it appears in the series. For example, Yung-jim Chang and Chang Yung-jim are both Mr. Chang, not Mr. Jim or Mr. Yung.

### Business Gifts

Gift exchanges between hosts and first-time guests in South Korea are common, though you won't find yourself on the endless treadmill of regifting characteristic of Japan. To preserve face for yourself and your Korean counterpart, let him present a gift to you first and then reciprocate. A typical gift Americans receive is red ginseng tea, highly prized in the ROK. In any event, the gift will usually be something locally made, a native craft or other item the host feels is representative of his country.

For Americans, the suggestions made in Chapter Three are suitable gifts. Logo gifts are fine, as long as they are good quality and not too expensive. Logo gifts should be practical—usually work-related—and impersonal. A bottle of good Scotch will also be welcomed.

If your company already has a supply of logo gifts that are regularly distributed, be sure they did not originate in Japan or South Korea for U.S. export. Do the same when choosing items from a premium supplier's catalog. Giving a Korean a gift made in his own country or in Japan may make a poor impression.

Koreans appreciate gifts that represent your part of the U.S. as well. One Texan gave his Korean colleague a western-style belt and says that he was delighted. Avoid gifts of food, which may not appeal to Korean tastes.

## Bowing and Shaking Hands

Traditional Korean bowing is complex and not necessary to learn. Shaking hands loosely is a common practice, or a slight ducking of the head will do for most bows. However, elderly people should be shown veneration by a deep bow of respect.

If you're a man who is introduced to a Korean woman, and she extends her hand to you, shake it. If not, don't offer yours. Thomas Kutzen recalls an embarrassing incident:

> I learned about Korean handshaking customs on my first day at work. I had just entered the bank in Seoul where I would have my office, and as soon as I was introduced to a female member of my new staff, I naturally reached out and shook her hand. She blushed fourteen shades of red and the entire department laughed.

American businesswomen in South Korea must do the extending first. While shaking hands is not mandatory for U.S. women, doing it may avoid confusion and embarrassment for native colleagues. While American women *are* accepted in Korean business circles, they are not an everyday sight, and few Korean women are decision makers. As bowing is commonly practiced between local men and women, with women bowing more subserviently, Korean male executives with whom you deal may be puzzled as to how to bow to a foreign woman who is being treated unusually—like a man. A handshake initiated by you is the simple solution.

## Negotiating Teams

Depending on the firm, you may deal with an individual Korean or a group. If you deal with a group, it's apt to be smaller than in Japan and may function more like negotiating teams in China, with conversations being two-way between you and the chief negotiator and subordinates taking notes, contributing information only when asked. Says an American veteran of such meetings:

> Korean groups don't usually work together as harmonious units in the Japanese tradition. Rather, the number of people present is more of a reflection of Confucian-style clanship, or extended family, as well as the stress on filial piety, which extends to boss-worker relationships as well as those in the home. In effect, you have a *family* of businesspeople. The family does have a hierarchy, but everyone may routinely participate whether his presence is relevant or not. This is quite unlike the situation in Japan, where every person at a meeting has a reason for being there.

## Negotiating Notes

Protocols, premeeting socializing, and preliminary small talk are similar throughout East Asia, South Korea included. What makes Koreans different from Japanese or Chinese is their willingness to be more direct, although they are not always as blunt as Americans tend to be. Koreans are less concerned with facework (although facework does enter negotiations), partly due to national character, partly because they are in a greater hurry to progress as individuals, as companies, and as a country.

Let your colleagues decide when premeeting pleasantries are sufficient. Koreans often segue into business subtly; be alert. Begin with a brief introduction concisely summarizing the issues you'll discuss. Don't be disconcerted if you're asked questions right away. Questions are a good sign. They indicate Koreans are attentive and interested in what you're saying. If your general remarks draw blank looks instead, don't worry about whether or not you've made yourself clear. Speaking slowly and avoiding American idioms, proceed to details, which may elicit a response.

Avoid hard sell, but don't be too roundabout and vague in making your presentation. Explain facts objectively. If you're still confronted by silence, pause and ask: "What information would you really like to know?" Don't ask: "Do you understand what I'm saying?" This is where face comes in. Be aware that even Koreans who are fluent in English may have difficulty understanding you for any number of reasons: rapid or slurred speech, American regional accent, etc. If you sense you're losing your audience, tactfully probe to learn why.

Don't be overly aggressive, dynamic, intimidating or intense in stating your case. Key points should be made with calm logic. An American who worked in Seoul adds: "The more you position a business proposal as an offering that can be accepted or rejected rather than one only a fool would refuse, the more likely Koreans are to respond favorably to it."

Koreans are like other East Asians in that they may say yes to indicate not that they necessarily agree with you but merely that they are listening.

If you're asked a question about information covered earlier, instead of getting frustrated, go back and develop the line of inquiry. This tells you that you're communicating and making progress, not merely fishing. Use that. Build on it. If a colleague simply wants you to backtrack to confirm one idea or expand on a single trend of thought, he'll let you know. You may not have to repeat the entire presentation from scratch.

Be sensitive to the *tone* of a meeting—what you see and feel as well as what you hear. When Koreans show curiosity, seize the opportunity and develop it. One U.S. negotiator explains:

> Koreans may disgress at any point in a meeting. Sometimes you'll get a signal that you missed the boat, or that the Koreans are done discussing business for the day. They will suddenly divert from shop talk back to the social chitchat preceding the session. If that happens, you'll be lucky if you can steer the conversation back to business. Once Koreans have decided that they're done, they'll let you talk on and on about nonbusiness matters until the conversation gets very dull.

While Koreans may be circumlocutious for face reasons, they have earned their nickname the "Irish of Asia." Lawrence V. Fairhall, who has lived in South Korea for over a decade, elaborates:

> The Koreans are a very open people, much more so than the Japanese. They *will* tell you no. Even outright arguing is not the loss of face in Korea that it would be in Japan. Koreans *will* speak quite frankly to you. One problem with trying to govern the country is that the people are so much like the Irish. If they don't like something, they're not afraid to tell you straight out. A Westernized Korean will get to the point without fuss. There's often little difference in doing business with a Westernized Korean than there is in entering an American office.

Be this as it may, face still affects communication and behavior, and

the forms it takes may be subtle. Observes Thomas Kutzen of Chase
Manhattan:

> If a Korean says: "Let me suggest Deal X," and you don't like what's
> proposed, it's best to show your dislike indirectly. Koreans are highly
> sensitive to people's feelings. They'll pick up on yours. They'll project
> theirs to you in the same way and expect you to be attuned to them.
> They may give their heads a little shake, or sigh, but what they really
> mean is: "We think we've got something better." Or they may be con-
> ceptualizing a solution you've proposed in a different way. The Japanese
> influence has not been entirely processed out of Korean business.

Yet Koreans still differ markedly from the Japanese. In addition to
their willingness to say no, they may interrupt you in mid-sentence, which
is most unmannerly in Japan. According to a Wall Street banker who was
stationed in the ROK:

> A very polite Korean, who is used to dealing with Westerners and who
> listens to you from start to finish without interrupting, probably feels
> that he's "handling" you—that is, managing or controlling the situation.
> In his perception, *he* has the upper hand, not you. However, if he
> interrupts you, it's often because his eagerness to get deeper into the
> discussion or refine a point in his understanding *overwhelms* him. When
> this happens, facework is ignored. Now he doesn't care who's on top.
> Americans are sometimes put off by such interruptions, but they're often
> good signs. To interrupt is to show eagerness, and eagerness implies a
> sincere wish to deal.

## Nonverbal and Other Forms of Communication

Koreans dislike noisy laughter, exaggerated gestures, and loud, overly
convivial behavior. Says former Korean Cultural Service director Tae-
wan Yu: "While we are straightforward, we shun rude outspokenness. We
value characteristics of an 'inner soul.' American businesspeople would
do well to send over to Korea cultured, softspoken representatives."

Koreans may avoid saying yes or no. Instead they will squint. If they
were leaning forward on their elbows while listening to you, they will sit
back in their chairs. They will crook their heads. But nothing may be
said. These gestures indicate that you have reached an impasse. In effect,
they skip a turn in the conversation and now it's your turn again to speak.
Try to make the same point from different perspectives. It may take several
versions to clarify an issue.

If leaning back in one's chair is a neutral position, leaning forward, with arms on thighs, hands capping knees, and eyes fixed on a document on the table shows genuine interest. Notes one old hand: "You'll rarely find a Korean, hands on knees, leaning forward and looking at what you're doing, being a passive, disinterested observer."

Even cigarette smoking can be significant. Sometimes Koreans will hold their cigarettes (a high percentage smoke) in a Germanic manner, with the thumb and fingertips, rather than between the index and middle finger. They will let the thread of smoke curl upward and drift around. It gives them an air of being pensive. This may be a natural motion, but often it's used as a conscious tactic. An American who frequently trades in Seoul says: "Koreans are not one-on-one with you when they're using cigarettes in this way. Symbolically, they're trying to stay on top of the situation. This is facework. If you smoke, you can reverse the tactic. You can use the same ammunition on the Koreans that they use on you."

When dealing with an older-generation traditionalist, it's polite to pass and accept documents, food or other items with the right hand, not the left. The fingers of the left hand, palm up, should be extended, lightly touching the right elbow, an old custom originating when Koreans wore long robes with wide loose sleeves that had to be folded or cupped so as not to spill or drag items across a dinner table or desk. When passing something to a traditional Korean who is your senior in age or rank, as a sign of respect, touch the left fingers to the right *wrist* instead of the right elbow. Korean women do this to show their humility to men. But American women should follow the rules for men. Confucian male-female etiquette, which persists among traditional Koreans, does not apply to U.S. businesswomen.

Making eye contact with Korean colleagues is important in meetings and at other times. It ensures attention, shows sincerity, and forms a subtle but significant bond between individuals. Without eye contact you may be treated as a nonperson in South Korea. On sidewalks you'll be impersonally bumped and jostled because pedestrians have no direct visual relationship with you. For the same reason, automobile drivers will behave aggressively, showing disregard for strangers on the road. But if you stop at a traffic light beside a Korean driver who was acting abrasively, and your eyes meet, he will nod, smile, laugh good-naturedly, and *then* give you the right of way.

## Social Customs

As in Japan, evening entertainment often plays a key role in Korean commerce. "Even more so with visiting Americans," says Tae-wan Yu, "since it would be both impolite and impolitic for foreigners who could improve the Korean economy to be left in a lonely hotel room evenings. Americans should make their preferences known. If you prefer cabaret to opera, say so. A Korean host will try to accommodate a visitor's wishes."

How you'll be entertained varies with the length of your stay. If you're in South Korea for only a couple of days, you may simply be treated to lunch or drinks; try to reciprocate before you leave. You probably won't be invited to a Korean home until a relationship is well-established. What you're more likely to experience as a newcomer is a visit to a *kisaeng* (pronounced "key-san") house.

## Kisaeng *Houses*

*Kisaeng* houses are restaurants serving traditional Korean cuisine and/ or nightclub drinkeries.

A traditional Korean meal is served in one elaborate course. It consists of many small dishes, some highly spiced. As is true throughout East Asia, the basis of the meal is rice; meat, poultry, fish, and such are accompaniments. In addition, *kimichi*—a vegetable pickle seasoned with garlic, red pepper, and ginger—is ever present; it's the national dish of Korea. Although the meal is eaten with chopsticks, Americans may be offered forks. Members of a dinner party help themselves to the assortment of foods. Unlike the custom at Chinese banquets, the host does not put food on the guest's plate, or vice versa.

Traditional drinks include *soju*, a clear fermented liquor reminiscent of the Chinese mao-tai; *jungjong*, similar to saki, the Japanese rice wine; ginseng wine, which is strong and sweet; and a brew called *takju*, a bit more potent than beer; beer is also available.

Koreans often assume that Americans don't care for their food. If you'd like to sample a traditional meal, speak up, or you may automatically be taken to a continental restaurant at a local Hilton. Just about the only thing Chinese, Japanese, and Korean cuisines have in common is chopsticks; even the rice is not the same.

No matter where you dine, you'll probably end up at a *kisaeng* house.

*Kisaeng* houses are similar to Japanese *karoke* bars (see *Night Clubs* in the chapter on Japan). The favorite drink is Scotch. Hostesses will join you at the table; at the better places, their relationship with guests is rarely other than platonic. Everyone takes turns singing songs. And the cost of the evening, while less expensive than in Japan, is still steep, often several hundred dollars.

Only yesterday, *kisaeng* drinking parties were the exclusive purview of men. Today, American women are invited to *kisaeng* houses as well, although Korean women (other than hostesses) will not be present.

Reciprocate an evening at a *kisaeng* house with a restaurant meal at your hotel. Traditional entertaining is best left to the natives. When playing host, your guests will probably be men; few Korean women are executives. Don't urge a Korean man to bring his wife along; it isn't the custom. Similarly, if your wife or husband is with you on the trip, it's up to the spouse to find something to do alone that night. In South Korea, evening entertainment is part of the negotiating process, and *only* negotiators should be present.

## Drinking Customs

Traditional Japanese and Korean drinking customs are not the same. In Japan, your glass will constantly be kept full to the brim. It's bad manners to leave a glass half empty. In Korea, a glass won't be refilled if there's still some liquid in it. Koreans will keep a watchful eye on your glass, and the moment it's completely empty they will promptly refill it. If *you* are pouring, it's bad manners to replenish a glass that's not entirely drained.

Westernized Koreans usually follow Western drinking customs. Traditionalists shake out the few drops that may be left in the bottom of a glass when they have finished its contents, then present the empty glass to someone at the table using two hands. Often the host will do this for the guest of honor. Then the host will refill the glass, holding the bottle with two hands. As the guest, you'll now have two glasses in front of you, your own and your host's. The proper response is to finish your glass and present it—after shaking it out—to the person who just gave you his glass, and then refill it, using both hands.

If you're the guest of honor being hosted by a group of Korean traditionalists, everyone may want to exchange glasses with you. This can leave you facing several glasses of Scotch and the prospect of a major hangover. It's not necessary to drink them all, but try to be a good sport. Says an American with plenty of Korean drinking experience:

> It's funny to watch an American and an East Asian when they first meet. Neither knows whether to bow or shake hands. It's also true of trading glasses in Korea. Most Korean businesspeople drink like Americans. But even those who might otherwise trade glasses may not because they know it isn't our custom. Still, it's always best to know what the local tradition is and if you can, play the game. It makes for better camaraderie all around, and that's good for business. If you see other Koreans in your party trading glasses, go for it.

## Conversation

Do some reading and you'll find much to discuss with native colleagues. By the first century A.D., Koreans were already keeping written records. By the seventh, they were making sophisticated astronomical observations. By the thirteenth, they had invented movable metal type— two hundred years before Gutenberg. By the sixteenth, they had created the first ironclad warship. In 1770, they produced their first encyclopaedia, a year before the *Encyclopaedia Britannica* was first published. This is only a sampling of what Koreans have accomplished in 5,000 years. Add to this the ROK's rise from agrarian poverty to a rapidly industrializing country in less than three decades, and it should be easy to keep social conversations alive.

While it's okay to talk shop at meals and *kisaeng* parties, avoid it when you've had a lot to drink. Like Japanese and Chinese, Koreans will hold you to your promises, whether or not you're sober when you make them.

Don't talk about local politics. It's forbidden by the government and may get natives into trouble. Avoiding political discussion is considered mandatory for national security.

If you come to South Korea from Japan, it's not necessary to keep your Japanese visit a secret, but don't dwell on it. Don't criticize the Japanese in order to curry local favor. Koreans will promptly spot this for what it is: patronizing, insincere, and a poor basis for trust.

# CHAPTER TEN

# Latins:
# The Other Americans

"We speak of Latin lovers. Latins love their individuality, their families, their friends, life, and business—in that order."

*An American operations manager*
*stationed in Caracas*

An international financial analyst, a native of Brazil, was asked how he
would advise American business travelers to Latin America. Without
hesitation he replied: "Stay home."

This gloomy prognosis prevails in the U.S. Some firms have aban-
doned their Latin American branches. Others, initially enticed by income-
tax moratoriums, the easing of import/export duties, cheap labor, and
other financial incentives have been scared off by what they read in the
newspapers, which bodes no good for profits.

But given the chronic economic, political, and/or military instability
in much of Central and South America, it may come as a surprise that
many Americans remain even in the most tumultuous of countries. Of the
seventy manufacturing subsidiaries or sales divisions of American corporations formerly operating in El Salvador, over half are still there, among
them Citibank, AVX Ceramics, Texas Instruments, Caess, Xerox, and
Kimberly-Clark. Wrote Fred R. Bleakley in the *New York Times* (March
25, 1984):

> When it comes to discussing the performance of his plant, Roberto
> Salazar, a general manager of AVX Ceramics, says, "I'm not modest."
> For each of the past three years, he says his parent company, the AVX
> Corporation of Great Neck, L.I., judged its El Salvador manufacturing

operation, which assembles electronic components for transistors and circuits, to be ahead of its eight other plants (in Israel, Ireland, Japan, Mexico, and the United States) in quality and production.

Meanwhile, other companies are *expanding* their Latin American operations region-wide. On July 24, 1984, Avis announced:

Despite a prevailing atmosphere of economic and/or political instability in most of Central and South America, Avis Rent-A-Car System has experienced a steady flow of car-rental business in the southern half of the Western Hemisphere, and plans a significant increase in sales and marketing efforts in 1984 and 1985.

Avis has licensees or joint-venture partners in Argentina, Brazil, Chile, Colombia, Ecuador, Peru, Uruguay, Costa Rica, Guatemala, and Mexico—as well as in both Nicaragua and El Salvador.

Nor are business opportunities in Latin America limited to large multinational firms. In 1981, Iowa-born Linda McGlathery, former deputy director of the Peace Corps in Guatemala, began a one-woman shop in the country exporting locally made textiles, fashion accessories, and crafts. The government of Guatemala has changed hands three times in six years by military coup, and there—as well as throughout macho-male-dominated Latin America—female entrepreneurs are rare. McGlathery, who employs local artisans who would otherwise be jobless, has since opened branch offices in Haiti and New York. She numbers Ralph Lauren and Neiman-Marcus amoung her U.S. clients, and has her future sights set on the fashion capitals of Europe.

The people behind success stories like these explain that long-term commitment and constant monitoring of shifting political and economic currents are among the keys to profitability in Latin America. But they also stress that understanding the business cultures of the region is equally vital. Most feel that such awareness is scant among U.S. businesspeople. As a result, many commericial opportunities that would be mutually advantageous to U.S. and Latin firms are ignored or negotiations fall through.

Such awareness begins by understanding common but often misused terms of regional reference that may themselves be highly sensitive issues south of the Rio Grande.

## Latin America

Latin America includes the Spanish-, Portuguese-, and French-speaking countries—excluding Canada—of North America, Central

America, South America, and the West Indies. The region is composed of twenty republics: Argentina, Bolivia, Brazil, Chile, Colombia, Costa Rica, Cuba, the Dominican Republic, Ecuador, El Salvador, Guatemala, Haiti, Honduras, Mexico, Nicaragua, Panama, Paraguay, Peru, Uruguay, and Venezuela. The term is also used to include Puerto Rico, the French West Indies, and other islands of the West Indies where a Romance language is spoken. Occasionally Belize (British Honduras), Guyana, French Guiana, and Surinam are considered part of Latin America as well.

## North America

The northern of the two continents of the Western Hemisphere, North America is usually thought to encompass *all* the mainland and related offshore islands lying north of the Isthmus of Panama, which connects it to South America. Some definitions, however, exclude Central America.

## Anglo-America

When Americans refer to North America they usually mean Anglo-America, used to describe only the U.S. and Canada. Mexico is part of North America.

## Middle America

Middle America includes Mexico and the republics of Central America.

## Central America

The narrow, southernmost portion of the North American continent, Central America is generally applied to the republics of Guatemala, Honduras, El Salvador, Nicaragua, Costa Rica, and Panama, and to the colony of Belize. However, Panamanians may consider their country a separate and distinct geopolitical entity from Central and South America. Note that Central America does *not* include Mexico. Mexicans consider their nation part of North America, and may take offense when other North Americans refer to their country as being Central American. As Mexicans see it, this is unneighborly disassociation.

## South America

The southern of the two continents of the Western Hemisphere, South America is politically divided into eleven independent countries—Argentina, Bolivia, Brazil, Chile, Colombia, Ecuador, Guyana, Paraguay, Peru, Uruguay, and Venezuela—as well as two colonies, Surinam (Dutch) and French Guiana.

## America

Named after the Italian navigator Amerigo Vespucci (1454–1512), America includes *all* the lands of the Western Hemisphere—North, Central, and South America. In English, *America* and *Americans* are commonly used to refer only to the U.S. and its citizens. However, among the peoples of the hemisphere whose native tongues are Spanish, Portuguese, and French, the terms refer to them as well. Technically, Canada and Latin America are part of America and their citizens are Americans.

This is not to suggest that Mexicans or Brazilians commonly refer to themselves as Americans; they don't. But this semantic hair-splitting may cause provocation among Latins when U.S. citizens refer to *themselves* as Americans and to their country as America, distinguishing them from Latin American natives and lands. This may be perceived as a superior attitude. In Mexico, you're not simply a North American, implying that Mexicans are something else. Refer to yourself as a North American *from the U.S.* South of Mexico, you *are* a North American, but not merely an American. Your country is the United States, not merely America.

## Portraits of a Businesspeople

For the 1986 World Cup soccer tournament to be held in Mexico, the Mexicans commissioned local artists to create an official mascot. The result was a cartoon character named *Pique*, which looks something like Speedy Gonzales of U.S. cartoons and comics. Pique's oversized sombrero, huge handlebar mustache, rumpled uniform, and dreamy expression raised outraged cries from Mexican nationalists who saw in the figure all the hated stereotypes ascribed to them by gringos to the north: the lazy, languid, siesta-loving Latin, slovenly, unsophisticated, and technologically backward, without a modern business care in the world.

In Mexico City, Caracas, São Paulo, Rio de Janeiro, Buenos Aires, and other Latin American commercial centers, such images are frequently as out of date as a Model T Ford. In fact, potentially anywhere in the region, Latin negotiators are apt to be highly intelligent, schooled in the latest technologies, elegantly dressed and mannered, probably more cultivated than the average American executive, and increasingly U.S.-educated, often with a good command of English.

Be this as it may, most Latins resist "Americanization." Not only are they culturally different from us (at least those of us who are not of Hispanic descent) and proud of it, but they are also culturally different from *each other*. Still, in fundamental ways they remain brothers under the skin, sharing traits uncommon among U.S. executives. Felix E. Forestieri, public relations director, Latin America, for Eastern Airlines, explains:

> Yes, there are wide differences among Latin businesspeople. But there *is* a general entity that can be called a "Latin American," regardless of which Latin country he is from—when contrasted to the businesspeople of other cultures, particularly that of North America. There does exist a common denominator that allows a Mexican and an Argentinian to sit down together and *feel* the same way about an issue.
>
> I am originally from the Dominican Republic. Now I am an American citizen. I have been dealing with the United States since I was eight years old. But despite the fact that I have been living in this country for fifteen years, there is still better communication between an Argentinian, or a Mexican, or *any* Latin American, and me, than there is between an Anglo-Saxon American and me.

Perhaps Forestieri's choice of Mexico and Argentina as examples was inadvertent, but it's significant because the two countries occupy opposite ends of the Latin American spectrum in ways that go beyond geography. Unlike most people of the region, Mexicans identify more closely with their Indian than with their Spanish heritage. In contrast, Argentinians are among the most European of Latin American peoples in their manners and mores. What is it about peoples as culturally diverse as these that allows them "to sit down together and *feel* the same way?"

## Society

Latin American societies have traditionally been two-class and highly stratified, and largely remain so. At the top of the social order is a small group of wealthy families that may be oligarchies, directly or indirectly controlling national governments, political parties, state-owned industrial monopolies, and major private-sector firms.

But the local elite may represent less than 1 percent of a national population. The majority of Latins are appallingly poor, uneducated, unskilled or semiskilled, and unemployed or underemployed. The rich few don't question the justice of this situation, and unless incited by revolutionary fervor, the poor resignedly accept their misery as inevitable. As the histories of Latin countries are infused with Roman Catholic cultural traditions, it's generally assumed that the rich are rich and the poor are poor because God ordained it.

However, as Latin American economies are increasingly shifting from traditional agrarian to modern industrial bases, educational opportunities have become more available to lower-class individuals who show intelligence and talent. They are needed to fill jobs like receptionists, typists, clerks, technicians, accountants, and managers. Hence, a middle class is growing in the region. But particularly at the lower- and middle-management levels, qualified personnel remain in short supply due to cultural bias. Among the wealthy elite, most forms of work are considered ungentlemanly and plebeian. And among the emerging middle class, management is thought to be a low-prestige occupation; medicine, law, and architecture score the most social points.

Aristocratic top executives or government ministers may negotiate with you at the outset, but not necessarily. Often the groundwork for negotiations with superiors is laid by middle-class middle managers, and they may have considerable influence with corporate higher-ups. In addition, your negotiating counterparts may be old-fashioned traditionalists, particularly in the less sophisticated and modern central and western parts of South America. They may not speak English, have had limited or no dealings with Americans, and may be unfamiliar with international commercial practice. However, such traditionalists may potentially be found anywhere in Latin America.

Yet the number of Latins who are Western-educated, English-speaking, and well-tutored in the modus operandi of world trade has significantly grown. They, too, may reside in Bogata, Quito, Lima, or Santiago, cities which are off the beaten path for many Americans. Many Latin business sophisticates are cultural hybrids. They adopt some Western methods and manners, but also manifest traditional native traits, among them personalism, machismo, the need to feel simpatico, and attitudes toward family, hierarchy and rank, face, space, time, and change. Your understanding of these characteristics may affect the outcome of negotiations.

## Personalism

A primary concern in Latin life is enhancing and protecting one's sense of self-esteem: *personalism*. Individual uniqueness is the Latin source of dignity as a human being. If self-esteem is low, a Latin may suffer an identity crisis that obliterates the importance of all else in life. As such, personalism must be preserved at all cost, even at the expense of business practicalities.

Latins express personalism in many ways. One is by aesthetic cultivation. While U.S. businesspeople may give professional concerns priority in life, Latins often don't. A government minister may be a published poet. A chief executive may be an amateur archeologist, with a collection of Mayan, Incan or Aztec artifacts. Such pursuits are not mere hobbies. They help to define one's personalism—what sets an individual apart from everyone else—and may rank higher in one's sense of self-esteem than professional accomplishments.

U.S. negotiators are often frustrated by a Latin's reluctance to talk shop right away. Instead a colleague may want to share with you what *he* considers paramount in life. The poet recites verses. The ornithologist takes you bird-watching. The archeologist displays his relics. By initially focusing on what we consider secondary avocational activities, a Latin tries to say: "First let me show you the civilized, cultured part of me— the *true* me, what is in my *soul*. Only then can you understand, or should care to know, my professional side, which is not who I *really* am. Without knowing my true self, how can we form the trust relationship mandatory to do business?"

One U.S. negotiator, a Latin American native, puts it like this:

> Doing business in Latin America is like getting married in a formal, old-fashioned way. First there's a period of courtship. It's a time of testing, a proving ground. If the two of you can manage to fall in love with each other, the rest becomes easier and negotiations take on a logic and momentum of their own. If you don't take the time for romance, the wedding will probably be called off. The business will go to a competitor who has the patience to cultivate a relationship first.

Personalism often enters Latin bargaining sessions in individual displays of charisma—a dynamism of personality calculated to elicit respect from others. In Latin America, respect is a source of personal power, and personal power translates into the ability to get things done.

But the ability to achieve and the quickness to do so may not go hand in hand as they do in the U.S. Latins can be circumlocutious, subjective rather than objective, emotionally intuitive rather than logically deductive, and unconcerned with the accuracy of data on which decisions are based. They can also be verbose. Opinions are often expressed in elaborate flourishes of verbal rhetoric that seem more like a politician's speech than an executive's discussion. The nature of a business relationship may be defined in terms of *ideals* rather than realities. Frequently the show is the thing; the process counts more than the result. Such symbolic displays of personalism can take priority over impersonal facts.

Americans often apply pressure, trying to cut through the Latin need to express personalism. Few succeed. A more effective tack is to understand that *you* have personalism, too—and *show* it. When a Latin bares his soul to you, he expects reciprocity, which U.S. businesspeople frequently avoid, because revealing cherished personal aspects of their lives and exposing weaknesses as well as strengths are usually considered unprofessional conduct here.

However, this communing of souls permits a Latin to become simpatico with you. Simpatico is a deep, sincere empathy that old friends share. It's the foundation for trust. It paves the way for becoming *compadres*—people who are so simpatico that their feelings of mutual trust, friendship, and loyalty approach that of family. Becoming simpatico takes time and may extend your trips to Latin America well beyond normal limits were negotiations being held in the U.S. But in the long run, it's the best insurance that agreement will be reached and project implementation reasonably efficient. Compadres don't let each other down.

## Machismo

Machismo is an exaggerated expression of masculinity originally coined to describe Latin men. The classic paradigm of machismo is the bullfight: a test of human grace, quickness, courage, stamina, power, and respect. Machismo calls for a proud, aggressive, competitive stance in all important social matters. Characterized by personal dynamism, zest for action, and physical, sexual, psychic, and political potency, it's a Latin trait aligned with personalism. They differ in that personalism refers to the human being; Latin women have personalism, too. Machismo is specifically concerned with *the man*.

However, aggressiveness and competitiveness, while present in other areas of life, are not normally seen in a Latin office. The sense of competitiveness instilled by athletics in American boys during their early years is not part of the upbringing of aristocratic Latin youngsters. As adults, their main motivation for negotiating may be to enhance personalism for themselves, their families, and their organizations by forming a relationship with a prestigious American firm. It's not necessarily for the profit potential of a given transaction.

The motivation of middle-class middle managers for dealing is not usually the prospect of career advancement that comes with a job well done in the U.S. Upward mobility, particularly in family-owned firms and family-controlled government ministries, can be difficult if not futile. Choice jobs are often filled by organizational outsiders: relatives or friends who are well-connected to decision makers. Promotion from within, based on individual ability and proven performance, is not the custom as it is here. Competition is pointless with nothing at stake.

What motivates mid-level negotiators to deal with you is a deep feeling of loyalty to their superiors or patrons. Loyalty is fostered by superiors through paternalistic benevolence and favors bestowed on subordinates. Hence, if you convince middle managers that your proposal will make *their* work more efficient (thereby benefiting their superiors and firms), they have reason to hear you out. By taking time to develop a simpatico relationship with them as well as with their patrons, you'll gain their support in selling your proposition upstairs.

## Social Connections

In Latin America, *whom* you know matters more than *what* you know. In U.S. business, a person who is a lone wolf can be successful, even powerful, and in fact the acquisition of power in our country may result in the increasing isolation of the individual who wields it. But few Latins want to be loners. A Latin without connections—family, friends, patrons—lacks the associative influence and power to get things done.

A Latin individual is the societal embodiment of all his ancestors and current human affiliations. The family derives or loses status by the achievements of its members. When a person does something laudible, by association personalism is increased for all family members. If a relative behaves shamefully, the stigma is borne by everyone bound to him by blood or other allegiance.

Separate networks of social influence are often interconnected by marriage or through mutual friends, business dealings, etc. As such, Latin society is tightly knit and mutually interdependent, more like an American political party than like our society as a whole, where even nuclear families may be loosely structured and informal, and extended-family ties weak. The intricate web of strong family connections that pervades Latin society can generate jobs, form informal courts of law, change or bend laws in formal courts, and provide financial security for the elderly or improvident.

Being accepted within Latin spheres of influence is possible for Americans, but it doesn't happen overnight. The key to acceptance is to become simpatico with native colleagues. Simpatico is based on friendship, and Latin friendship takes what many North Americans consider unbusinesslike priority in life, and may result in unprofessional inefficiency.

For example, Latin employment practices are often not based on merit but on friendships and kinship ties. A person who is well connected may be given an important job before a better qualified but unconnected applicant is considered. Because the human element takes priority over performance, superiors are reticent to fire subordinates for incompetence, laziness, tardiness, and most other reasons other than being disloyal. Latin American organizations may practice what in effect is lifetime employment, although it's not the formal policy that it is in Japan.

So strong are family and friendship bonds that a manager's first obligation is to the people to whom he feels allegiance, not to an abstract organization, as is true in the U.S. A Latin will work hard for his company or ministry less out of loyalty to it than out of duty to his patron—often his immediate superior. Similarly, if the needs of the organization conflict with the needs of people to whom one is obligated, family and friends come first.

This is the tightrope Americans must walk to succeed in the region. In the U.S., you may see your identity as being part of the XYZ Company. But in Latin America, you must show empathy, sympathy, and loyalty to the *human beings* of local XYZ organizations with whom you negotiate. It's the relationship between people, not corporations, that counts. To initiate and maintain it, you may have to do things that the home office would normally frown upon, like take more frequent and longer business trips to socialize and develop trust, bestow "favors" (such as business intelligence) that a Latin colleague can parlay into social or professional prestige, and show patience when deadlines are missed. Friendship in Latin America usually requires more than superficial displays like hosting a dinner, giving a gift, or playing golf.

## Hierarchy and Rank

Understanding the dynamics of Latin American superior-subordinate relationships is critical to negotiating success. Latins are raised from childhood to have a strong sense of social place. Society is rigidly stratified because it's God's will, and upward mobility is difficult because individual destinies are in God's—not human—hands. The main ways to improve one's lot in Latin America are by having clout with people of influence, and—to a growing extent—by having an education.

Latins are reared to respect the key male authority figures in their lives. Early figures are male relations: fathers, grandfathers, and uncles. Later, respect is extended to include a patron, an employer, an immediate superior, or a forceful, dynamic leader. This respect is not developed by empirical observation, as is customary in the U.S. Rather it's inherent, a natural outgrowth of the Latin admiration for personalism and machismo in others, and the need to belong to an influential social network to derive self-identity.

Respect for hierarchy and rank is the basis for *face*. To keep, save or gain face, top executives may not consult underlings to gather sufficient and accurate data needed to make informed decisions. Instead, decisions may be based mainly on intuition, not facts. An intuitive decision is automatically best because of the status of the person who makes it. He's given the credit for having wisdom beyond the comprehension of subordinates; because of his high rank, he's closer to God.

Decisions are commonly announced with a flair inspired by personalism. Such dramatics are calculated to reinforce the feeling that the decision is right and the decision maker is worthy of respect. If, later, the decision turns out to be wrong, it was due to God's mercurial will. The human decision maker is not blamed; because of respect for his status it's taken for granted that *anyone* in the same situation would have made the same mistake.

In bargaining sessions subordinates will often withhold what may be better-informed opinions that contradict the greater wisdom of their chief negotiator or not speak at all unless specifically addressed. Partly they are present to assimilate information you convey. But they may also be asked to attend meetings to increase the personalism of the chief negotiator in your eyes by their sheer numbers, by showing deference to him, and by supporting his judgments without question.

This does not mean middle managers don't know right from wrong, that they are powerless to change a top executive's mind, or that *you* are powerless to influence them to that end. But reevaluation happens offstage. Without implying disrespect for the judgment of superiors, you must gently, delicately, and indirectly convince subordinates that the course your company prefers is best for all concerned. If you succeed—and the process can't be rushed—they in turn will use circumlocution and tact to sway a superior, trying to bring him around to a line of thinking you've persuaded them is right.

Decision makers in Latin America *do* hear out subordinates privately, at an appropriate time and place. Sometimes they must—and know it— if they are mere figureheads who rose to the top through connections rather than by knowledge, ability, and performance. Often it's not so much the *content* of the information as *how* the information is conveyed that concerns them most.

### Time

Just as there's a Muslim notion of fatalism regarding Arab time, so there is a Catholic concept of fatalism governing Latin time. Time is minutely divisible and controllable in the U.S. Moreover, it's a sign of professionalism for an executive here to accurately predict how long a given job will take to do, and to have the power to speed up time if a usual deadline is not fast enough. The American Puritan ethic dictates that through hard work deadlines can be met. But time is not money in Latin America; it's not a tangible commodity that can be saved, spent, or easily manipulated to suit human whim. Latins don't naturally believe that where there's a will there's a way. The only will that counts is God's. If something does not get done "on time," logic dictates that God's will overrules personal desire, always an unpredictable but possible event.

The notion that everything ultimately is in God's control discourages forethought among many Latins. Thus, expressed intentions may be perceived as deeds actually done with no mental projection into the future to compare promises made with the ability to keep them. In addition, because family and friends take priority over business, a deadline commitment may be superseded by conflicting, more important obligations to people to whom one owes allegiance. If this becomes necessary, it too is the will of God.

Your best assurance that U.S. schedules will be met in Latin America is to take the time to become a person to whom a Latin feels allegiance. This is done by conveying your humanity, sincerity, loyalty, and friendship, not by stressing profits. It's also essential to accept the normal pace of business life in the region. For example, Latin courtesies and protocols are formal, elaborate, and extensive, and because of the Latin stress on good interpersonal rapport, everyone—even casual acquaintances who are merely passersby on the street—is entitled to more than a mere wave or nod that for North Americans is sufficient acknowledgment. As a result, Latin businesspeople are chronically running late.

There are, however, exceptions to this rule. In major commercial centers like Mexico City, São Paulo, and Buenos Aires, as business cultures become more internationally homogenized the pace of negotiations is becoming brisker and more efficient. In fact, there may be marked differences in negotiating styles among Latins of different cities in the same country, even ones that are only a few hundred miles apart like São Paulo and Rio de Janeiro in Brazil. Explains Patrick J. Oliver, vice-president, Latin America and Florida Division, for Pan Am:

> The business community in Rio has a more genteel mentality. The climate is hot, the business pace is more leisurely, and courtesies are more elaborate. The climate in São Paulo is more moderate, and the business atmosphere is more akin to that of a major U.S. city. Rio is the image we all have of Latin America. You must be simpatico. You must talk for an hour about everything *but* business. You drink lots of coffee. You may not even get around to talking shop on the first call. But that approach doesn't work in São Paulo. Paulistas are as busy as executives in New York. And they want to *project* an image of efficiency. Often they get impatient if you take more than a minute to say hello. They want to get down to business right away.

Despite what is generally true, be aware that executives *anywhere* in Latin America—including Rio—may expect brisk, modern efficiency in your business approach. Don't prejudge Latins you have yet to meet, and who, like businesspeople everywhere, defy stereotyping. Distinguishing between a slow, cautious traditionalist and a Latin executive in a rush is fairly easy. If you look for clues as to what your presentation style should be, you'll find them, and your effectiveness as a negotiator will be improved.

## Women

American women bound for Latin America and the superiors who send them tend to worry about whether they will be sexually harassed and able to gain credibility in what is a world of macho men. For many North

Americans, machismo conjures extreme and extremely distasteful images, like a woman innocently walking past a construction site evoking catcalls, hooting, wolf whistles, and profanity from nearby men. However, these are not the sort of men you'll face in a Latin American office. Latin business sophisticates are usually well-groomed, well-mannered, well-schooled, and quite polite. Among the impoverished lower classes, with which you'll have little or no contact, machismo may be blatant and coarse. But among upper-class decision makers, it's a subtle projection of a refined, cultivated persona. Most U.S. businesswomen find it refreshing and pleasant.

Still, you may get sexual signals even from Latin America's polished upper crust. It's common even for married Latin men to keep mistresses, and some are ever on the alert for new sexual conquests. Warning signs include prolonged eye contact, legs touching under the table, elaborate compliments on your beauty, attempts to cast and keep you in the role of a tourist rather than a professional—by endless talk of local sights, scenery, and shopping, avoiding business—and invitations to serve as an evening escort, just the two of you.

Even these activities are not necessarily related to sex. But the more they persist, the more they begin to mask sexual overtures. Businesswomen who know the region well say it's easy to sense instinctively which is which. You probably will get compliments from Latin men. Enjoy them, but relate social conversation in the office to business. Stress that you're not merely a woman but a businesswoman, a competent professional with a job to do. Yes, your hotel is quite comfortable, thank you, and the desk in your room is large enough to do work after hours. No, you haven't had a chance to go shopping or sightseeing yet; hopefully you can find time when your job is done. While maintaining eye contact is a sign of sincerity between Latin men, a look of professional attentiveness and one of sexual attraction is a distinction most women are quick to draw, and if the former turns into the latter, break it off. At such times, for example, snapping open an attaché case makes a definitive statement.

If you're alone rather than a member of a negotiating team, and are invited out for the evening, don't go with only one male escort if you're concerned about sexual complications. If a Latin man is married, request that he bring his wife, or invite a group of men to join you; there's safety in numbers. Spending an evening alone with a Latin man does increase the odds of having a pass made, but it will probably be subtle and indirect, not overt. Exaggerated displays of masculinity hide feelings of inferiority; Latins are as eager to be rejected as Americans are. If your manner makes it clear that your sole purpose is business, Latin men will usually get the message and not press.

Ironically, a problem American women often don't consider and sometimes should is the reverse. Latin men can be handsome and alluring: sun-bronzed, dressed in dashing white, and eminently civilized. Still, don't succumb to a Latin executive's charm if you value your professional credibility.

## Business Customs

How do you pave the way for success in Latin America? Thoroughly research local political, economic, and cultural environments. Compile dossiers on prospective client firms and their top executives. Don't assume you're dealing with U.S. businesspeople in a U.S. environment. Take time to know your market and target your wares to it. Reduce risk by testing goods that are already proven sellers in the U.S. rather than trying to launch new products. Approach the manager in an organizational hierarchy who most acutely feels the need you're going to meet, which is not necessarily a corporate officer; it may be more effective to work your way up the chain of command. Be patient; don't expect immediate results. Be professional, but don't be afraid to show your humanity as well; Latins want to see it. Be prepared to regularly reinforce a business relationship once it has begun through *personal* contact, rather than taking it for granted after agreement is reached. Otherwise a contract may not be worth the paper it's written on. You may have to travel to Latin America several times a year to show your face, socialize, and reestablish trust, even though such trips may not be mandatory for purely business reasons.

### Test Marketing in Puerto Rico

Since doing business in Latin America usually takes longer than it does here, U.S. firms are ever on the lookout for ways to speed up the profit-making process. A favorite tack is to use Puerto Rico as a test market, and, if results are positive, to proceed with full rollouts in other Latin nations.

Many Americans consider Puerto Rico an ideal test market for Latin America as a whole because it's conveniently close to the U.S., cutting travel cost and time. It's free of most trade barriers, due to the commonwealth's affiliation with the U.S. And, after all, Puerto Ricans are "typical" Latins. They speak Spanish. They show traits like personalism and machismo. Their society is like other Latin societies in that it has a coterie of aristocratic elite, a small but growing middle class, and a poor majority. Roman Catholic mores permeate local life, as they do elsewhere in the region.

Thus, if it sells in Puerto Rico, it will sell in Mexico, Brazil or Argentina—or so our business thinking often goes. Unfortunately, despite some similarities, Puerto Ricans can be significantly different from other Latins. Being more Americanized, they identify more closely with the U.S., or at least are more *aware* of current events and trends here. As such, they are often more receptive to the marketing strategies of U.S. firms than are natives of Latin nations less involved with our country. In fact, the farther south of the Rio Grande a country is, the less U.S. influence tends to be felt.

In addition, the term *Latin* is not a synonym for *Spanish* as many Americans think. The culture of Brazil has Portuguese, not Spanish, roots. In Argentina and Chile, where Spanish is the first language of the land, the second language of educated people may be French, German or Italian, not English, and the influence of Western Europe is more pervasive than that of the U.S.

Puerto Rico is not the foolproof, low-cost shortcut to regionwide success that Americans often suppose. Positive test results there should not be generalized. Instead, they should indicate only that *further testing* may prove successful in other Latin countries; it may also fail.

## Dress

In tropical climates Latin businessmen may sport elegant white suits, but Americans should pack what they would normally wear at home in comparable temperatures when meeting with conservative people. Light-colored, monochromatic suits—always with ties—are acceptable daytime office wear when it's hot. Men should not remove their jackets unless Latin colleagues have already done so, and only then after asking permission. In cooler weather, dark suits—black, gray or navy—white shirts and black shoes make a good impression everywhere. Evening socializing may be formal. Check with a Latin trade organization in the U.S. or your local representative (see Chapter Three) to see if you'll need a tuxedo.

American women should wear their best business clothes. The few Latin female executives and the wives of affluent businessmen are as fashion-conscious as Parisians. Like Frenchmen, Latin executives have discerning eyes and notice small details like the quality of wristwatches, other jewelry, leather goods, and even pens. Be picky about what you pack.

Don't dress to emphasize your femininity. Stress your professionalism, and your femininity will be apparent without destroying your credibility as a woman who can do a man's job in a man's world. Get advice before you leave to see if you'll need a formal gown as well as a cocktail dress for evening wear. Evening outfits should not have low-cut necklines and should be at least knee length. Look smart but not too sexy; Latin men may read more into it than you had in mind.

## Collateral Materials

When promotional literature and other documents are translated for Latins, several mistakes are often made.

Don't give Brazilians literature translated into Spanish rather than Portuguese, the native tongue; this is insulting.

Don't assume that Spanish words with identical spellings have identical meanings throughout Latin America; many don't. The Parker Pen Company designed ads for a ballpoint pen called *Bolla* to be marketed in the region. The dictionary definition of *bolla* is simply "ball." However, depending on the country, *bolla* may also mean a revolution (in the anarchistic sense), a lie, or an obscene gesture. Luckily Parker caught the error in time. Other companies don't; lost sales and tarnished images may result.

A professional translator would have spotted the problem with a word like *bolla*, but most U.S. firms don't use pros. Instead they have a Spanish-speaking employee do the job. Often these people write no better Spanish than Americans write English. And it doesn't follow that a native of Mexico or Puerto Rico will know what *bolla* means in Colombia, Argentina or Chile. To avoid confusion and possible insult, hire a pro.

When communicating intercontinentally by mail or telex, it's courteous to answer a Latin's message in the *same* language in which it was written, be it Spanish, French or English, even if you know the author is fluent in English. If a Latin prefers to communicate in English, he'll do it.

## Communicating by Telephone and Mail

Negotiations in Latin America can take a long time not only for cultural reasons but also because local telephone systems may be poor.

The individual you're trying to reach may not even *have* a telephone. And sometimes making a connection can take an hour or an afternoon. Moreover, Latins consider the telephone inappropriate for long business discussions; it's too impersonal. They mainly telephone to ask simple questions that require uncomplicated answers or to arrange personal meetings for more detailed talks.

If you leave a telephone message with a secretary or assistant, don't assume it will be delivered, or relayed accurately, or if it is conveyed accurately that it will necessarily elicit a return telephone call. Some Latins are very good about returning calls, others aren't. Be persistent. If perseverance doesn't pay off, you don't need a return call to get the message.

Latins usually exchange business cards, but it's not always done. If not, ask for one. Trying to track down a person's address, telephone number or telex number in Latin America when you're back in the U.S. can be more of a hassle than you'd believe.

Send letters by *registered* mail. They are more likely to reach addresses. You'll also improve the chances of correct delivery if you note addresses as Latins do, putting the zip code (if one exists) *before* the city, not after the country.

If you telephone Latin America from the U.S., call person to person, not station to station. With bad connections and receptionists not speaking English, your colleague's name may be the only thing you say that's understood.

## Appointments

Latin decision makers are dependably busy; prior appointments are a must. Natives work on two different schedules. Traditionalists begin the workday early, before 9:00 A.M. They take a long lunch break from noon till about 3:00, with the meal eaten at home followed by a siesta. On returning to the office, they work late, often till 8:00 in the evening or beyond. If a colleague takes a siesta, don't call him then; it's an invasion of privacy. Appointments are best scheduled for late in the afternoon, after he's had his nap.

The second schedule is like ours. Work starts at 9:00 A.M., lunch is around noon, and the day is done at 5:00 P.M., with no afternoon nap. Latins who work modern hours are probably most reachable an hour or so before lunch. Learn in advance which schedule a company you're trying to contact is on, as well as the hours individual decision makers keep; they may not be the same.

While you're expected to be on time for meetings, Latins are often late. You may be kept waiting for a few minutes or an hour. See *Appointments* in the chapter on Western Europe for what to expect and how to behave. The important rule to observe is not to lose your temper. If it's any consolation, many American executives are kept waiting; you're not the first. If you want the business badly enough, you'll remain calm and relaxed and take it in stride.

## Protocols

Handshaking customs and forms of address are the same as those discussed in Chapter Four for Latin Europeans.

## Negotiating Teams

In bargaining sessions, you'll either deal with a single individual; a group composed of a superior and his subordinates, whose influence with the chief negotiator should not be underestimated, even though they may be passive listeners in meetings; or a group of top executives who are decision-making peers. Peers pose the most problems.

American negotiating teams are usually interdisciplinary. Members each have a different expertise to contribute and are united in overall purpose. Latin teams may be quite the reverse. Members may be present not because they are knowledgeable about the issues to be discussed but because they are charismatic or powerful in the organization. In other words, a Latin negotiating team may be assembled not on the basis of competence but on the basis of personalism.

Unfortunately, personalism is an innately noncomformist trait. Latins use personalism to *separate* themselves from others in order to attain individual uniqueness that commands respect and becomes a source of power. Personalism is founded on fantasy and idealism, not on reality and pragmatism. It's subjective, not objective. It encourages Latins to behave dramatically. This intensifies one's charisma. Personalism discourages respect for uncolorful facts.

Thus, the concepts of personalism and team unity are often mutually exclusive. Personalism precludes teamwork, because each member tries to gain and hold the center stage to enhance his own self-esteem at the expense of team goals. Says a former U.S. State Department official: "We often found it harder to get Latins to agree with each other than it was to get them to agree with us."

What can you do about this? Not much. Be aware of it and if it happens, be a patient audience. The fervor of Latin personalism is usually in direct proportion to the scope of the transaction being negotiated. At the highest levels of business and government, it's most intense. However, it's best to discuss the possibility of Latin interteam wrangling with your superiors before leaving the U.S. Many home-office decision makers find it hard to believe this sort of thing actually happens, and may unfairly suspect their own negotiators of simply being the wrong people for the job.

## Presentation Style

It's customary to be served coffee after hands are shaken, business cards exchanged, and seats offered. Don't refuse coffee, as a rejection of hospitality is a symbolic rejection of a Latin host. You're apt to drink a lot of coffee in Latin America. Use the occasion to decide on an effective presentation style.

Your host will help you choose a style by giving you clues. Normally, nonbusiness matters are discussed while drinking coffee, permitting both parties to get to know each other better as people rather than as professionals. A Latin traditionalist will be in no particular hurry to talk shop. You may spend from fifteen minutes to a half hour discussing the weather, local sights, sports, world affairs that are not personally sensitive, and other safe subjects. Talk of families is not a safe subject unless your colleague introduces it first.

In this situation, relax, take the opportunity to reveal your personality, *listen* as well as talk, try to draw your counterpart out, and put company deadlines and pressures out of your mind for the moment; glancing at your watch will only be counterproductive.

You may not get around to serious or any business discussions at your first meeting, or possibly your second or third. Subsequent meetings may take place out of the office—in a café, at a restaurant, strolling through a local park. Be cool. Traditional Latins will introduce shop talk when they are ready, which usually means when they decide they like you well enough to consider a serious relationship. Conscious ploys to make yourself seem *more* likable will be pegged for what they are: insincere. Don't mistake slowness and caution for lack of intelligence. Don't force the issue by bringing business up yourself. It's uncivilized to be overeager, provoking suspicion and alienating your host.

When you finally do get a sign to begin, it's best to position your

offer in humanistic, idealistic terms. Remember: You're beginning a court-
ship that will hopefully end in marriage. Your colleague may be as interested in enhancing his prestige and extending his power through the
relationship you propose as in making money. As an American, you
represent the United States; often this fact alone has social-point potential.
And power is gained by forming a new alliance with a true friend—that
is, a person who can be called upon to bestow favors, feels a sense of
mutual obligation, and is loyal. That's what prolonged socializing is all
about: seeing if you have the seeds of these qualities in you.

While some Latins you meet will represent variations on this theme,
others will be modern business sophisticates who will exude busyness,
efficiency, and intelligence. During coffee, social chitchat may last only
a few polite moments, and your colleague may ask what's on your mind
professionally before you finish your cup. At this point, the guidelines
for making an effective presentation in Northern Europe are the ones to
use.

### Negotiating Notes

Negotiating success hinges on personalizing business relationships.
Many U.S. businesspeople understand the dictionary definition of *personalize* without appreciating its deeper implications for Latins. One of
them is time. Explains a Latin executive who works in the U.S.:

> It is insulting and condescending to Latins for North Americans to bluntly
> state: "Our product is the best." Even if it *is* the best. This is too
> aggressive. It is better to take a softer approach: "Here is our product.
> This is how we do business. We know your business methods are dif-
> ferent. But we think there is an opportunity here for us to work *together*."
> Always the stress is on forming a relationship, on working together, not
> on the opportunity to improve profits by 10 percent. You must think
> long-term. You must be future oriented. To succeed in Latin America,
> you must look ahead five, maybe ten years, something not often done
> in this country.

Another commonly overlooked aspect of personalization is a feeling
of *genuine sincerity*, not merely playacting, something to which Latins
are acutely sensitive. Says a U.S. corporate officer who was born in South
America, and will be called Valdez because he requested anonymity:

> You look at Valdez now in his fancy American office and at Valdez out
> in the field. They are two different people. In the field, I am honestly,

visibly *enjoying* what I am doing. I am appreciating the weather. I am walking slower. I am feeling *good*. I am not in the U.S. I am someplace else. And being in a different environment, I take on a different persona. If Latins perceive that what you are doing is only for work, you will fail. They will not trust you.

Most importantly, sell *yourself* first, not your company. A company is an abstract entity. Latins cannot *see* it. What they can see is *you*. I sell Valdez. I sell the fact that I am a likable, intelligent, reliable, efficient, and effective individual. Sure, I have flaws. As I get to know my Latin colleagues better, I show them my flaws. No one is perfect. Accepting imperfections is part of what goes into relating to people as human beings.

Once I have sold myself, then I proceed to sell my organization. Where does it stand among other players in the marketplace? Our company is large, but it is not the biggest in our field. So I must position myself. I say that bigger doesn't necessarily mean better. I explain that we can provide top-quality services. Latins want to know how we were able to develop that kind of quality. In their minds, only the biggest companies have the financial resources to really achieve excellence. I tell them about the makeup of our organization, what our corporate *culture* is. This they can understand and relate to: quality that is the product of human talent and dedication.

U.S. businesswomen have an additional credibility roadblock to overcome because they are of an untraditional sex. Harriet Mouchly-Weiss, chairman of Ruder Finn & Rotman International Partners, observes:

In my experience, Latins will take you seriously, but they will also take note that what they are hearing is coming from a woman, which may change things somewhat. Latin business culture is based on the fact that women have not been part of the managerial workforce. Therefore women are inexperienced in business. Latin men will wonder if they can really trust what you say as a result.

You have to show them that you have the experience and technical backup. You must convince them to believe by the authoritative tone of your voice and the factual content of what you're communicating, regardless of which sex is the source. You must demonstrate that you know your business, that you've done it, are doing it, know how to do it.

Don't talk about "our company," as Americans are prone to do. In Latin America, it's the *individual* who counts, not the group, not the company. Speak in "I's," not "we's." Let your colleagues know that *you* are personally responsible for X, Y, or Z accomplishments. Define what your job actually is, where you fit into the corporate hierarchy, what stature you have. Once Latin men have a sense of your "place," and begin to realize you're a person who has achieved, who is experienced, accomplished and corporately important, then business is business and it becomes easy to keep the discussion on a strictly professional level.

Old-fashioned Latins prefer indirection and circumlocution to blunt statements of bottom-line fact. Often they are reticent to give you a frank no for an answer. This is considered impolite. Instead what you may get is elaborate rhetoric that circles around an issue at hand. Yet traditional Latins *will* tell you no if time permits them to do so in a way that they consider decorous so as not to disappoint you, especially if they like you. If you're sensitive to this possibility, you can tactfully draw a colleague out until a wishy-washy reply becomes a concrete response.

Stubbornness is another characteristic of personalism and machismo. Latins dislike compromise, the bedrock of U.S. negotiating style. To Latins, compromise means giving something up. Personalism dictates that one must jealously guard all one has, giving nothing up. Machismo causes Latins to feel that compromise has negative implications and is a sign of masculine weakness. To compromise is to be passive not active, sacrificing personal honor and integrity. Keep this in mind when developing your bargaining strategy; as much as can be predicted, decide what you're willing to give the Latin side with no strings attached to get what you want.

## The Decision-making Process

In Westernized Latin hierarchies, decision making works similarly to that of the U.S. Even when you deal with a company president or government minister, if the decision requires technical input from subordinate specialists a decision maker refers it to lower-ranking experts and generally follows their advice. However, in less modern organizations—often those owned or controlled by ruling families—decision making is apt to be centralized and arbitrary. Traditional Latin decision makers may be unwilling to share information with their peers or with lower-ranking personnel, for to do so would be to give up personal power. Seeking counsel from those who may be better informed about specific issues concerning a larger decision is thought to be undignified. With old-guard Latins, how effectively you appeal to individual identity and dignity may take priority over the lucrativeness of a transaction, influencing the decision of whether or not to deal.

## Lawyers and Contracts

Throughout the region, laws are harsh and rigidly enforced but are made flexible behind the scenes by having relatives and friends capable of influencing the system from within.

Cross-cultural training expert Alison R. Lanier elaborates in *Update: Venezuela*:

> We break a minor law relatively easily (speeding, etc.) but once caught most of us do not try to tamper with the legal machinery. We think it bad to "use influence" or to "buy off the court." However, we build some leeway into the law. We are generally not arrested if we are going only 1 mph over the limit—we can talk our way out of minor problems *if the law has not started to grind*. With most South Americans it is exactly the opposite. There is no leeway whatsoever in the *law*; even a fraction of a violation is caught up. However, Latin leeway starts after the arrest, with family pressures, payoffs, deals of all kinds. This is a fundamental cultural difference. It can lead to great emotional reactions on both sides in any given case. (Intercultural Press, Chicago, 1981)

Family pressures, payoffs, and deals of all kinds can work to the advantage of U.S. negotiators who, by forming a trust relationship with Latin counterparts, in effect become part of an extended family. Just as Latins may expect favors from you, as part of the mutual obligations of friendship you can request favors in return; one of them is legal clout. Says Pan Am's Patrick J. Oliver:

> Americans are quick to ask: "Is it legal?" In Latin America, the answer, of course, is nearly always "no." But Latins have a law for every occasion. If they really want to do business, they will find a law that permits them—and you—to do just about anything you desire. Particularly if you're dealing with the government and the transaction is one that will benefit the nation, somehow, somewhere, there will be a law to accommodate it, as this is precisely what developing countries seek.

As the desire to do business is predicated on trust, it affects the nature of traditional contracts. While contracts between U.S. businesspeople and U.S.-educated, Westernized Latins may be detailed legal instruments, often they merely express the character of a commercial relationship in terms of idealistic principles; they don't address specific details of process, timing, and legal responsibility. These are subsequently negotiated on an ad hoc basis between concerned parties throughout the relationship.

This is not to say that lawyers are unimportant in Latin America. They can be vital, particularly for their knowledge of how to make local laws specifically prohibiting certain actions more pliant, as well as who to approach—and how to approach them—to achieve a desired result. Their role as mediators in negotiations to amicably settle disagreements is also significant. However, their primary purpose is to make it easier to do business, not to complicate matters that are already complex. In Latin America, a lawyer does not represent mistrust.

### Body Language

Latins are anything but aloof and insensitive. Paradoxically, considering machismo, Latin men are more "feminine" than American men in that they are a more tactile people. Touching is an important form of communication in Latin America. It's a sign of sincerity. Among old friends or even mere acquaintances who are passersby in the street, a casual wave of the hand by way of recognition and greeting is an insufficient display of warmth. A handshake may be accompanied by a shoulder or upper-arm squeeze, or a one-armed embrace called abrazo in Spanish. Or a handshake may be replaced or followed by a double abrazo: a two-arm hug. But a handshake with a loose grip lasting about twice as long as an American handshake is probably what newcomers will receive, whether you're a man or a woman.

When conversing, expect to be touched frequently. This may include lapel fingering, chest or shoulder tapping, and arm squeezing. Latins talk with their hands to emphasize points, ensure your attention, and express their personalism.

Touching implies a different concept of space from that of Americans, who are physically unable to touch each other due to normal conversational distance. Latins consider our preferred 18 to 21 inches to be outside their sphere of psychic influence. As discussions grow more animated they will move in to a distance of only 2 or 3 inches, so that you face each other practically nose to nose and have no choice but to look directly into each other's eyes.

Such mannerisms make many U.S. businesspeople uncomfortable. Often it destroys their concentration and they are unable to think. But there's nothing sexual implied in these displays of physicality. If you flinch, stiffen, tighten your lips, grind your teeth, retreat, look away, or show any other form of annoyance, it will be interpreted as insincerity and rejection. If necessary, role-play with a friend or spouse before leaving home and it will begin to feel more natural.

You'll also notice a difference in spatial perception in how Latin offices are arranged. Walled offices are often not status symbols, as they block a person's view of his staff. This too is personalism at work. To keep an eye on one's underlings is to show authority. A department head's desk may be in the middle of a small open room with the desks of subordinates clustered around it. What Americans consider crowded, Latins may feel is spacious. When this public layout exists, presentations may take place in separate rooms reserved for receptions and private discussions, or you may have to wend your way to a colleague's desk and make your pitch before his staff. For this reason, it's best to keep presentations as simple as possible, doing without visual aids that don't fit comfortably on a desktop.

## Social Customs

American expatriates stationed in Latin America who form close relationships with natives in business and government may be invited to their homes, but it's not a privilege readily extended to transient business travelers. It's even rarer for first-time visitors who are complete strangers to receive such invitations. A typical Latin American house is walled and womblike. It suggests concern for privacy and security, and a sense of disconnection with the outside world—even neighbors. Such is the sanctity of family in Latin America. The family is everything. You're either a family member or friend or a part of the great blurry mass of people composing "everyone else." It's a closed, protected world to which those who are unknown or unaccepted are denied entry.

Don't feel insulted if you're not invited to a Latin home right away, or feel it's a sign that your business prospects are not good. It's simply a natural, culturally inculcated caution. If your relationship deepens with subsequent trips and with regular communication in between, an invitation home will eventually be extended.

### Entertaining

Business entertaining is usually done at restaurants, private clubs, and nightclubs rather than at home. Breakfast meetings are not found in Latin America. Even lunch invitations should not be extended unless you know your colleague works a nine-to-five day. If he goes home for a traditional siesta, nothing should interrupt it.

Lunch is usually a Latin's main meal. Dinner is late, eightish at the earliest, and restaurants may be full at midnight. Be prepared to stay up late. If you're the host for dinner, ask a male guest if he'd like to bring his wife along, leaving it up to him to decide. Notes a native of the region:

> It is important to invite the wife because you want her to like you. Wives are influential people in Latin America. They are not the second-class citizens that many Americans suppose. A wife can make or break a business deal. If you make a good impression, she will help you sell your company to her husband.
>
> Also, if a wife is left alone at home, and the husband is out with you until eleven o'clock at night, she will not believe that he is really doing business. She will think he is fooling around with another woman. When he comes home, he gets static: "Why are you paying more attention to someone else than you are to me? You should be giving *me* more attention."
>
> It becomes a contest. Suddenly you find that you have inadvertently inserted yourself between a Latin man and his wife. You will create disharmony by not inviting the wife. In Latin America, you can be 99 percent sure that a wife is not going to give her husband the benefit of the doubt that he stayed out late because he was attending an innocent business dinner.

U.S. businesswomen who are alone and cautious should think twice about inviting a Latin man to dinner unless he's accompanied by other members of his firm; otherwise the invitation may be misconstrued. You should also be wary of accepting invitations from Latin men that don't include wives (assuming the men are married). If you're traveling alone and feel it's appropriate to be the hostess, invite a man to lunch or late-afternoon drinks. Have an excuse for not accepting a dinner invitation afterward, should one be offered. Jet lag is popular and hard to debate.

To create a good impression, order locally made wines, beers, and liquors. Imported liquor can be expensive and may cost your host more than he planned to spend. Native wines are dependably national prides. To order foreign labels is tactless. Latin women are demure in their drinking habits, preferring wine or aperitifs to hard liquor. American women can drink what they want, but it's best to follow the local example. Regardless of your sex, getting drunk is vulgar to the region's business elite.

## Conversation

Mealtime and other out-of-office conversation is best confined to nonbusiness subjects, unless your colleague introduces shop talk. Such occasions are mainly for mutual revelations of personalism. While you should not ask a Latin about his family if he doesn't mention it first, it's okay to talk about your family, especially children if you have them. As many Latins plan to send their children to U.S. schools, questions you can answer on the subject helps to establish a personal bond. Other acceptable topics of conversation include your hobbies, your aesthetic interests, or any local or national pride—a historical site, an architecturally imposing building, the beauty of a local park, etc. The more you can demonstrate your breadth of interests beyond business, the more you'll impress a Latin as being a person who is civilized. Avoid the subject of politics, yours or his. If a Latin brings the subject up (and he may), ask questions, keep your opinions to yourself, and let him do the talking.

## Social Gifts

Good-quality corporate mementoes are fine to give on initial visits, when something more personal would be out of place. A bottle of brand-name Scotch is a suitable intermediate gift. But as your relationship develops, more thoughtful gifts become appropriate. As Latins will try to share with you what really matters to them in life early on in conversations, it makes choosing a gift well-matched to the recipient that much easier.

Gifts that are intellectually oriented are appreciated—fine classical records, works of literature, especially poetry, and so on. Gifts for wives are well-received if they are not too intimate, although women have more latitude here than men, particularly if they have met a male colleague's wife and know her taste in perfumes, handbags, and such; gifts like these, however, are inappropriate for men to give, unless the presentation is to a group of wives at a dinner party hosted by you. Gifts for children are always safe. Whatever your kids want, their kids want.

Be cautious about giving the latest technological gadgetry made in the U.S. without sounding out your Latin colleague on a previous trip; it may create an unintended impression of American superiority. Most gifts recommended in Chapter Three will do.

Gift-giving taboos include handkerchiefs (suggesting tearful occasions, such as funerals), knives of any kind, including letter openers (implying the severing of a relationship), and books by Spanish authors from Spain—even greats like Cervantes and Lorca—which may remind Latins who are intensely proud of their independence of their former colonial oppressors.

# APPENDIX:

## Where to Get Professional Help

For more on cross-cultural negotiating, this selected list of organizations is worth considering. Each will send you free promotional literature as a basis for making further inquiries.

### Foreign Language Lessons

While there are many excellent language schools, these are cited because their facilities are not limited to one region or city of the U.S. The addresses below are corporate headquarters.

**The Berlitz Schools of Languages of America**
Research Park, Building O, 1101 State Road, Princeton, NJ 08540;
   (609) 924–8500
Over 200 locations worldwide, with at least one in most major American cities.

**Inlingua**
551 Fifth Avenue, New York, NY 10176; (212) 682–8585
Over 200 locations worldwide, with at least one in most major American cities.

## Michel Thomas Language Centers
60 East 42nd Street, Suite 1560, New York, NY 10017; (212) 688–8400

Locations in New York, Washington, DC, Miami, Beverly Hills, Los Angeles, Encino, and London.

## Interpretation and Translation Services

The following are either industry organizations that will send you membership directories or private companies. In addition, the language schools previously listed also provide interpreters and translators.

## The American Association of Language Specialists
Suite 9, 1000 Connecticut Avenue, NW, Washington, DC 20036;
(202) 298–6500

## The American Society of Interpreters
1629 K Street, NW, Suite 5117, Washington, DC 20006; (301) 657–3337

## The American Translator's Association
109 Croton Avenue, Ossining, NY 10562; (914) 941–1500

## Technical Translation International
500 Fifth Avenue, Suite 200, New York, NY 10036; (212) 719–3550

## Intercontinental Bureau of Translators and Interpreters
285 Madison Avenue, New York, NY 10017; (212) 689–8810

145 Natoma Street (at New Montgomery Street), San Francisco, CA 94015;
(415) 495–0265

## Cross-Cultural Training for Business Travelers and Expatriates-to-Be

The first five organizations listed conduct *only* private training programs customized for individual corporate clients, usually with groups of managers as trainees. In addition to private customized training, Ellen Raider International offers public programs in which individual managers from different firms are trained together.

## International Council to Management
American Graduate School of International Management, Glendale, AZ 85306;
(602) 978–7115

**Business Council for International Understanding Institute**
The American University, 3301 New Mexico Avenue, NW, Suite 244,
  Washington, DC 20016; (202) 686–2771

**Intercultural Relations Institute**
2439 Birch Street, Suite 8, Palo Alto, CA 94306; (415) 328–0800

**Renwick and Associates**
7333 East Monterey Way, Suite Four, Scottsdale, AZ 85251;
  (602) 949–0130

**Moran Stahl & Boyer**
355 Lexington Avenue, New York, NY 10017; (212) 661–4878

**Ellen Raider International**
752 Carroll Street, Brooklyn, NY 11215; (212) 499–2612

## Books and Films

**Intercultural Press**
P.O. Box 768, Yarmouth, ME 04096; (207) 846–5168
The largest publisher of mail-order books for businesspeople on cross-cultural training subjects. Most titles are unavailable in book stores.

**Copeland Griggs Productions**
3454 Sacramento Street, San Francisco, CA 94118; (415) 921–4410
Offers four short cross-cultural training films in color. The series, called "Going International," includes: *Bridging the Culture Gap*—on cross-cultural negotiating conflicts; *Managing the Overseas Assignment*—on common work-related problems; *Beyond Culture Shock*—on adjusting to life abroad; and *Welcome Home, Stranger*—on the readjustment problems expatriates face on returning to the U.S.

# INDEX

---

Accounting firms, 29
Advertising, 35, 57–58, 83–84. *See also* Collateral materials
Age, American, 37, 51, 159
Aggression, American, 11–12, 20, 55, 86, 213
Airport: flight plans, 63, 64, 67; getting met at, 67–68; regulations, 33
Alcohol, 40, 51; in East Asia, 161, 204–205, 241, 242, 244, 259–261; in Europe, 100–102; as gift, 61, 108, 132, 206, 254, 289; on intercontinental flights, 65; in Latin America, 288. *See also* Drinking customs; Toasts; Wines
Algeria, 112, 124
Altitude, 40
America, defined, 265
American Association of Language Specialists (TAALS), 43
American business styles and traits, 9–16
American businesswomen, 36, 50–52, 56, 66–67; in Arab countries, 50, 51, 123–124, 126, 138; in China, 51–52, 224; in Europe, 51, 78, 79, 98, 99, 100, 102, 103; in Japan, 36–37, 51, 201; in Latin America, 263, 274–276, 277–278, 283, 288; in South Korea, 51, 254, 258, 260
American Export Development Mission (1978), 38–39
American Society of Interpreters, 43

American Translators Association, 43
Appointments: in Arab countries, 119–120, 122–123, 127–129, 135, 144; in Europe, 82; in Latin America, 279–280
Arab countries and Arabs, 9, 26, 33, 61, 110–147; American businesswomen in, 50, 51, 123–124, 126, 138; American image of, 110; behavioral styles and customs of, 114–124, 126–147; body language of, 141–143; business cards in, 129, 135; business customs in, 124–143; business hours in, 128–129; collateral materials in, 130–132; conversation in, 140–141; decision-making process in, 138–139; defined, 111; dress for, 126–127; drinking rituals, 121–122, 135–136, 145; entertaining in, 143–147; handshakes in, 132–133, 135; hospitality in, 121–122, 136, 145, 147; houseguests in, 143–147; and Islam, 111, 115–118; negotiating styles in, 138–143; presentation style in, 135–137; pre-trip research for, 124–125; privacy of, 120–121; table manners in, 145–146; and time, 118–120, 122–123, 127–129, 135, 144; types of businesspeople in, 111–115; use of names in, 134, 139–140; visas for, 125–126; weather in, 126, 127; women, 120–121, 131, 144
Arab Gulf, 111–112, 121, 134, 139

*295*